Rife Original Frequencies (1936)
&
The Mysterious Nemescope

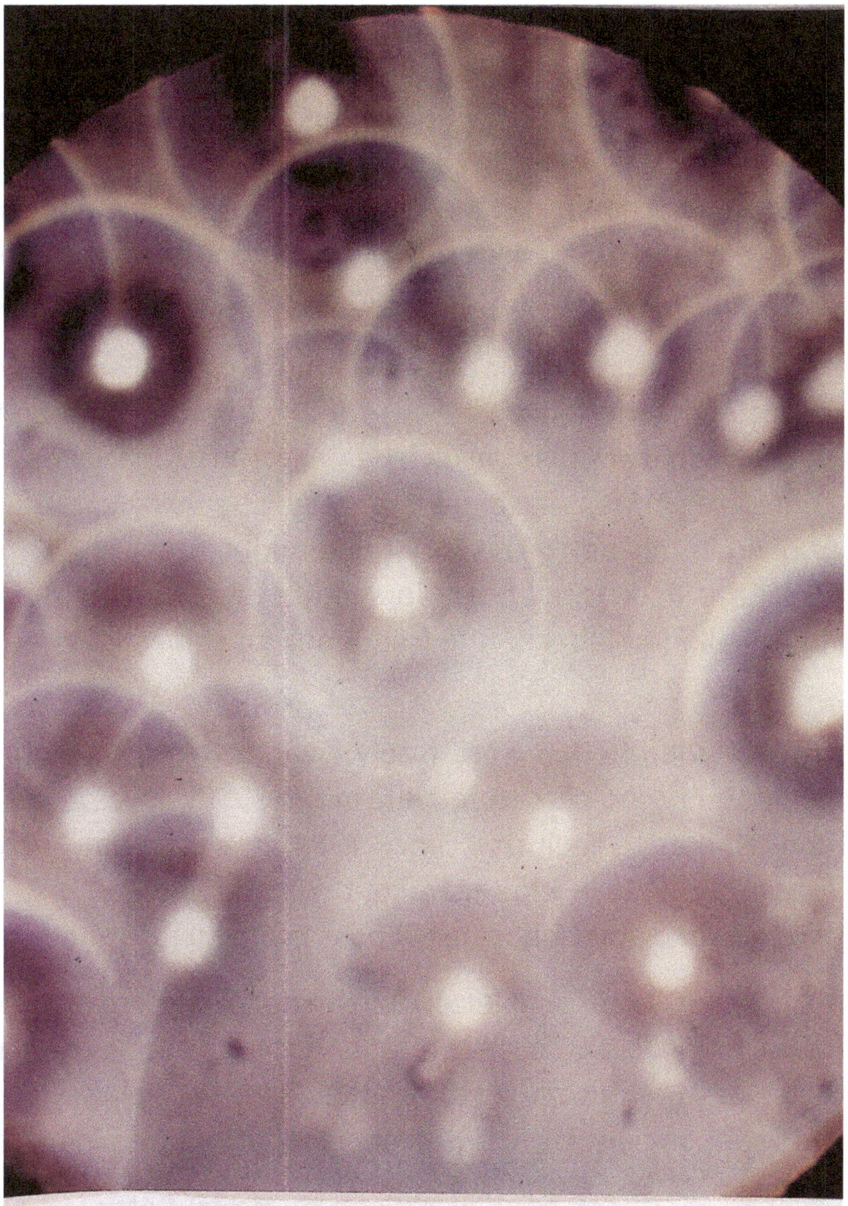

ENZYME OF PAPAYA: Mark the difference in size, the outskirt rings always overlapping the nuclei of the other enzymes.

By
Steven A. Ross Ph.D.

Publisher: Less Complicated, Inc.
PO Box 20756
Sedona, AZ 86341

© 2022 by Steven A. Ross

ISBN: 978-1-7356749-2-6

Except as permitted by U.S. Copyright Law, no part of this book may be reprinted, reproduced, transmitted, or utilized in any form by electronic, mechanical, or other means, now known or hereafter invented, including photocopying, microfilming, and recording, or in any information storage or retrieval system, without written permission from the publishers and author.

Disclaimer: The information contained within this book is not intended as a diagnosis or recommendation of therapy for any health condition that the reader might have. You should always consult a health professional if you have a question. Although there are various machines that might be using similar technologies to those mentioned in this book, this is not an endorsement of any product existing on the market. This book is not an endorsement of a wide range of health devices that have been called or labeled Rife frequency machines, devices, techniques, or whatnot!

The materials included herein were freely given to me in 1984 by John Crane of San Diego, California, who befriended Rife in the 1950s. I was given permission and without stipulation as to their use. Since 1984, I have openly lectured and made presentations around the world regarding the Royal R. Rife story. These materials are copies from the original laboratory books of Royal Rife and Dr. Elmer Nemes.

In my possession: 500 personal letters of the doctors corresponding with Rife, in both microfilm, originals and hard copies; newspaper clippings, magazine articles, journal articles dating from the 1930s and 1940s. In our possession are the Guest Books of the various scientists and doctors who visited Rife in his laboratory.

The Nemescope Laboratory book was given to me by Betty Lee Morales through her will.

Acknowledgements

I would like to acknowledge my wife, Deborah Cambio, who has come into my life, through time, in time. She has brought wisdom, beauty, integrity, love, laughter, and fun into my life. If it had not been for her encouragement and support this book would not have been written.

I want to acknowledge Betty Lee Morales for her trust in leaving the Nemescope materials for my caretaking.

I want to thank Daniel Kluz, my dear friend, who volunteered to edit this work to be the grammatically correct and smooth reading book that it is. I appreciate his support and diligent work on my behalf for more than 35 years.

Special thanks to Ramsey Lucas for his cover artwork.

Finally, it is important for me to acknowledge the unseen spiritual entities that have provided me the guidance and support, not only in finding the Rife Universal Microscope, but have encouraged me throughout my life to see the richness and beauty of the true underpinnings of the physical life.

Table of Contents

Introduction

For the first time in print, Dr. Steven A Ross presents the laboratory notebook of frequencies from the Rife Research group along with the original photographs taken through the incredible Nemescope, developed by Dr. Elmer Nemes.

In Part 1, you will find Rife's original frequencies discovered through the Universal Microscope in 1929-1935 as well as the heretofore unpublished typewritten pages, in Rife's own words, explaining what he discovered during his research.

Part 2, The Nemescope, will include the purported photographs of atoms and atomic bonds; photographs of the virus of cancer; photographs of a virus associated with Leukemia; virus associated with Multiple Sclerosis; photographs of the polio virus; enzymes; magnetic flux lines and many other interesting and informative photographs.

In 1933, Royal R. Rife invented his Universal microscope that allowed the discovery of specific frequencies that would devitalize or destroy microbes and viruses that were the cause of more than 60 diseases and illnesses. The Universal microscope was thirty times more powerful than ordinary light-source microscopes obtaining a magnification of 60,000 diameters. Dr. Ross has possessed this one and only microscope as well as hundreds of original documents and laboratory notes from the Rife laboratories in the late 1920s – 1940s.

Dr. Elmer Nemes developed his Nemescope, that saw down to the atomic level, in the early 1950s. The Nemescope was 60 times more powerful than the Rife microscope and allowed pictures of the energy bonds between atoms, the viewing of magnetic flux lines around the poles of magnets, and live photographs of the virus of cancer at 3.5 million diameters. The Nemescope was stolen in the mid-1950s with only Nemes' notebook of images, taken through the Nemescope, still surviving and in the possession of Dr. Ross. Were these the first pictures of atoms? Are these the pictures of the cancer virus?

IRON NUCLEATE: By shorter wave length, more magnification and resolution, showing the basic atomic and molecular groupings, representing not only more emitted spectral lines from the iron nucleate atom, but "energy lines," revealed by magnification of structure and internal resolution, towards the nucleus of the atom.

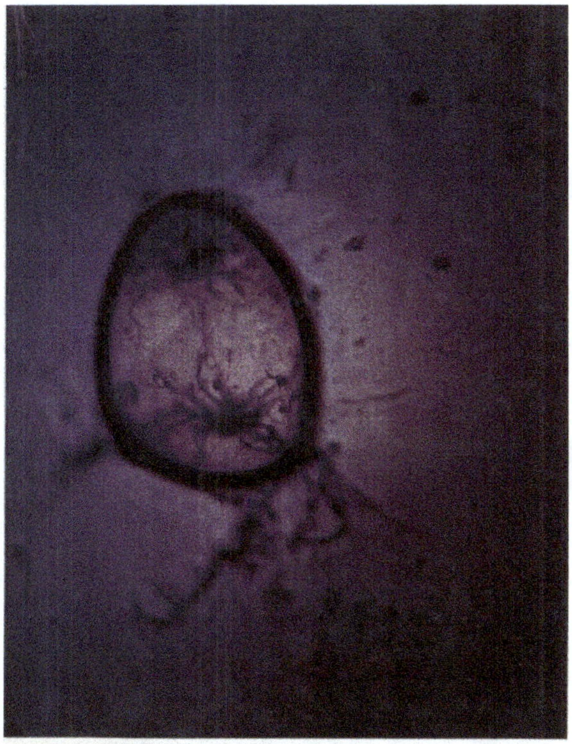

CANCER VIRUS: Spherical particles in the urine of a known cancer victim, showing intra-particle morphology.

PART 1

The Rife Universal Microscope

The Universal Microscope of Royal Raymond Rife

Royal Raymond Rife, Jr., was born May 16, 1888, in Elkhorn, Douglas County, Nebraska. According to a notarized statement made by his aunt on April 24, 1939, "I am the aunt of Royal Raymond Rife and at the time of the death of his mother Ida May Rife, when he was about 8 months old, his father brought him to me and I raised him and brought him up as though he was my own, although I never formally adopted him. He lived with me continually from the time he was 8 months of age until the year 1905 and I have been constantly in touch with him ever since." Signed, Nina Culver (Rife) Dryden, Rancheita, San Diego County, California.

Although he was not a medical doctor, Rife started his first research working on tuberculosis. Rife believed that that something was taking place with the disease below the level of the bacterium. This need to create greater magnification was the impetus to create microscopes that could see viruses. Rife was the first researcher known to have isolated and photographed the tuberculosis virus.

Royal R. Rife's microscopes remain the most powerful light-source microscopes ever invented. Rife's Universal microscope is the most powerful of all the microscopes. The research team working with the microscopes in the 1930s included researchers from the Mayo Clinic, Northwestern University, Johns Hopkins University, the USC School of Medicine, the University of California, and several other prestigious scientific institutions. Using Rife's microscopes, medical discoveries were made at the Mayo Clinic and Northwestern University, and the Universal microscope received high praise from the California Institute of Technology.

The Smithsonian Institute, in its 1944 report, devoted more than 12 pages to the Universal Microscope. Through this high-powered microscope, the researchers visually pursued the theory that everything in the universe vibrates, including viruses, bacteria, germs, and other micro-organisms. If they could find the right resonate frequency, then the elements that lead to cancer and 60 other diseases and illnesses might be destroyed like a glass shattering. Would they find this theory was sound without harming the normal healthy cells? If they did find that it worked, wouldn't the world of science and medicine come running to their doorstep? Who wouldn't want an effective medical approach to stopping cancer and other diseases utilizing physics?

When Rife developed his first Rife microscope in the 1920s, he was able to achieve documented magnification of 8,000-17,000 diameters while all other microscopes were achieving approximately 1,800X magnification. At the time, 1,800 was considered the theoretical limitation for any light-source microscope, but Rife's device was ten times greater than all other microscopes in use in the 1920s and 1930s.

His microscope was examined and utilized by the top scientists and medical researchers of the day. By 1934, Rife had developed his Universal Microscope that was able to achieve magnification of nearly 60,000 diameters. Rife's microscopes were light-source microscopes as they utilized light as one of the sources for magnification. We contrast this with the term *electron microscope* which was developed in the 1940s. Although electron microscopes were able to bring tremendous magnification, no live specimen could be examined through an electron microscope. The specimen is placed in a vacuum, then bombarded by electrons. Both these principles destroy the life of any specimen. This is an important difference from light-source microscopes, which do allow viewing of live organisms without harm.

The most important point to be made is, with this increased magnification, Rife's research group was able to see and make important discoveries regarding cells, microbes, viruses, and other elements that no other researchers on the planet were able to see. A good analogy would be if you compare a telescope to a pair of binoculars. How much more detail and distance could you see with between ten and thirty times more power? Through Rife's microscopes, which allowed him to watch live viruses, Rife was able to observe them changing forms, thus proving that microbes and viruses have the ability to change from one form to another depending upon the medium they are in.

Due to the unique properties used in the construction of Rife's microscope, most notably the use of Risley counter-rotating quartz prisms in conjunction with light illumination, every microbe, bacteria, and virus would glow in a unique color that was specific to that particular organism. Rife's group saw that every time they were looking at slides of a specific disease, the same color would be present for that particular organism. They achieved this by using various modes of lighting to bring each virus into visibility in their natural colors. Rife first turned to this technique of using light to stain the specimens because he realized that the molecules of the chemical stains used under normal microscopic analysis were much too large to enter into the structures he sought to examine. Also, the usual process of staining used in microscopy is sometimes lethal to the specimens being examined.

Color is a rate of vibration. Different vibrations lead to different colors. Every element in nature has its own unique color characteristics. For example, scientists can tell what elements exist within different stars in the galaxy based on the analysis of the color signature that appears with a device known as a spectroscope. Chemists and manufacturers can know what chemical reactions take place and what elements are present due to the Fraunhofer lines – the colors – that are present during any mixtures that take place.

So, it was not unusual for Rife's group to be able to discover that microbes had their own unique color or vibrational signatures. Not only was Rife using higher magnifications, but principles previously unknown to science where he was mixing light and color sources. In sound it is called *heterodyning*. You take one sound and add it to another sound to derive additional sounds. It had never been done with light as Rife devised.

Once Rife's group discovered that they had unique frequencies visible in microbes, bacteria and viruses, as denoted by the unique colors that were present through the microscope, utilizing laws of physics, the researchers knew that had discovered each microorganisms resonant frequency. The researchers were aware that glass shatters when it is subjected to a specific frequency? Not all glass present in an area will shatter, but only the glass that resonates exactly with the frequency that is generated. In addition, think about two cars speeding head on toward each other at the same speed. When they meet they will cancel out each other.

Armed with these concepts, Rife's research team set out to find frequencies that could be beamed or projected toward microorganisms that would destroy them, neutralize them, render them harmless, or devitalize them. They would call each specific frequency the MOR, or Mortal Oscillatory Rate, of the microorganism.

On their path to discovering the resonant frequencies, and since they were looking with microscopic depth unavailable to any other scientists before then or now, they found that different frequencies also had the effect of mutating different organisms from one class to another. That is, a benign microorganism could mutate from its state to become a deadly pathogen just from being subjected to a frequency. This mutation was called *pleomorphism* and had been hotly debated in medicine regarding whether it was possible.

The following two articles, "The Rife Microscope or Facts and Their Fate" by Royal Lee and "Invisible Ultra-Violet Life Frequencies Made Visible" by Mark Gallert, provide insight of the magnitude of Rife's discoveries.

The Rife Microscope or "Facts and Their Fate"

"FACTS do not speak for themselves, but must be spoken for,"* is an axiom too rarely admitted.

In the world of health and disease, there are despotic influences that take incredible pains to hide facts that would explode their control over current theories and practices. It was a Harvard professor who defined a medical education as, "The warping of unsuspecting immature minds into a meticulous system of commercial superstition."

It seems that the commercial drug and food interests have seized upon the mistakes of the pharmacologists, who long ago limited the useful and available drugs or remedies for disease, the weapons of the doctor, to poisons and poisons exclusively. (See Lee Foundation Reprint No. 25A for the complete story.) That has put the medical profession of the civilized world in a frightful spot. They find themselves today treating starvation and deficiencies of mineral foods and vitamins WITH POISONS instead of with the physiologically correct nutrient principle. Their victims die after this treatment of symptoms instead of causes has produced misleading spells of remission of their starved state. Ten to twenty years is chopped off the life span of most people as a consequence. All because SOMEBODY is actively promoting the continuance of that mistake, and other mistakes, of pharmacologists, to protect their special racket.

What are the OTHER mistakes? One is the idea that germs are causes of disease instead of the result of wrong food and wrong environment. Rosenow, one of the most alert and outstanding of our recent bacteriologists, announced in 1914 in the Journal of Infectious Diseases, Volume 14, that he had established the fact by experimental investigations that bacteria are not of themselves deadly or dangerous, but are rather a primitive and potential form of life, able to modify itself very quickly to changing environments. Bacteria are beneficent or dangerous according to the host, according to the surroundings in which they live, even as you and I would be entirely different in character and in health if brought up under other conditions.........

*Krebs, Krebs & Beard, in *Medical World*, July, 1950

Dr. Rosenow summed up the situation as follows: "It would seem, therefore, that focal infections are no longer to be looked upon merely as a place of entrance of bacteria, but as a place where CONDITIONS ARE FAVORABLE for them to acquire the properties which give them a wide range of affinities for various structures." In other words, the disease has been caused previously by injury of one sort or other, resulting in degeneration of protective tissues and a weakening of the protective mechanism in general. Then, when the soil has been prepared (by the patient), the appropriate bacterium is generated and becomes parasite upon its natural habitat, just as in the case of the flies and the manure ... (See, "The Philosophy and Science of Health", E. E. Rogers.)

This was not compatible with the plans of organized medicine, or with the plans of some power higher than this (Drug & Food monopolies??), so it was never given any public recognition. No text book on bacteriology mentioned this important principle, unless to say it was not true.

Later, another great research man went further, and showed that one micro-organism could be converted to another. For instance, colon bacillus into typhoid, by altering the environmental biochemistry. What happened to him?? That is a long story. Not only was his remarkable work studiously ignored, but any medical doctor who made use of his practical discoveries to treat patients was immediately stripped of his privileges as a member of the local medical association. By a fluke of fate, an article describing some of the work of this man accidentally got published in, "The Journal of the Franklin Institute", of Philadelphia, a non-medical journal where the censorship was not so well maintained. But, the proper influence was soon brought to bear, and no copies of this article are commonly available. What is the name of the investigator, and the name of the article?? It is, "The New Microscopes", by R. E. Seidl, M. D. & M. Elizabeth Winter.

The fact that important commercial interests connive to suppress valuable discoveries which might hurt their business was well illustrated by the recent article in, "Reader's Digest", in which the suppression of information about the nickel-cadmium storage battery has been so effective for the last forty years, during which American battery users had spent vast sums for short lived lead batteries, in total ignorance of the existence of a battery that was ten times as durable and reliable, and freely available to European motorists.

(Cont'd on inside of Back Cover.)

Rife's obliteration from public view was no less efficient. Here is his story, as well as I can give it at the moment:

Mr. H. H. Timken, the motor axle magnate, employed Rife at his San Diego winter home garage as a chauffeur and mechanic. Finding that Rife was working as a hobby on a new system of optics for high power magnification, Timken realized that he was on the trail of something big, and set up a foundation with an endowment fund to finance Rife's researches, and built him a laboratory on the Timken grounds. Rife proceeded to justify Timken's generosity with a vengeance, the Franklin Institute report offering only a short review of what had been accomplished. With his 150,000 power microscope that made live germs visible as clear as a cat in your lap, Rife showed that they:

1. Gave off a monochromatic wave length of invisible ultra-violet light, at all times during their life.
2. That by superimposing another beam of monochromatic ultra-violet, he could produce a heterodyne beam of visible light.
3. That by subjecting the germ to a short wave frequency of the correct value, the germ immediately disintegrated.
4. That by subjecting test animals that had been given lethal doses of pathogenic germs, he could invariably save their lives by subjecting their bodies for a few minutes to the proper single wave length of electrical energy.
5. That by altering the environment and food supply, friendly germs such as colon bacillus can be converted into pathogenic germs such as typhoid.
6. That there are only about ten different classes of germs, within each class conversion from one form to another is a matter of environment.

But, when he announced his findings his troubles started. Local medical doctors who recognized the value of Rife's discoveries, and tried to apply them to their clinical work, soon found their relations with the local medical society cancelled. Rife was called a quack. No doctor was permitted to use his apparatus or methods on penalty of ostracism.

No medical journal was ever permitted to report on Rife's work. This one by the Franklin Institute slipped by the censors, since this organization is not medical but supports general scientific activities. But that mistake was soon rectified, it appears, as there is still no general knowledge of Rife's epoch-making discoveries. Again, the iron curtain of Fishbein is effective. By the way, Fishbein is still active on this most important job for the monopolists, He is editor-in-chief of the "Index Medicus", the American source index for everything medical, and associate-editor of the "International Medical Index", published by Elsevier in Holland. As such, he is in a position to determine what the doctor will find out about any subject in medicine, and what he will not find out. We can give you a list of various subjects on which this censorship is rigorously applied. (Any evidential support for homeopathic medicine, for osteopathy or chiropractic manipulation for example.) Only the treatment of disease with synthetic drugs is carefully reported. Botanicals are played down, foods as remedies are almost as taboo as Rife's work. Trace minerals have been proven to be the key to the cause and cure of undulant fever for ten years, but not a trace about the work in any of Fishbein's censored medical journals. (See Lee Foundation Reprint 25A for information on the official definition of a medical remedy for disease, how it excludes automatically any vitamin, nutritional mineral or enzyme, and Reprint No. 41 for more on undulant fever.) (Both free on request.)

REPRINT NO. 47

Lee Foundation for Nutritional Research
Milwaukee, Wisconsin 53201

"**NOTE:** Lee Foundation for Nutritional Research is a non-profit, public-service institution, chartered to investigate and disseminate nutritional information. The attached publication is not literature or labeling for any product, nor shall it be employed as such by anyone. In accordance with the right of freedom of the press guaranteed to the Foundation by the First Amendment of the U.S. Constitution, the attached publication is issued and distributed for informational purposes."

NEW LIGHT ON THERAPEUTIC ENERGIES

Compiled and Summarized

by

MARK L. GALLERT, M.D., M.SC.

JAMES CLARKE & CO. LTD
31 QUEEN ANNE'S GATE
LONDON, S.W.1

INVISIBLE ULTRA-VIOLET LIFE FREQUENCIES MADE VISIBLE

Microscopes constructed on entirely new principles have been invented and developed by Royal Raymond Rife, a scientist and biologist. These new microscopes have led to many discoveries regarding:

(*a*) The characteristics of bacteria and virus micro-organisms.

(*b*) Factors leading to the production or transformation of various micro-organisms.

(*c*) The role of bio-chemical changes, in encouraging or retarding the growth of harmful micro-organisms.

In this section we shall first consider briefly the new features of the Rife Microscopes, and then summarize the discoveries that have occurred through the use of these instruments.

1. THE RIFE MICROSCOPES

With these outstanding optical devices, resolution up to 31,000 diameters and magnification up to 60,000 diameters is obtained, with a number of advantages over the electron microscopes—the only other devices known at the present time which reach such high magnifications.

The results obtained from the Rife microscopes are due principally to the use of three principles of physics in a manner completely new to the field of optics:

1. A method of selecting a portion of the frequency spectrum of light for use in viewing specimens.

2. A method of heterodyning light to bring micro-organisms of various invisible ultra-violet colours into the visible light frequency range.

3. The attainment of very high magnification and resolution through an ingenious method for keeping the optical rays parallel in the instrument.

Considering each of the foregoing principles in turn:

1. *Selecting a Portion of the Frequency Spectrum*

It is well known that a beam of light passed through a prism is broken up into the colour spectrum, and since different colour-components of the beam are displaced by differing degrees, the beam emerging from the prism is spread out over a relatively wide area. The visible colours can be seen un-aided, but beyond the red component of the beam there is an invisible beam of infra-red and beyond the violet component there is an invisible area of ultra-violet frequencies transmitted by the prism if it is made of material such as quartz which permits the transmission of ultra-violet.

In the Rife microscopes, circular, wedge-shaped, block-crystal quartz prisms are used to polarize the light to be sent through the scope. By means of a revolving adjustment or control, the portion of the spectrum sent through the prisms is selectable, so that a narrow band corresponding to any colour from infra-red up through the visible colours and then through the entire ultra-violet range in narrow steps, can be selected for use in illuminating the specimens. The importance of this unique feature will be evident later.

2. *Heterodyning Light*

We will first explain the term "heterodyne" and then show its application to light as developed by Rife. It is an observed fact in physics, and a principle constantly used in radio and in work with sound, that when two different frequencies of vibration are produced, they inter-act upon each other to produce two new frequencies—one of which is the *sum* of the two original or fundamental frequencies; the other is the *difference* between the two originating or fundamental frequencies. Suppose, for example, that in the range of sound, a tone of 400 cycles per second and another tone of 600 cycles per second is produced. The resulting new frequencies will then be 200 cycles (the difference between 400 and 600 cycles—and 1,000 cycles for the other new tone, the sum of 400 and 600 cycles.

So far as is known, Rife was the first individual to apply this principle to the field of light. The visible frequencies range from about 436 trillion oscillations per second at the red end of the visible spectrum, to about 732 trillion oscillations per second at the violet end of the visible spectrum. An oscillatory rate faster than 732 trillion times per second results in a beam which is in the invisible, ultra-violet range. The ultra-violet band occupies several octaves of vibration, as compared to the visible spectrum which occupies less than one octave of vibration. . . . (The upper limit of an octave has twice the vibratory rate of the lower limit of the same octave.) So the range of the vibratory light spectrum invisible to the human eye is larger than the frequency range of the light spectrum which the eye can perceive.

The process of heterodyning light is accomplished by bringing an invisible, ultra-violet beam of, for example, 1,200 trillion oscillations per second into contact with another equally-invisible beam of say, 1,700 trillion oscillations per second; the difference between the oscillatory rates of the two originating beams results in the production of a light beam having an oscillatory rate of 500 trillions per second, which is within the range visible to the human eye.

In the past, many micro-organisms could only be observed if stained with a chemical. Some micro-organisms never became visible with other microscopes, because no suitable stain could be found for them. One of the prime advantages of the Rife microscopes is that Rife found many of the micro-organisms having no colour in the visible light range—their frequency characteristic is such that they have a "colour" in the invisible, ultra-violet range. By the use of the heterodyning principle in his microscopes as mentioned, the micro-organisms of ultra-violet colours are brought into the visible light range in their natural state, without the use of any stain. This method also brings into visibility the micro-organisms which had not responded to any known stain, and all micro-organisms can be viewed in their natural live state—a very considerable advantage, since the use of a stain kills the micro-organism. In fact this is the only microscope yet known by which ultra-high magnification can be used to view organisms in their living state, for the beams from electron microscopes instantly kill any living organisms.

3. *Achievement of Very High Magnification through Optical Means*

In the ordinary microscope, the rays of light refracted by the specimen enter the objective and are then carried up the tube in supposedly parallel rays, but in practice these rays converge after a certain distance, cross each other, and then diverge, resulting in distortion and a limit on the amount of magnification obtainable, since the rays by ordinary means cannot be kept parallel for a sufficient distance to pass them through several series of lenses. In the Rife microscopes, specially-designed quartz prisms are inserted into the tube at frequent intervals to counteract the tendency of the rays to diverge from parallel. This enables three matched pairs of oculars to be used in the universal microscope, the largest which Rife has constructed, permitting the attainment of the extraordinarily high powers of magnification and resolution that we have already mentioned. The supposed limit on magnification arising from the dimension of a wavelength of the light used for viewing the specimen, has been transcended by Rife, partly through the utilization of ultra-violet light which is composed of wavelengths of shorter dimensions than those of visible light, and partly by other means. Many technical details of the instrument are contained in the article *The New Microscopes* by R. E. Seidel, M.D. and M. Elizabeth Winter, published in the February, 1944, Journal of the Franklin Institute. That article has recently been reprinted by the Lee Foundation for Nutritional Research, Milwaukee 3, Wisconsin, and published as their Reprint #47.

2. DISCOVERIES RESULTING FROM THE USE OF THE RIFE MICROSCOPES

1. *Frequency Characteristics of Micro-organisms*

The adjustment or control mechanism in the Rife microscopes, for selecting the frequency band of light sent up through the lenses, has already been mentioned. In the use of these instruments, it is found that the control setting differs for every different type of bacteria and virus, and that for any particular type of bacteria or virus the setting is always the same. This means that each different type of bacteria and virus has its own characteristic life frequency which it emits, and by "tuning" the microscope to that frequency of light, the micro-organism becomes brilliantly visible without the use of any chemical stain.

In the use of the Rife microscopes it has been found, for example, that Bacillus Typhosus is always a turquoise-blue; Bacillus Coli is mahogany-coloured; Mycobacterium Liprae is always a ruby shade; the filter-passing form of virus of tuberculosis is an emerald green; the virus of cancer (one of the discoveries made possible by the Rife microscopes) is purplish-red, etc. Different colours are of course representative of different frequencies of light.

2. *Observations of Micro-organisms not shown by Other Microscopes*

Because of the unique characteristics of the Rife instruments as already described, they permit observation of micro-organisms which other microscopes are unable to show. Among the discoveries thus made, have been virus organisms present in poliomyelitis and cancer.

3. *New information regarding the relationship between Micro-organisms and Their Chemical Environment*

The cancer virus which was isolated by Rife, and which he terms BX virus, induced cancer growths in 104 successive generations of albino rats. During the course of the extensive experiments performed with this virus, it was found that with a slight change in the chemical media for the culture, a larger virus resulted, termed BY. Another slight change in the chemical media, and the virus is transformed into a monocyte. With still another change in the chemical environment, the monocyte becomes a fungi, and with a still further slight change, the fungi turns into Bacillus Coli! Then if the Bacillus Coli is kept in a certain media for a year (the time required for metasteses), the BX virus again appears! The changes in the chemical environment required to effect these transformations are very slight—in fact it is stated that an alteration of four parts per million in the media will transform the harmless B. Coli into the deadly B. Typhosus. These changes can be made to occur in as short a period as forty-eight hours.

It is Rife's belief that all pathogenic (disease-producing) micro-organisms are divided into ten groups, and that any micro-organism can be converted into that of any other within its group, by changing the chemical environment, sometimes by as little as two parts per million. From the above it can be seen how slight metabolic changes in body tissues can induce a micro-organism of one group to change into another micro-organism within the same group. The Rife work provides interesting support for, and visual confirmation of, the Naturopathic theory. In contrast to the Allopathic view, Naturopaths hold that the important factor in fighting disease is the vitality of the patient and the strength of the general constitution, and that if these can be supported and the body chemistry kept balanced, germs need not be a concern.

4. *Use of Selected Frequencies of Radiation to Destroy Specific Micro-organisms*

To quote from the article in the Journal of the Franklin Institute:

> "Under the Universal (Rife) Microscope, disease organisms such as those of tuberculosis, cancer, sarcoma, streptococcus, typhoid, staphylococcus, leprosy, hoof and mouth disease, and others may be observed to succumb when exposed to certain lethal frequencies peculiar to each individual organism, and directed upon them by rays."

The frequencies referred to in the above paragraph are in the radiowave band, and the most effective method of administration has been found to be the use of these differing frequencies of radio waves to pulse the current of a vacuum tube similar to an X-ray tube but partially filled with helium, so that none of the destructive X-ray radiations are emitted. The beam or rays from this new type of tube is directed at the micro-organisms under consideration. This work is in the laboratory stage, and is of interest mainly because of the principles involved.

Once it was proven, by the use of the Rife microscopes, that each type of micro-organism has its own particular life frequency or rate of vibration in the light band, it became a logical corollary that for each type of micro-organism there is also some frequency radiation or rate of oscillation that will be destructive to the organism.

In the field of radionics, for example, the theory has long been maintained that each virus, bacteria or type of toxin has its own frequency of radiation or tuning, and that these frequencies provided a key to tunings which could be used to destroy the virus or bacteria—however with Rife's work it is now possible to prove the correctness of the theory, by observation with his special microscopes which show the destruction of any micro-organism when the appropriate frequency of radiation is applied.

The Laboratory Notes of Royal R. Rife

The following laboratory notes describe the frequencies associated with Rife's original frequency devices comprised of old radio tubes; each frequency was passed through a glass tube filled with a particular gas. The following pages of frequencies are not intended to be used for the named conditions. These are the frequencies Rife utilized in the 1930s and which appear in the Rife laboratory book.

The following pages are produced exactly and in the order that they appear in Rife's original laboratory notes.

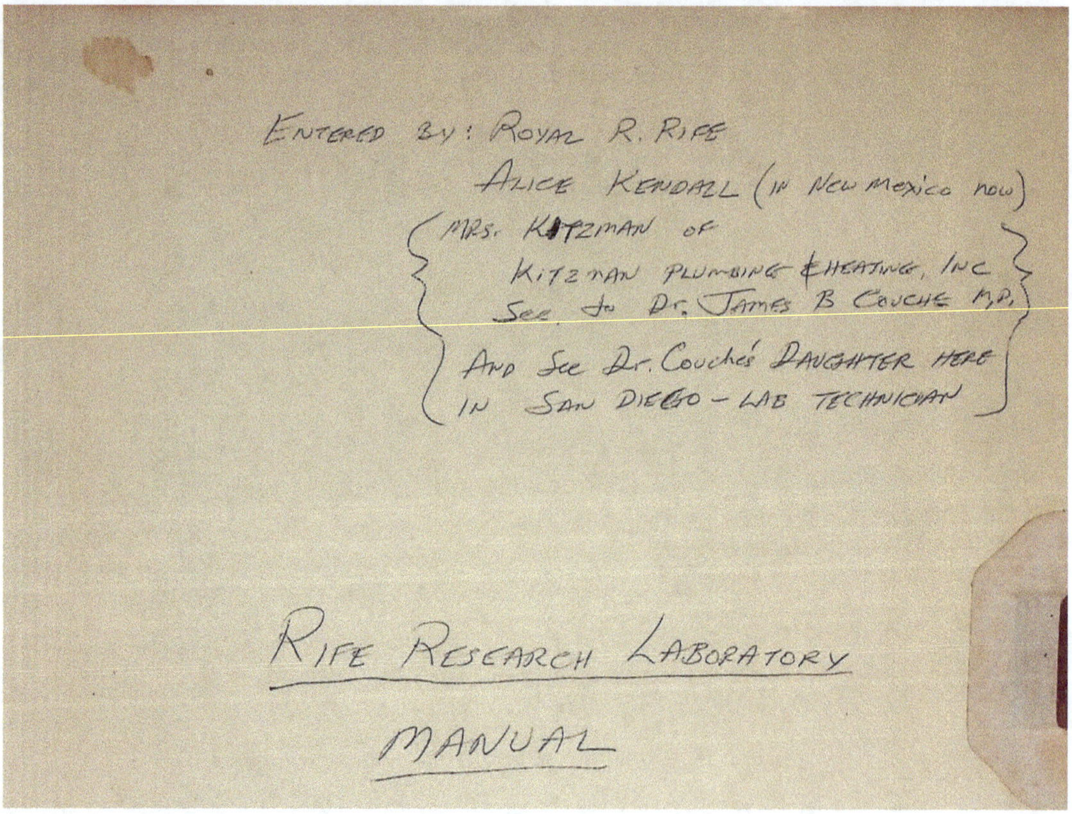

ENTERED BY: ROYAL R. RIFE
ALICE KENDALL (IN NEW MEXICO NOW)
MRS. KITZMAN OF
KITZMAN PLUMBING & HEATING, INC
SEE TO DR. JAMES B COUCHE M.D.
AND SEE DR. COUCHE'S DAUGHTER HERE
IN SAN DIEGO - LAB TECHNICIAN

RIFE RESEARCH LABORATORY
MANUAL

49

RIFE RESEARCH LABORATORY

Tumor Classification (HISTOLOGICAL)

Group I Connective tissue

(a) Fibroma composed of connective tissue
(b) Chondroma " " cartilge
(c) Chordoma " " tissue of Chorda dorsalis
(d) Osteoma " " bone
(e) Myxoma " " mucous tissue
(f) Lipoma " " fat tissue
(g) Angioma " " blood vessels
(h) Lymphoma " " lymphatic tissue
(i) Sarcoma a cellular tumor composed of anaplastic tissue of any of the above types.

Group II Muscle Tissue - Myoma And Myosarcoma

(a) Leiomyoma composed of smooth muscle tissue
(b) Rhabdomyoma " " striated " "

Group III The Elements of The Nervous System

(a) Neuroma composed of nerve fibers
(b) Neuroma ganglionare composed of nerve fibers and ganglion cells.
(c) Glioma composed of glia tissue
(d) Neuro-epithelioma composed of neuro epithelium.

Group IV Endothelium Endothelioma

Group V Endothelium, Pavement Or Glandular

(a) Papilloma a tumor of pavement epithelium, with supporting tissue in normal arrangement.
(b) Adenoma a benign tumor of glandular epithelium, with supporting tissue in normal arrangement.

RIFE RESEARCH LABORATORY

Tumor Classification (cont)

(C) Epithelioma, or Epidermoid Carcinoma a tumor of epithelium in atypical arrangement

(d) Carcinoma a tumor of glandular epithelium in atypical arrangement

Group VI Complex Tissues

(a) Simple mixed tumors composed of more than one type of neoplastic tissue, named according to composition, as chondro-epithelioma, adeno sarcoma.

(b) Teratoma composed of tissues and organs of one, two, or three germinal layers, monodermal, bidermal or tridermal types.

(c) Embryoma composed of tissues from three germinal layers in more or less orderly imitation of a fetus.

RIFE RESEARCH LABORATORY 51

Treponema Pallidum - Spirochaete of Sypilis
(Schaudin and Hoffman) (1905)
(Syphilis)

Motile
Flaggelated
Can be cultured
Length - 3.5-15.5 u : breadth - 0.33-0.5 u

Polarity
+ anode
- cathode X
Death rate in milliamperes - D.C. 80
Influence of X ray slight
" " Ultra Violet Ray none
" " Infra Red " none
Thermal death point 39½ C 24 hours
Filament voltage 10
" amperage 31
Plate voltage 307
Cycles per second 900,000
Wave length of Super regeneration of audion tube 108 Met.

RIFE RESEARCH LABORATORY 52

Baccillus Tuberculosis
(Koch) (1882)
TUBERCULOSIS

Non motile
" flaggelated
" sporogenous
" liquefying
" chromogenic
aerobic
acid resisting
Highly pathogenic
Length - 1.5 - 3.3 μ : breadth - 0.2 - 0.5 μ

Polarity
+ anode X
- cathode
Death rate in milliamperes 168
Influence of X ray none
" " Ultra Violet ray retards culture growth (5 hrs.)
" " Infra Red " slight
Thermal death point 42½ C - (24 hrs.)
Filiment voltage 9
" amperage 21
Plate voltage 1138
Cycles per second 583,000
Wave length of super regeneration of audion tube 554 meters

RIFE RESEARCH LABORATORY

Micrococcus Gonorrhea
(Neisser) (1879)
(Gonorrhea)

Non motile
" flaggelated
" sporogenous
" liquefying
" chromogenic
aerobic parasitic coccus
Pathogenic for man only
Length - 1.6μ : breadth - 0.8μ

Polarity
+ anode X
- cathode X
Death rate in milliamperes 8 3/10
Influence of X ray none
" " Ultra Violet ray slight
" " Infra Red " stimulates growth
Thermal death point 39C. (24 hrs.)
Filiment voltage 12
" amperage 40
Plate voltage 453
Cycles per second 600,000
Wave length of super regeneration of audion tube 1990 Meters

RIFE RESEARCH LABORATORY

54

Baculus Leprea
(Hansen) (1879)
(Leprosy)

Non motile
" flaggelated
" sporogenous
cultivable on special media
parasitic
acid resisting
Length – 1.4 – 3.3 μ : breadth – 0.2 – 3.5 μ

Polarity
+ anode X
– cathode

Death rate in milliamperes 53
Influence of X ray slight
" " Ultra Violet ray stops growth in lesion in 4½ hrs.
" " Infra Red " none
Filament voltage 6
" amperage 19
Plate voltage 127
Thermal death point 42 C (24 hrs)
Cycles per second 743,000
Wave length of super regeneration of audion tube 90 Meters

RIFE RESEARCH LABORATORY 55

Actinomyces Bovine
(Longenbeck) 1845 (Bollinger) 1846
(Actino mycosis)

Non motile
" flaggelated
" sporogenous
parasitic
pathogenic
aerobic and anaerobic
Long thread-like chains - 0.3 - 0.5 μ in thickness.

Polarity
+ anode X
- cathode X
death rate in milliamperes 12 2/10
Influence of X ray slight
" " Ultra Violet ray stops culture growth in 45 min.
" " Infra Red " slightly retards growth
Thermal death point 40 C (24 hrs.)
Filiment voltage 5
" amperage 16
Plate voltage 140
Cycles per second 678,000
Wave length of super regeneration of audion tube 1607 Meters

RIFE RESEARCH LABORATORY 56

Baccillus Typhosus
(Eberth) 1880 (Gaffky) 184
(Typhoid Fever)

Non liquefying
" chromogenic
" aerogenic
motile
flaggelated
aerobic and anaerobic
Length – 1.3–2.4u : breadth – 0.5–0.8u.

Polarity
+ anode
– cathode X
Death rate in milliamperes 28
Influence of X ray none
" " Ultra Violet ray stops motility in 21 min.
" " Infra Red " stops growth in culture in 50 min.
Thermal death point 39½ C. (24 hrs.)
Filiment voltage 8
" amperage 21
Plate voltage 135
Cycles per second 900,000
Wave length of super regeneration of audion tube .345 Meters.

RIFE RESEARCH LABORATORY 57

Micrococcus Catarrhalis
(Seifert) and (Kirchner) (1890)
(Catarrhal inflamation)

Small ovoid granule
non motile
" sporulating
" flaggellated
" liquefying
" chromogenic
aerobic and anaerobic
Length 2. u. : breadth 1. u.

Polarity
+ anode X
− cathode
Death rate in milliamperes 75
Influence of X ray none
" " Ultra Violet ray none
" " Infra Red " none
Thermal death point 47 C 24 hrs.
Filament voltage 9
" amperage 54
Plate voltage 700
Cycles per second 1,800,000
Wave length of super regeneration of audion tube. 175 Meters

RIFE RESEARCH LABORATORY 58

Bacillus Coli Communis
(Escherich) (1885)
(B. Coli)

Non chromogenic
" liquefying
" sporogenous
motile
flagellated
aerobic and anaerobic
Length 1.3 μ : breadth 0.4-0.7 μ

Polarity
+ anode X
- cathode none
Death rate in milliamperes [illegible] 7
Influence of X ray none
" " Ultra Violet ray stops motility in 5.3 min
" " Infra Red " slight
Thermal death point 45C 24 hrs.
Filiment amperage 21
" voltage 5
Plate " 240
Cycles per second 683,000 443
Wave length of super regeneration of audion tube 1050 Meters.

RIFE RESEARCH LABORATORY 59

Bacillus Pestis
(Yersin) and (Kitasato) 1894
(Bubonic Plague)

Non motile
" flagellated
" chromogenic
aerobic and anaerobic
minute diplococcoid
Length 1.5-2 µ ; breadth 0.5-0.75 µ

Polarity
+ anode X
- cathode X
Death rate in milliamperes 140
Influence of X ray none
" " Ultra Violet ray increases culture growth
" " Infra Red " none
Thermal death point 48 C 24 hrs.
Filiment voltage 6
" amperage 55
Plate voltage 375
Cycles per second 160,000
Wave length of super regeneration of audion tube 585 Meters.

RIFE RESEARCH LABORATORY

Bacillus Tetani 60

(Nicolaier) 1884 (Kitasato) 1889

(Tetanus)

Non chromogenic
flagellated
Sporogenic
liquefying
motile
anaerobic

Length 2.4 μ; breadth 0.3-0.5 μ

Polarity
+ anode X
− cathode X

Death rate in milliamperes 64

Influence of X ray none

" " Ultra Violet ray stops growth in 82 min

" " Infra Red " slight

Thermal death point 51 ½ C 24 hrs.

Filament voltage 6

" amperage 30

Plate voltage 140

Cycles per second 700,000

Wave length of super regeneration of audion tube 19,000 Meters.

Bacillus diphtheriae
(Klebs) 1883 (Loffler) 1884
(Diphtheria)

Non motile
" flagellated
" chromogenic
" liquefying
aerobic
purely parasitic
Length 1.5-6.5 μ : breadth .3-.8 μ

Palarity
+ anode
- cathode X
Dearth rate in milliamperes 175
Influence of X ray slight
" " Ultra Violet ray - stops culture growth in 4½ hrs.
" " Infra Red ray none
Thermal death point 45C 24 hrs.
Filiment valtage 9
" amperage 18
Plate valtage 585
Cycles per second 800,000
Wave length of super regeneration of audion tube .275 Met.

RIFE RESEARCH LABORATORY 62

Bacillus Anthracis Symptomatici
(Ballinger) and Freser) date?
(Symptomatic Anthrax)

Non chromogenic
motile
flagellated
liquefying
aerogenic
anaerobic
Length - 3.5u : breadth - 0.5 - 0.6 u.

Polarity
+ anode X
- cathode
Death rate in milliamperes 71
Influence of X ray none
" "Ultra Violet ray motility stops in 72 sec.
" " Infra Red - slight
Thermal death point 49½ C 24 hrs.
Filament voltage 5
" amperage 27
Plate voltage 224
Cycles per second 400,000
Wave length of super regeneration of audion tube 18,000

RIFE RESEARCH LABORATORY 63

Bacillus Anthracis
(Pollander) 1849 (Davaine) 1863
(Anthrax)

Non motile
" flagellated
" chromogenic
sporogenous
liquifying
Length- 5.20 μ : breadth 1-1.25 μ

Polarity
+ anode X
- cathode X
Death rate in milliamperes 75 D.C.
Influence of X ray slight
" " Ultra Violet ray stops growth in culture 2½ hrs
" " Infra Red " none
Thermal death point 45C 24 hrs.
Filament voltage 12
" amperage 48
Plate voltage 695
Cycles per second 900,000
Wave length of super regeneration of audion tube. 1100 Meters

RIFE RESEARCH LABORATORY 64

Diplococcus Pneumoniae
(Sternberg) 1880 (Pasteur) 1880
(Pneumonia)

Non motile
" flagellated
" sporogenous
" liquefying
" chromogenic
aerobic and anaerobic
slightly elongated diplococcus

Polarity
+ anode
- cathode X

Death rate in milliamperes	12
Influence of X ray	none
" " Ultra Violet ray	stops culture growth in 64 min.
" " Infra Red ray	retards growth in culture
Thermal death point	47C 24 hrs.
Filiment voltage	9
" amperage	26
Plate voltage	1100
Cycles per second	1,200,000
Wave length of super regeneration of audion tube	785 Meters.

RIFE RESEARCH LABORATORY 65

Diplococcus Intracellulous Meningitides
(Weichselbaum) 1887
(Spinal Meningitis)

Non motile
" flagellated
" sporogenous
" chromogenic
" liquifying
aerobic and anaerobic

Polarity
+ anode
- cathode X

Death rate in milliamperes	110 D.C.
Influence of X ray	none
" " Ultra Violet ray	slight
" " Infra Red "	none
Thermal death point	48C 24 hrs
Filament voltage	11
" amperage	29
Plate voltage	870
Cycles per second	927,800

Wave length of super regeneration of audion tube 167 meters

RIFE RESEARCH LABORATORY 66

Bacillus Mallei
(Loffler and Schutz) (1882)
(Glanders)

Non motile
" flagellated
" Sporogenous
" liquefying
" chromogenic
aerobic and anaerobic
Length 1.5-3μ: breadth 0.25-0.4μ

Polarity
+anode X
- cathode

Death rate in milliamperes 95
Influence of X ray none
" " Ultra Violet ray none
" " Infra Red " none
Thermal death point 50°C 24 hrs.
Filiment voltage 9
" amperage 127
Cycles per second 986,000 927= Plate voltage
Wave length of super regeneration of audion tube 407 meters.

RIFE RESEARCH LABORATORY 67

Spirillum Cholerae Asiaticae
(Koch) 1884
(Cholera Spirillum)

Motile
flagellated
liquefaying
parasitic
aerobic and anaerobic
non-sporogenous
" chromogenic

Polarity
+anode X
- cathode X
death rate in milliamperes 74
Influence of X ray none
" " Ultra Violet Ray slight
" " Infra Red " none
Thermal death point 43 C
Filament voltage 12
" amperage 26
Plate voltage 187
Cycles per second 851,000
Wave length of super regeneration of audion tube 312 met.

RIFE RESEARCH LABORATORY 68

Bacillus Typhi Murium
(Loffler) 1889
(Typhus Murium)

motile
flagellated
aerogenic
non sporogenous
" liquefying
" chromogenic

Polarity
+ anode
− cathode
Death rate in milliamperes
Influence of X ray
" " Ultra Violet ray
" " Infra Red "
Thermal death point
Filiment voltage
" amperage
Plate voltage
Cycles per second
Wave length of super regeneration of audion tube

RIFE RESEARCH LABORATORY 69

Bacillus Influenzae
(R. Pfeiffer) 1892
(Influenza)

Non motile
" flagellated
" sporogenous
" liquefying
" chromogenic
aerobic

Length 0.5 u : breadth 0.2 u

Polarity
+ anode
- cathode X

Death rate in milliamperes 120
Influence of X ray none
" " Ultra Violet ray slight in slowing growth
" " Infra Red ray none
Thermal death point 50C.
Filament voltage 11
" amperage 7
Plate voltage 250
Cycles per second 1,674,000
Wave length of super regeneration of audion tube 154 met.

RIFE RESEARCH LABORATORY 70

Koch-Weeks Bacillus
(Koch) and (Weeks) 1895
Contagious Conjunctivitis

non motile
" flagellated
" sporogenous
" liquefying
" chromogenic
aerobic and anaerobic
Length - 1.2 μ : breadth 0.25 μ

Polarity
+ anode X
- cathode X
Death rate in milliamperes 89 D.C.
Influence of X ray none
" " Ultra Violet ray none
" " Infra Red " none
Thermal death point 42 C.
Filament voltage 12
" amperage 8
Plate voltage 900
Cycles per second 1,206,000
Wave length of super regeneration of audion tube 148 meters

Staphylococcus Pyogenes Aureus
(Rosenbach)
(Staphylococcus)

Non motile
" flagellated
" sporogenous
liquifying
chromogenic
aerobic and anaerobic
diameter - 0.7 μ

Polarity
+ anode
- cathode X
death rate in milliamperes 89 D.C.
Influence of X ray none
" " Ultra Violet ray retards growth in culture
" " Infra Red ray stimulates " " "
Thermal death point 40 C.
Filament voltage 12
" amperage 18
Plate voltage 1,100
Cycles per second 998,740
Wave length of super regeneration of audion tube 540 meters

RIFE RESEARCH LABORATORY 72

Streptococcus Pyogenes
(Rosenbach) date?

Streptococcus

Non motile
" flagellated
" sporogenous
" liquifying
" chromogenic
aerobic and anaerobic
diameter – 0.4 – 1 u

Polarity
+ anode X
– cathode

Death rate in milliamperes 120 D.C.
Influence of X ray none
" " Ultra Violet ray retards growth in culture
" " Infra red ray none
Plate voltage 921
Filiment voltage 8
" amperage 9
Cycles per second 1,241,000
Wave length of super regeneration of audion tube 142 met.
Thermal death point 50 C.

RIFE RESEARCH LABORATORY 73

Bacillus Typhosus Filterable virus:
Rife & (Kendall) 1932 passes W: K medium

motile small ovoid granule
highly plastic
visible only with monochromatic light
angle of refraction 4.8—
color by chemical refraction turquoise blue
length. breadth

Polarity
+anode X
– cathode

Death rate in milliamperes 128. D.C.
Influence of X ray none
" " Ultra Violet ray slows motility
" " Infra Red " none
Thermal death point 41C 24 hrs.
Filiment voltage 11
Plate voltage 1,100
Cycles per second 9,680,000
Wave length of super regeneration of audion tube 21½ met.
Filiment amperage 49

RIFE RESEARCH LABORATORY 74

Bacillus Coli Filterable virus

R.Sc.X (Kendall) 1932 passes W: K medium

motile ovoid granule
highly plastic
visable only with monochromatic light
angle of refraction 7° +
color by chemical refraction dark brown
length: breadth

Polarity
+ anode X
– cathode X
death rate in milliamperes 86. DC.
Influence of X ray none
" " Ultra Violet ray none
" " Infra Red " stimulates growth
Thermal death point 43 C 24 hrs.
Filiment voltage 12
" amperage 30
Plate voltage 980
Cycles per second 8,581,000
Wave length of super regeneration of audion tube. 27 Meters.

RIFE RESEARCH LABORATORY 75

Streptococcus Poliomyelitis Filterable virus
Rife &? (Rosenow) 1932 passes N
Chick infusion broth

non motile spherical granule
highly plastic
visable only with mono chromatic light
angle of refraction 8.3+
color by chemical refraction Redish Brown
length breadth

Polarity
+ anode
− cathode
death rate in milliamperes
Influence of X ray
" " Ultra violet ray
" " Infra Red "
Thermal death point
Filiment voltage
" amperage
Plate voltage
Cycles per second
Wave length of regeneration of audion tube

51

RIFE RESEARCH LABORATORY

76

Research On Baccillus "X"

The B. X was isolated from ten differant cases of Breast Carcinoma by Dr. R. R. Rife at the Rife Reseatch Laboratory in San Diego (Point Loma) California. It was carried through forty four transplants on "K" media in all ten instances.

The technique used in the isolation of this organism is, in brief, as follows; Blocks of tissue, taken under the most sterile conditions, were transfered into "K" media (previously examined for sterility). These were then placed under the direct influence of an argon filled gas tube, working under five thousand volts, for twenty four hours; then were placed in water baths, with two inches of vaccum, and incubated at 37.5° C. At this time the delicate shine of growth is noticeable. From this point on as many as desired transplants can be be made without repeating the foregoing operations.

The "B" X" is a filterable virus which filters through the W Berkfeld filter. It is a small ovoid granule, highly plastic, and visable only with mono chromatic light. The angle of refraction is 12 3/10 — and the color by chemical refraction is purple red. The length of the organism is 1/15 u and its breadth—1/20 u. It carries an attraction to the cathode pole. Its death rate in milliamperes is 175 d.c. The X ray and Infra Red have no influence on the organism but the Ultra Violet ray slows up its motility. The thermal death point is 42°C for 24 hours, the filiment voltage is 10, and the filiment amperage is 86. The plate voltage is 928, and its electronic oscillating rate is 11,780,000 cycles per second. The wave length of super regeneration of Audion tube is 17 6/10 meters.

RIFE RESEARCH LABORATORY

Research On Baccillus X (continued)

An innoculative serum was prepared by combining in a mixture, the transplants from the ten original growths with a 20 to 1 dilution of normal saline solution.

On Aug 3, 1933 1/10 CC. of the above serum was innoculated into the breasts of two sets of white rats. One set consisting of two pregnant females with one control, and the other of two young females and one control. The serum was injected directly under the epidermus of the breasts. The animals had been kept in quaranteen for a period of ninety days and were normal in every respect at time of innoculation. Seven days later the innoculated rats developed lesions (superficial) in the thyroid region and on the shoulders. These lesions varied in size and severity on succeeding days. The controls remained normal. On Aug 21, the control of the pregnant female set gave birth to two young; one died. The delivery of the innoculated pregnant females was still delayed, and the temperatures of all the innoculated animals rose from 1 to $1\frac{1}{2}$° F. The lesions increased in area and density, and one focus in particular was decidedly excavated. On Aug 22 one of the infected rats presented 5 young, and the other until this day has remained barren, the swelling of the abdomen which evidentally was occupied by the young having gone down and returned to normal. In the offspring of the infected mother, two developed the identical type of lesions on the surface of the thyroid region. One of these grew otherwise normally and in the other the growth was stunted. The latter developed a severe growth on the upper portion of the right side of the jaw which consumed most of the normal tissue. The teeth were badly malformed, and grew very long, curving inward and deep into the throat. These were shortened by surgical operation. During this entire period the controls

53

RIFE RESEARCH LABORATORY

Research On Baccillus "X" (continued) 78

c. remained normal. x

On Aug. 28x a set of male rats consisting of the same number were innoculated as in the females. The same type of epidermal faci develaped, the control remaining normal. On Sept. 5, one of the males was posted and revealed no pathology. A lesion was exised from the shoulder of the other ~~infected~~ innoculated male.* On Sept. 14, the Baccillus "X" was recovered and identified in the media. The lesions on all the innoculated rats vary in size and density from day to day and in some cases clear up and break out in other portions of the epidermus.

*tissue placed in "K" media and run through the original method of technique.

RIFE RESEARCH LABORATORY

Research On Baccillus "X" (continued) 79

It has been demonstrated by experiment that the B. X exists in two cycles, which may be classified as forms A and B. Form A applies to B.X in its ultra filterable cycle. In this stage the organisms theoretically exist in malignant tissue. Examination of the fresh filtrate preperation of malignant tissue under 20,000X magnification, using any known system of illumination, fails to reveal the precence of living bodies

However, after a special method of cultivation, involving the use of the Argon Ray and Vaccum conditions, the afore mentioned filtrate in K medium contains swarming myriads of the visable cycle - form B. The B.X in this form may be seen under 17,000X magnification (using monochromatic illumination) as a highly plastic ovoid granule - purple-red in color.

Since experiments show that the Baccillus X in form A exists in malignant tissue, it is theoretically possible to change its cycle to form B by application of the Argon Ray and Vaccum conditions. After the cycle change has been accomplished (in theory), the application of the osocillatine ray at a cycles per second vibration of 11,780,000 should completly destroy the B.X in the malignant tissue.

RIFE RESEARCH LABORATORY Sarcoma 80

Operation And Investigation Of Tumors In White Rats (2/14/4)

The tumor was located beneath the epithelial tissue covering the left side of the chest.

The duration of the operation was 55 minutes; during which time the animal was under ether anesthesia.

The tumor weighed 60g. and was of the Lipoma type. It was removed under sterile conditions and placed in glycerine immediatly after the operation.

Three portions of tissue was removed from the center of the tumor. A tube of sterile "K" media was innoculated with one portion. Another was sent to Dr. Foord for histological examination, and the third was ground in a sterile mortar containing sterile normal saline solution. The contents of the morter was next passed thru a Berkfeld "W" filter and examined under 11,000 X magnification.

The fresh filtrate under the microscope revealed numerous ovoid granules, purplish red in color, and resembling the B.X in morphology. The organisms are non-motile.

RIFE RESEARCH LABORATORY 81

Bacillus X (Cancer) Carcinoma
(Rife) 11-20-32

Filterable Virus: Passes W: K Medium

motile small ovoid granule
highly plastic
visable only with mono chromatic light
angle of refraction 12 3/10
color by chemical refraction Purple-red
length - 1/15 u : breadth 1/20 u

Polarity
+ anode
- cathode X
Death rate in milliamperes 175 D.C.
Influence of X ray none
" " Ultra Violet ray slows motility
" " Infra Red - none
Thermal death point 42C. 24 hrs.
Filiment voltage 10
" amperage 86
Plate voltage 928
Cycles per second 11,780,000
Wave length of super regeneration of audion tube 17 6/10 met.

RIFE RESEARCH LABORATORY 82

Herpes Encephalitis Filterable virus
(Rosenow) 1932 passes N
brain broth infusion

non motile
highly plastic
visable only with mono chromatic light
angle of refraction 14-
color by chemical refraction Brilliant Choral Pink
length breadth

Polarity
+ anode
– cathode
Death rate in milleamperes
Influence of X ray
" " Ultra violet ray
" " Infra Red "
Thermal death point
Filiment voltage
" amperage
Plate voltage
Cycles per second
Wave length of super regeneration of Audion tube

RIFE RESEARCH LABORATORY

Solution For "K" Media

Tyrode Solution

NaCl	8.0 grams
KCl	0.2 "
$CaCl_2$	0.2 "
$MgCl_2$	0.1 "
Na_2HPO_4	0.05 "
H_2O (distilled)	1,000 c.c.

Add sufficient $NaHCO_3$ to bring reaction of finished medium to PH 7.4

K(dry) 0.50 – 200 mg. use 6 c.c. tyrode

Locke Solution

NaCl	9.0 grams
KCl	0.42 "
$CaCl_2$	0.24 "
$NaHCO_3$	0.1 "

I

R. R. Rife

I have never made claims or statements that virus was the causitive agent in cancer. But I know it is. I have isolated it directly and produaced it back into the experimental animals and produced all the symptoms of the disease. We recovered from the resulting tumor all the true pathology of neoplastic tissue.

The therpy that I have experimented with is electronic frequency. That ismerely a transition frequency. It is the same frequency as the bacteria. The frequency of each bacteria is absolutely individual. They run through a very large goumet. Some of them are very broad, and long, some not so short. None of them are what we call ultea-short wave, that I have found as yet.

I do not say that every frequency that I have found through the field of photogenic organism is a true frequency. There is a possibility that many of those are harmonics.

I have in my file over 20,000 tissue section slides. They do not amount to much as far as the virus of cancer is concerned. They show something, but they do not give the virus of cancer. Later I found it.

When I first started work on this thing, way back in 1921, it was my presumption that when the causitive agent of malignancy would be found, it would be found to be caused by micro-organism; and not unlikely a so-called non-pathogenic organism which we have with us at all times.

I developed the first microscope for the work of studying these tissues. In our microscope we use a rotating wedge-shapped quartz prisms. As the intense needly point beem of light is passed thru the condenser and up into the optical system of the microscope, we rotate the prisms at different degrees of refraction. In this way we produce a frequency of light that is in coordination with the chemical consitituents of the virus under observation. This is the same as polarized light, but it is not polarized light. We cannot use polarized light for it takes in everything. We segregate that down with what we term a variable mono-cromatic beam. In this way we find the proper color or index of light refraction, and we bend that beam thru its angle until we find a frequency that shows this virus in its own true chemical characteristics. We find its predominate chemical factor and its radicals.

We work on only the predominate of course, because that is the one we see. ~~So we put the filterable form of the~~

We come back to the field of species again. With my best methods and techniques of staining I had found nothing. Then by using the "K" media made of a tyrode solution which is a basic nine elements of salt and pig-gut dessicated and de-hydrated. This media has a faculty of transforming micro-organisms into what we term the transitional state. In this particular state after 36 hours we found granular particles that are a virus from this organism, free swimming in the state. We also found them in the ends of the rod forms, so that they will refract to a proper color of index light refraction. We know that we can transplant this culture

III

from one to the other back and forth thru our berkfelt filters, and we can produce the symptioms of cancer. But we do not see the virus. In the transitional state it sheds virus. The virus will produce cancer.

We work on only the predominate one of course, because that is the one we see. We put the filterable form of the bacillus typhosus, as an example, under the microscope. We set the prisms at eht proper degree of refraction for that particular chemical constituent of the virus and the micro-organism is brought into focus. This material has gone thru a triple filteration of "W" berkfield filters. It is just like a drop of dew, but we see there beautiful terquoise blue bodies swimming thru the field brilliantly. If we turn the prisms 1/10 of a degree we have a perfectly blank field. The bacillus typhosus produces the turquoise color.

If we put the filterable form of the colon bacillus which belongs to the same group as the bacillus typhosus, and there we have a redish brown hue. When we put the b-x, or cancer virus as we callit, we see a pruplish red organism that is highly motile.

Now if the bacteria that we are isolating is from a motile organism the virus is always motile. For instance you take the virus of T.B. It is non-motile; because its a non-motile organism.

When we take b-x that was isolated directly from an unulcerated breast mass, put it into the animal, and we recover the organism back again. If we can do it a hundred times consecutuvely with the same technique then it may mean something. After the 100 consecutive times it can be placed on the records.

Now we alter the media. We no longer have what we call a b-x. We have a b-y. This will no longer pass the "W" berkfeld filers. We use a much courser percocity known as the the N. This is like either a dyatomis or a porchiline filter.

If we alter the media again we see a mono-cocoid organism. This organism can be seen with a good research microscope. With the proper staining method. We stain this organism. We find it only in the mono-cites of the blood. The monocites are the only other cells which have no figiscitosis. When we

When we alter the media once again we come from the fluid media into out hard base media. We use either asparagus or tomato with our agur. Asparagus is better. We no longer have a b-x or a b-y. but we have a cryptomyses pleomorphium fungi, with all its 14 stages, clear from the original highfee form the spores and asca-spores, on down the line. Any one of these can be thrown back in 24 hours into a b-x by putting it back on a "K" media, capabable of producing the disease.

If we allow the cryptomoses pleomorphium to stand for a period of metastasis, one year, as a dormant stock culture, there have been cases where when planted back to its own individual asparagus base media, we no longer have a crypto-mysis, plagomorphium fungi, or a b-x or a b-y, or a mono-cocoid organis. We do have with every known lab test in the world, a coli bacillus, or an organism that was isolated from an unulcerated human breast mass.

I worked a great deal on tuberculosis. I isolated a virus from t.b. which I consider is what is here-to-fore known as "Poison molecule of Vohn" which was isolated some thirty years ago by Vohn of Ann Arbor. He did not isolate the organism but he isolated a chemical particule. Koch originally isolated the virus of t.b. He produced the vacines and anti-toxines that would kill the bacilli of t.b., but would kill the specimin also. Simply because with any known method of means that you release from this t.b. virus you release this so-called poison monicule of Vohns. It reacts upon the dead bodies of the rod form of t.b. and produces toximia and death.

We finally found an electronic frequency that we were experimenting with that would kill these bacteria. We found the frequency of the virus of t.b and we found the frequency of the rod form of t.b. which we had known for several years. We found that if we used the two of them simultaneously, or one right after the other, over the same carrier wave, that the patient got well. and the guina pig got well, but if we used either frequency individually we either killed the animal or we did nothing. They must be used together.

There are several information services on the Internet that give a very skewed and less than accurate account of the work of Royal Rife. One source states that Rife purportedly built a microscope, but nobody could understand what they were viewing. They go on to say that there were some strange colors that nobody could identify. We include a few original letters from Rife's files that should provide a good indication at what the true experts believed about the Universal Microscope of Royal Rife.

MANUFACTURERS OF
HIGH GRADE
OPTICAL INSTRUMENTS

SPENCER
BUFFALO
U.S.A.

Spencer Lens Company

Factory, Buffalo, N. Y., U. S. A.

SOUTHERN CALIFORNIA BRANCH:
605-6 BEAUX ARTS BUILDING
1709 WEST EIGHTH STREET
LOS ANGELES, CALIFORNIA

PHONE: DUNKIRK 7575

LOS ANGELES, CALIFORNIA.
November 27, 1931

Mr. Roy R. Rife
712 Electric Bldg.
San Diego, Calif.

Dear Mr. Rife:

Just a short personal line to tell you that you have made a very favorable impression on the scientific people in and around Los Angeles. We recently heard about a demonstration that you made at the California Institute of Technology and many of my friends connected with the educational institutions have spoken to me about the demonstration. It certainly has them all "agog."

I also wish to extend to you my sincere thanks for the very kind interview and time that you gave to a very dear friend of mine, namely, Dr. Charles Chamberlain of the University of Chicago. Dr. Chamberlain is well liked and loved by all who know him and you have made an old man very, very happy.

With kindest personal regards, and assuring you of my best wishes for your success, I am,

Yours sincerely,

Lyle D. Potter

LDP-GEA

UNIVERSITY OF CALIFORNIA
THE GEORGE WILLIAMS HOOPER FOUNDATION
SECOND AND PARNASSUS AVENUES
SAN FRANCISCO

March 6,1934.

Dr. R. R. Ryfe,
708 Electric Building,
San Diego, Calif.

Dear Dr. Ryfe:

I am still "dreaming" about the many things you were kind enough to show me last Saturday. As soon as I can tear myself loose I will accept the privilege of coming back and bringing with me some of the agents which produce disease. The tumor which I brought with me in the two rats is Hyde 256 carcinoma. I hope it will be of some use to you.

With kindest regards and best wishes, I am,

Sincerely yours,

K. F. Meyer

C O P Y

UNIVERSITY OF CALIFORNIA
The George Williams Hooper Foundation
The Medical Center
SAN FRANCISCO

October 18, 1935

Dear Doctor Johnson,

The copy of the results of your test of the Rife ray on typhoid organisms would appear to establish conclusively the efficiency of it to kill these organisms in the tissues. If the ray should prove equally efficient in killing other pathogenic microorganisms, it would be the greatest discovery in the history of therapeutic medicine.

I have obtained material from one breast carcinoma, from which the cultures were negative for Cryptomyces. The tumor was diagnosed by the pathologist as a scirrhus (fibro-) carcinoma, and may not have been a suitable case. I will discuss with you this case and the whole matter when you come up next week.

Doctor Meyer is ill, and we have been fearful that he had contracted a laboratory infection with some of the diseases he is working. However, this morning his temperature is down and he is feeling better.

Yours truly,

E. L. Walker (Signed)

PART 2

The Nemescope of Elmer Nemes

Who Was Elmer Nemes?

Very little information exists concerning Dr. Elmer Nemes. What we can share are small bits and pieces of his life as reported in publications. Note the conflicting accounts of his death. The following quotes were taken from *Science & Mechanics* magazine and *Magnets* magazine.

"Dr. Elmer P. Nemes, a 44-year-old Hungarian-born physician presently living in Beverly Hills, Calif."

"The inventor of the Nemescope was a brilliant brain surgeon. His name was Elmer P. Nemes and he ran the Nemes Research Laboratories, 4207 West Third Street, Los Angeles, California during the middle 1950's. Unfortunately, he was also an alcoholic. He was killed in a drunken brawl in San Diego in the early 60's – he had hit rock bottom, and stayed there."

"The person responsible for revealing this story to me is the grand lady of health and nutrition, Betty Lee Morales, 80, a longtime resident of Topanga and an individual with unbridled curiosity who has been involved in thousands of research projects during her lifetime. She and her husband were directly responsible for the remarkable photographs from the Nemescope screen, that you see on these pages, and her incessant curiosity spurred the inventor to extra efforts."

"We lost track of the stolen machine in New York," Betty Lee explained, "and the technology has lain dormant all this time."

"Who stole the machine? What role did the secretive segments of the United States government play? Betty Lee herself was involved with the Central Intelligence Agency in its earliest years after WWII, and while representing Dr. Nemes she worked directly with the late Congressman Craig Sheperd of San Bernardino, who had arranged a major appropriation for in-depth and clandestine research on the Nemescope just prior to its theft and subsequent disappearance."

"Research and development of a microscope of the type discussed was carried out by Dr Elmer Pierre Nemes during the 1941 to 1964 timeframe. Unfortunately, he met with an untimely death and left behind research records which are both incomplete and severely lacking in detail."

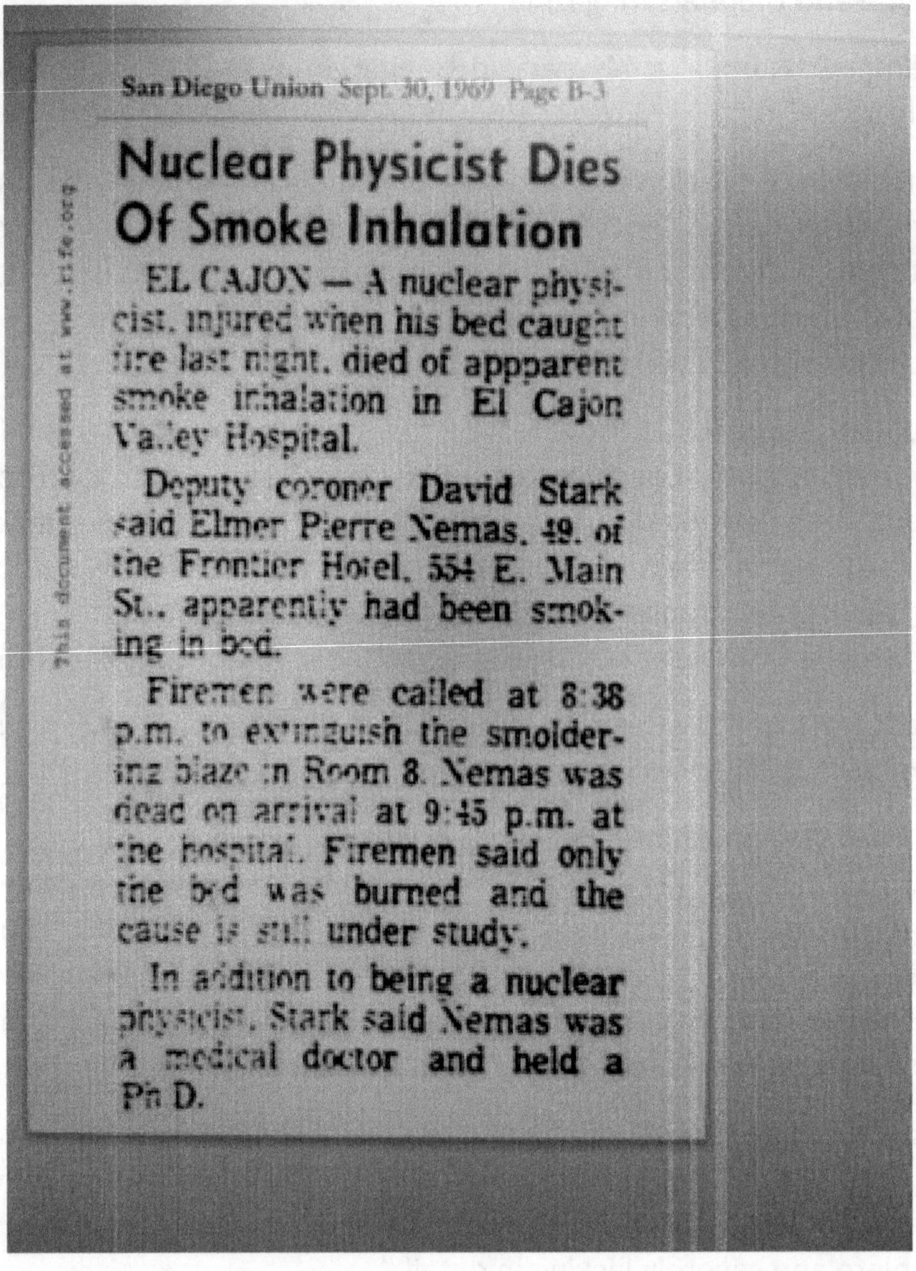

San Diego Union Sept. 30, 1969 Page B-3

Nuclear Physicist Dies Of Smoke Inhalation

EL CAJON — A nuclear physicist, injured when his bed caught fire last night, died of appparent smoke inhalation in El Cajon Valley Hospital.

Deputy coroner David Stark said Elmer Pierre Nemas, 49, of the Frontier Hotel, 554 E. Main St., apparently had been smoking in bed.

Firemen were called at 8:38 p.m. to extinguish the smoldering blaze in Room 8. Nemas was dead on arrival at 9:45 p.m. at the hospital. Firemen said only the bed was burned and the cause is still under study.

In addition to being a nuclear physicist, Stark said Nemas was a medical doctor and held a Ph D.

This document accessed at www.rife.org

The Nemescope Built by Elmer Nemes

The following articles appeared in Science & Mechanics magazine published in January 1964 and Magnets magazine published in September 1986. Both articles had a brief background on Elmer Nemes as well as discussing some of the mechanical and scientific aspects of his Nemescope.

The intent of this publication is to share the photographs taken through the Nemescope and preserved in the Nemes Laboratory notebook. The book of photographs is in the possession of the author, Steven A. Ross, who received the book from Betty Lee Morales, a close friend of Nemes and in prior possession of the photographs.

MAGNETS
New Racing Engine Kit from FORD!
SCIENCE
& MECHANICS
NEW
Hot-as-Sun
Fuel for
Star Travel!
PHILCO'S
AMAZING
GUN-AIMING
HELMET!
FIRST
Photos of
the Atom!
The Wonderful
Manure Battery!
AIM BY LOOKING!
FIRE BY BLINKING!
Make a Power
Tool from a
Food Mixer!

By David Legerman

FIRST PHOTOS OF THE ATOM!

A REVOLUTIONARY new scientific instrument has been invented that penetrates to the heart of matter, the atom, and photographs it in color! The incredible microscope is called the Nemescope, and it is the culmination of years of research by Dr. Elmer P. Nemes, a 44-year-old Hungarian-born physician presently living in Beverly Hills, Calif. Prior to the development of the Nemescope, the most powerful magnifying instrument known to science was the electron microscope. But this has several drawbacks, not the least of which is that it produces black-and-white or grey shadow photos with very little internal structure shown. The

This incredible microscope can photograph atoms, viruses, and enzymes to show inner structure

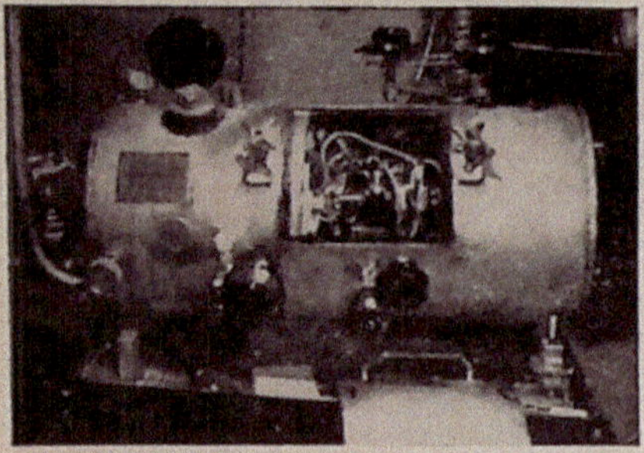

PROTOTYPE of Nemescope is tank-like case shielded with lead. Side lid slides back to reveal the second stage and specimen area.

electron microscope has an effective magnification of about 60,000X which can be further magnified photographically. However, there is no penetration of the structure of the examined material; nothing can be seen inside the surface. The Nemescope, which uses a ray of much shorter length than the electron, possibly below even the neutron range, gives beautiful penetration and resolution of internal structure.

The new microscope costs a fraction of the electron microscope and requires specimen preparation no more complicated than that required by a simple optical microscope. In addition to producing photographs of subatomic structure in color, the Nemescope can also project the image on a screen or reproduce it via television.

The secret of the Nemescope begins with the theory that if you can cause radiation of any substance, it will emit an image that can be converted to light, magnified, and photo-

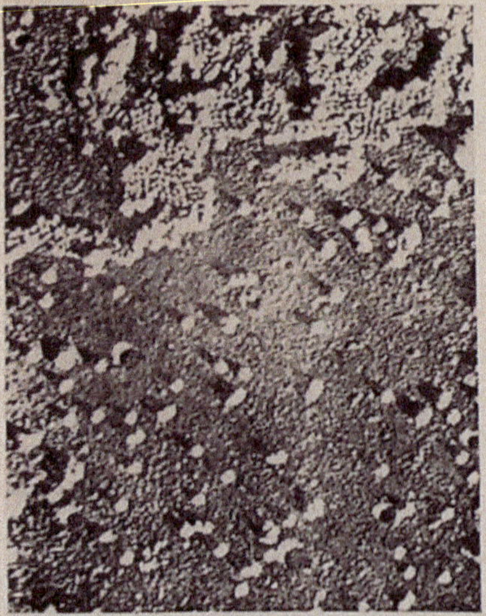

POLIO VIRUS photographed by electron microscope shows what appears to be solid beads, no internal structure. Photo is black/white.

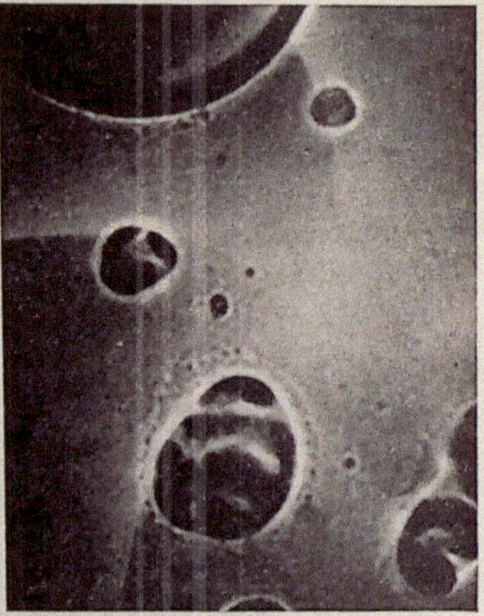

NEMESCOPE PHOTO (original in color) shows internal structure of polio virus. Chain of dots around oval mass are the basic toxins.

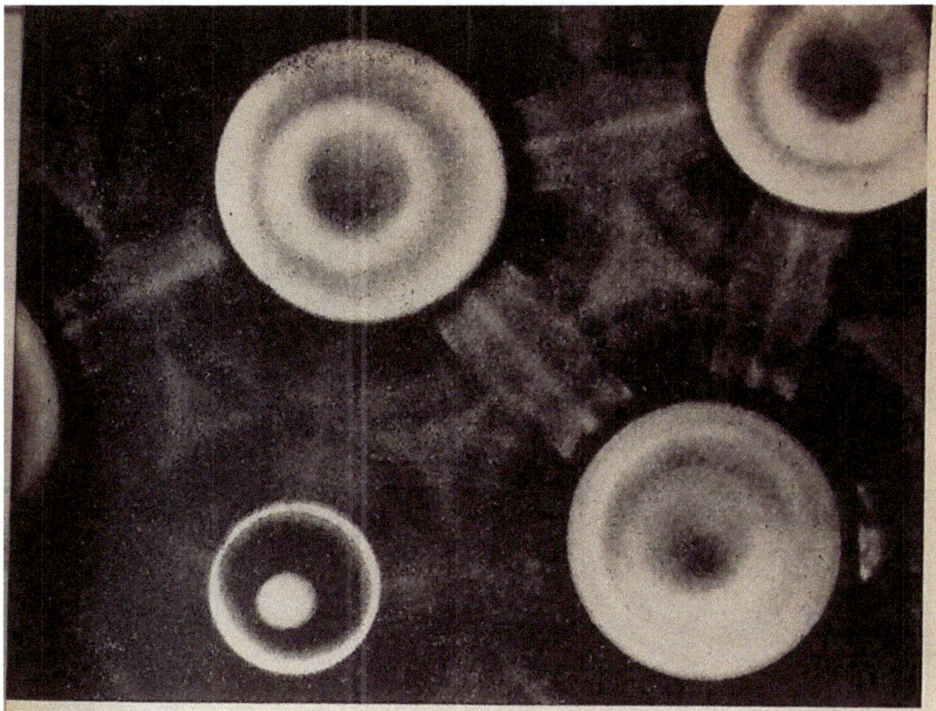

REMARKABLE resemblance to Rutherford model of the atom is shown in this photo of iron atomic and molecular grouping. Note "energy lines" extending from atoms' nuclei.

graphed in color corresponding to its spectrum characteristics. Any solid, liquid, or gas could be excited by radioactivity in this manner and would respond by emitting at its own resonance frequency an image in true color, form, and spectrum.

Working on this theory, Dr. Nemes constructed his first model, a tank-like case shielded with lead that was a maze of knobs, wires, pipes, and cables. At first all controls were hand-manipulated, but the Nemescope is now ready for electrically driven controls with motors that have recorded movement intervals of 1/75,000th of an inch.

A full explanation of how this remarkable instrument works would take many pages (it includes more than 20 original patents) but here is a brief outline:

1. The first unit is a cold cathode lamp with multiple units separately charged. The filaments are preheated by an input of 18 volts amplified to 608 volts at the emitting end. This cathode gun acts as the primary source of illumination and bombarder of the specimen to be examined.

2. The second unit is a condenser under vacuum with molecular nitrogen injected. In the condenser circuit are placed two radium guns each yielding 5,400,000 electron volts. The condenser includes a coil which carries by interchangeable switch from 240 megacycles to 35,000 megacycles in magnitron arrangement which hits the specimen to agitate or excite the molecular structure.

3. The resulting stream of energy is converted into light in the front orthicon tube, actually consisting of two tubes which pick up resonance frequencies in the high ranges. After amplification, the imaging orthicon emits a picture on the screen in color corresponding to the nature of the substance under examination.

Results obtained with the Nemescope have been no less than astounding. In 1955, working with patients in the hospitals of Mexico

(*Continued on page* 120)

ASSEMBLE THIS ALL BAND BATTERY SHORT WAVE RADIO FOR $9.95!

LISTEN AROUND THE WORLD—UP TO 12,000 MILES AWAY! Ships, Aircraft, Voice of America, Russia, London, Australia, Amateur, Citizens, Police—Also USA Broadcast. 5 WAVEBANDS ½ to 40 MC Calibrated tuning dial. Wt. only 3 lbs. WONDERFUL FOR EVERYONE. SEND ONLY $2.00 (cash, ck, M.O.) and pay postman $7.95 C.O.D. postage or send $9.95 for P.P. delivery. Complete Basic Kit includes all parts less tubes. EZ Instructions. Order yours now. Available only from:
WESTERN RADIO Dept. BRW-1 KEARNEY, NEBR.

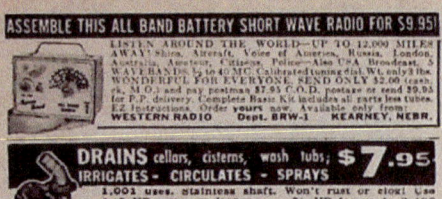

DRAINS cellars, cisterns, wash tubs; $7.95
IRRIGATES - CIRCULATES - SPRAYS

1,001 uses. Stainless shaft. Won't rust or clog! Use 1/6 HP motor or larger . . . ¾ HP for up to 2,400 GPH; 450 GPH 80' high; or 1800 GPH from 25' well. 1" inlet; ¾" outlet. Coupling included free. . $7.95
HEAVY DUTY BALL-BEARING PUMP. Up to 5,200 GPH; or 3,000 GPH from 25' well. 1¼" inlet; 1" outlet. $12.95
Postpaid if cash with order. MONEY BACK GUARANTEE
Centrifugal and Gear Pumps in All Sizes
LABAWCO PUMPS, Belle Mead 31, New Jersey

Shrinks Hemorrhoids New Way Without Surgery Stops Itch – Relieves Pain

For the first time science has found a new healing substance with the astonishing ability to shrink hemorrhoids and to relieve pain — without surgery.

In case after case, while gently relieving pain, actual reduction (shrinkage) took place.

Most amazing of all — results were so thorough that sufferers made astonishing statements like "Piles have ceased to be a problem!"

The secret is a new healing substance (Bio-Dyne®)—discovery of a world-famous research institute.

This substance is now available in *suppository* or *ointment form* under the name *Preparation H®*. Ask for it at all drug counters.

STORIES FOR MEN

A book of the most fantastic stories, photos and illustrations you've ever seen; at least not since you used to pass them along on typewritten pages back in the "good old days". Straight from the rare originals with every detail intact, every description vivid! Your complete satisfaction guaranteed!

- MIDGET & THE DUCHESS
- YOUNG LADY & HER DOG
- I WAS CAPTIVE TO SIX WOMEN
- DAY WITH TRAVELING SALESMAN and many others,

SENSATIONAL BARGAIN PRICE $1.98 ppd
LIMITED EDITION
Rush cash, check or M.O. Sorry no COD's.

PRIVATE EDITIONS
BOX 69856, DEPT. B-21
LOS ANGELES 69, CALIFORNIA

First Photos of Atom

(*Continued from page 69*)

City, Dr. Nemes succeeded in making pictures of cells from the blood and urine of cancer patients which established a relationship between human cancer and a virus.

In 1957, enzyme battery research started by Dr. Nemes resulted in another breakthrough when for the first time enzymes were resolved under a microscope. Through the Nemescope enzymes can be classified and identified. When we realize that enzymes are the chemical catalysts of living matter and that viruses share with bacteria the responsibility for most infectious diseases, a microscope that will enable man to study more closely these ultra-microscopic substances is indeed a boon to mankind.

Another exciting discovery made by the Nemescope is in the field of metallurgy. Behavior of metallic alloys under bombardment by the Nemescope has indicated that the present makeup of widely used alloys must be revised and new techniques developed to insure more stable bonding elements. Where the electron microscope showed perfect molecular alignment, Nemescope photos showed fault lines and distinct weaknesses among bonding elements.

Metal failure of hull welds or pipe welds may have been the cause of the sinking of the *Thresher*. It's obvious that a closer look at the behavior of metals in the atomic or molecular regions must be made. The Nemescope, with its great magnifying and resolving powers, will probably furnish the answers to these questions, as well as the answers to how materials behave when exposed to vacuum, ions and electrons, and the electromagnetic radiation known to exist in outer space.

Nemescope photos of the structure of the atomic nucleus are beautiful in their resolution. Perhaps the most surprising and exciting sight is how the atomic particles are connected by "force lines" or bands of energy. Nemescope photos of sub-atomic structure have an amazing similarity to Rutherford models of the atom—those three-dimensional models of vari-colored balls held together with pencil-thin rods. Leukemia particles and the common cold virus, when photographed by the Nemescope in full color, have a precision of structure that can, perhaps, be appreciated only by a research scientist or laboratory technician.

What lies ahead for this revolutionary

microscope? Of all the wonders of the sub-atomic world it has revealed, perhaps none is more important than the enzyme battery work mentioned above.

Nemescope research has determined that certain classes of enzymes can withstand radiation of 50 to 100 R or more. Theoretically, the harmful effects of radiation could be controlled by enzymatic protective radiation.

But more important, the particle energy for enzymes is not only radiation resistant but it is directly charged with the total amount of energy created artificially through bombardment under the Nemescope. By storing and converting this energy, it is possible to release it for use to create heat, electricity, or a harmless radiation.

Looking ahead, we may anticipate a new, golden age of low-cost, sub-atomic energy for the underdeveloped areas of the world that cannot afford the high cost of atomic or hydroelectric systems.

And some day, space ships traveling on enzyme power may take us to the stars, thanks to a remarkable new instrument of earth-bound science—the Nemescope. ■

Shoot Where You Look

(*Continued from page 75*)

to the system is a device that picks up the movements of the human head and the more delicate movements of the eyes and translates them electronically into instructions to guns and rockets. Invisible infra-red light is reflected from the cornea of the eye. As the eye moves, the light is reflected at varying angles which can be measured. The resulting information is fed into a weapons control system. Reaction time is cut from the conventional two seconds to one fifth of a second.

If both eyes could be instrumented, says Walter Wasserman, manager of Philco's Bio Technology Laboratory, there is no reason why human vision couldn't be used as a range finder. In other words, wear an aiming helmet, focus on a far-off object, and the distance would be computed automatically.

Connect this with miniaturized electronic controls in your car, for instance, and many highway accidents would become things of the past. This is merely one of the intriguing possibilities of this fascinating development that integrates man and machine. ■

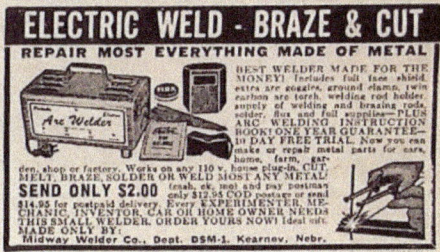

CLOGGED SEWERS

SAVE COSTLY PLUMBING REPAIR

PATENTED CUTTERS CLEANS 1" TO 12" PIPE with Power

★ FREE BOOK Tells How To Clean All Drains

Valuable advice on removing Roots, Grease, Detergent, Rags in TOILETS, SINKS, URINALS, BATHTUBS, SHOWERS, HOUSE-TO-STREET SEWERS, SEPTIC LINES. Get rid of foul odors. Do your own rodding or start your own Business. Receive FREE SKETCH of Plumbing Pipeline in average Building. Save Plumbing Bills. Tear this Ad out now and write your address beside it for helpful FREE BOOK on Power and Hand Units. No Agent will Call. (Chicago Phone Kildare 5-1702) MILLER SEWER ROD, DEPT. SR, 4642 N. CENTRAL AVE., CHICAGO 30, ILL.

ELECTRIC WELD - BRAZE & CUT

REPAIR MOST EVERYTHING MADE OF METAL

BEST WELDER MADE FOR THE MONEY! Includes full face shield, extra arc goggles, ground clamp, twin carbon arc torch, welding rod holder, supply of welding and brazing rods, solder, flux and full supplies—PLUS ARC WELDING INSTRUCTION BOOK! ONE YEAR GUARANTEE—10 DAY FREE TRIAL. Now you can make or repair metal parts for cars, home, farm, garden, shop or factory. Works on any 110 v. house plug-in. CUT, MELT, BRAZE, SOLDER OR WELD MOST ANY METAL!

SEND ONLY $2.00 (cash, ck, mo) and pay postman only $12.95 COD postage or send $14.95 for postpaid delivery. Every EXPERIMENTER, MECHANIC, INVENTOR, CAR OR HOME OWNER NEEDS THIS SMALL WELDER. ORDER YOURS NOW! Ideal gift. MADE ONLY BY:
Midway Welder Co., Dept. DSM-1, Kearney, Nebr.

Planer•Molder•Saw!

Now you can use this ONE power feed shop to turn rough lumber into high-value moldings, trim, flooring, furniture . . . ALL popular patterns.

RIP...PLANE...MOLD...separately or all at once by power feed . . . with a one horsepower motor. Use 3 to 5 HP for high speed commercial output.

LOW COST . . . You can own this MONEY MAKING POWER TOOL for only . . . . $30.00 down payment

Send coupon today

BELSAW POWER TOOLS 954 Field Bldg., Kansas City 11, Mo.
Send me complete facts on the MULTI-DUTY Power Tool. No obligation.
Name ______
Address ______
City ______ State ______

MAGNETS
Vol. 1, No. 9
IN · YOUR · FUTURE
September 1986
$25.00
Single Issue
Mysterious
NEMESCOPE
Views of Magnetism?

Letter from editor/publisher

Tom Valentine

This month's lead story should make heads spin. It might not have a lot to do with permanent magnets at first blush, and I'll admit to stretching a point to fit into our new format, but here's some of my thinking on the "Nemescope."

The point I have allegedly stretched is the showing of the "energy fields" between the iron nucleates on the cover and the shot of apparent magnetism on page 12.

Colors are matched to the elements in the Nemescope scheme. The color of the energy in the Jade plant juice is different than the color of the permanent magnet field around the screws and coming off the small magnet. We don't know whether the magnet was alnico or ferrite, but probably ferrite. Now, would alnico have reflected a different spectrum? Would the fields from SmCo or Nd-Fe-B show up as different colors? If not, why not? If so, why?

If for no other reason than to study the variations in magnetic flux fields, and perhaps electromagnetic fields, we need to recreate this remarkable machine.

But magnets were only part of the marvel. The Nemescope had the ability to show living things as they lived and breathed, so to speak. It's too bad those excited early experimentors did not take photographs of Nemes-screened bacterium for us to see how they show up. That living cancer virus is certainly ugly enough to be convincing. These photos certainly should create a sensation. I hope so. Your comments are wanted.

If biologists as well as engineers and physicists, are not entranced by this story, I'm living in a weird society. The Nemescope potential most assuredly must stimulate mental saliva in hundreds of specialty areas.

Now, the obvious!

What happened to the Nemescope? How did such a promising invention get tossed down Orwell's "memory hole?" Do we have another one of Valentine's juicy "conspiracy" yarns?

Perhaps we have.

No one can really shed any little light on what little is known of the Nemescope's vanishing act, but the fact that it vanished after a burglary shortly after upper crust people in government and industry were informed about it makes one wonder.

The mystery isn't nearly as fetching regarding another acclaimed microscope of the past, which has also been relegated to the "memory hole," even though it is still available. This was the Royal Rife "tuned light" microscope. **MAGNETS** is in contact with the individual who has access to the only working Rife microscope in existence and we will attempt to investigate the subject.

The problem with any "conspiracy" being attached to the apparent suppression of the Rife scope and the theft and disappearance of the Nemescope is one of "motive." Why would anyone want to suppress instruments that could see more clearly into the micro world?

It is not the job of **MAGNETS** to delve into the mystery of why the Nemescope vanished without a trace. It is, however, my opinion that **MAGNETS** is playing a proper role in attempting to publish enough information so that those enterprising minds stirred to action may re-invent this fascinating instrument.

Meanwhile, **MAGNETS** is also busy with the practical permanent magnet world and many of you will be delighted to know that in our October issue we'll have bales of data on magnet materials and electric motor design and manufacture. The response from the industry has been very good. We will have some papers never before published on the subject of new materials and motor design.

Finally this, a most reliable source has sent me some data that indicates our scientific genii are barking up the wrong tree when it comes to the alleged ozone layer demise in Earth's upper atmosphere. My source suggests that chemists should not be tackling a problem that is "magnetic" and not "chemical."

Watch for this future report.

Remarkable Nemescope Made Living Pictures Of the Micro-World

Copyright © 1986 MAGNETS In Your Future Magazine

(Editor's note: This is the kind of story that thrills even a crusty old journalist who has spent nearly 30 years scrounging around "unorthodoxy" in an effort to dredge up facts that cause consternation; in an effort to provoke the "I'll be damned!" response from readers. In the mid-70's I wrote about the Royal Rife microscope — a microscope that is still weaving its way around the pages of underground and off-the-beaten-path journals. The "tuned light" microscope of Royal Rife, who was financed by the Timken steel dollars, was a beauty, no doubt — but when compared to the Nemescope, the Rife device is a mere pretender. This is one of those stories that this editor rates among his top 10 all-time yarns. ***MAGNETS*** *magazine is the perfect forum for this story. We are on the cutting edge of the most exciting technology of all — the phenomena of permanent magnetism — and we have an audience that has already indicated an ability to be open and critical at the same time; to be scientific and awed as well.)*

By Tom Valentine

The inventor of the Nemescope was a brilliant brain surgeon. His name was Elmer P. Nemes and he ran the Nemes Research Laboratories, 4207 West Third Street, Los Angeles 5, California during the middle 1950's. Unfortunately, he was also an alcoholic. He was killed in a drunken brawl in San Diego in the early 60's — he had hit rock bottom, and stayed there.

His invention, the Nemescope, which we are detailing on these pages in an effort to entice others to recreate this vitally important work, was stolen from a store called the Bryn Camera Shop on Melrose Avenue in 1957, ending a remarkable series of experiments and demonstrations. The device was in the shop to have an electric field finder installed.

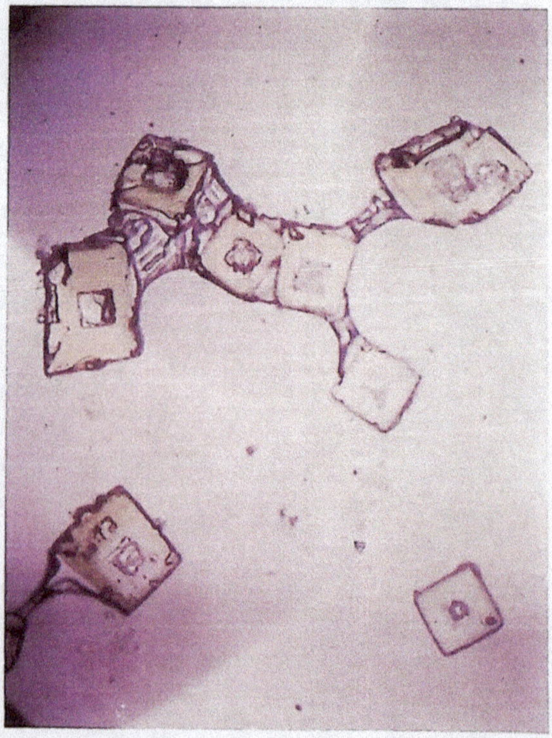

4

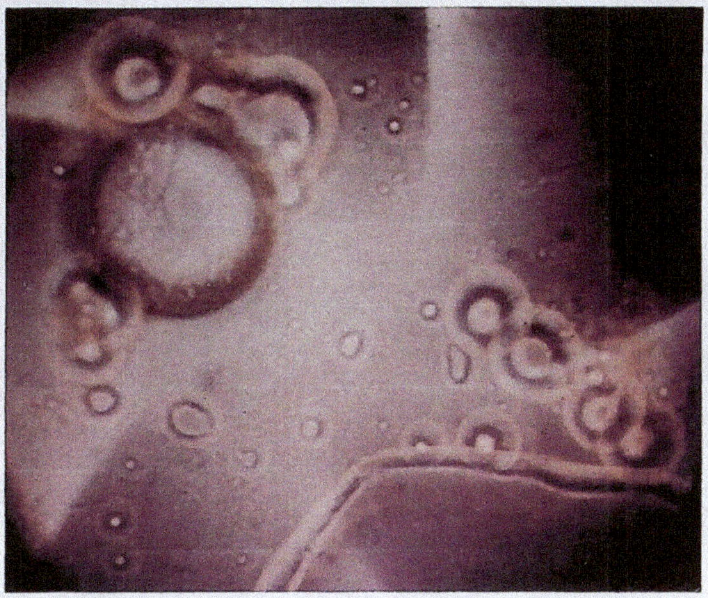

Enzymes in action were projected from two different specimens of carrot juice. In the photo above, the enzymes were active and could be viewed as they moved about on the screen and catalyzed or did what enzymes are said to do. The photo below was taken from a "commercial" carrot rather than an "organic" carrot and the enzyme was shown to be practically brimming over with substances, presumed toxins.

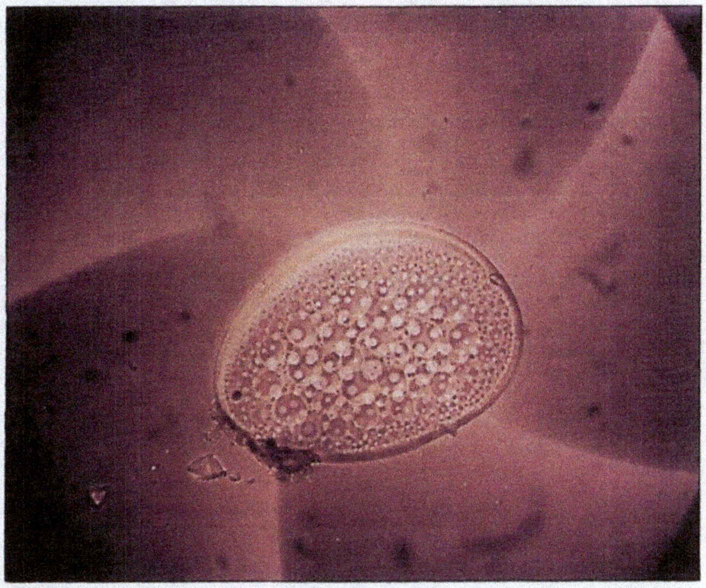

5

Continued from page 4

The person responsible for revealing this story to me is the grand lady of health and nutrition, Betty Lee Morales, 80, a long time resident of Topanga and an individual with unbridled curiosity who has been involved in thousands of research projects during her lifetime. She and her husband were directly responsible for the remarkable photographs from the Nemescope screen, that you see on these pages, and her incessant curiosity spurred the inventor to extra efforts.

"We lost track of the stolen machine in New York," Betty Lee explained, "and the technology has lain dormant all this time."

Who stole the machine? What role did the secretive segments of the United States government play? Betty Lee herself was involved with the Central Intelligence Agency in its earliest years after WWII, and while representing Dr. Nemes she worked directly with the late Congressman Craig Shepherd of San Bernardino, who had arranged a major appropriation for in-depth and clandestine research on the Nemescope just prior to its theft and subsequent disappearance.

The photographs in this issue were taken directly off a 12-foot by 12-foot screen where the images danced energetically in full color. The Nemescope projected motion pictures of the microworld onto the screen. Every object, in a medium of distilled water on a quartz slide, projected it's own natural colors — no dyes were needed. The photo on the opposite page, for example, is a picture of molecules of iron nucleate from the juice of a Jade plant, squeezed for the filming experiment on the spur of the moment by Betty Lee. The iron nucleates were linked together with a sparkling, vibrant energy that formed patterns on the screen as the living juice was photographed and projected.

"The flowing lines of force were clearly visible and very symmetrical," Betty Lee explained, "but later, when the life forces in the juice evidently died, there was no energy. The emissions of energy were silver and gold luminescent and traveled, apparently at the speed of light."

The Nemescope photos and explanations on these pages speak for themselves. Now, how did these pictures come about?

Nuclear magnetic resonance had been firmly established a few years before Dr. Nemes began his experiments with "radiation potentials, wave lengths of emitted quanta and color spectra."

Here is Dr. Nemes' summary of the invention:

"The specimen which is to be examined by the multiple source microscope, is bombarded, for example, with two sources of energy. One of these sources is energy at a frequency which approximates the frequency of one of the radiation potentials of the material forming the specimen, and the other source produces energy at a frequency which is slightly different from the first frequency.

"The energy from the first source impinging upon the specimen causes the atoms to be excited and to emit quanta of energy of a frequency which is dependent upon the frequency of the energy of the first source. The energy from the second source serves to spread out the frequency of the emitted energy over a range of frequencies so that a colored light effect is produced. The colored light effect, which is a highly magnified image of the specimen being examined, may then be photographed.

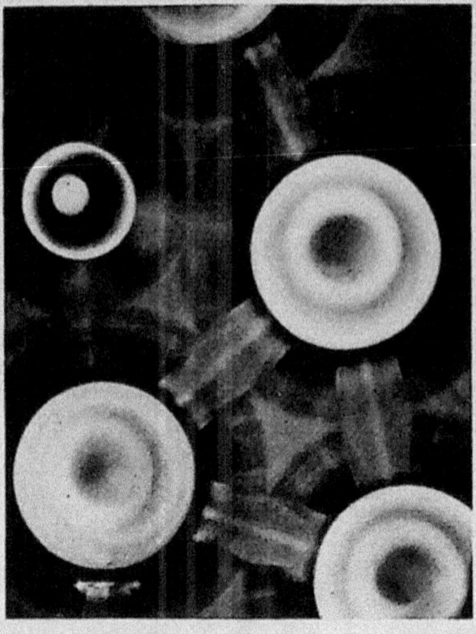

ON THE COVER

A Nemescope reproduction of the "iron nucleates" found in a specimen of Jade plant juice taken from the immediate environment and scoped. The symmetrical "lines of force" between the nucleate cores was said to be "vibrantly alive" when first shown on the screen. After some time passed the "energy" departed and the active lines left the screen.

"If desired, for photographic purposes, the spectrum which is emitted by the specimen being examined may be intensified by ultra-violet or visible light, comparatively long wave radiation. This combined light pattern is then enlarged by a conventional optical system and projected on the screen or some other suitable device and the composite is photographed by a camera."

Betty Lee's description may add to our perspective. "The device was an emission-type microscope — it depended upon resolution, not magnification. An electron microscope might get to 16,000X in magnification, but not have much resolution. You can compare the images of a gold grid taken with an electron microscope and with the Nemescope. (Photos on page 28). We projected images that were 5 million X."

Betty Lee's recollection of the key feature of the device is as follows:

"Dr. Nemes designed a radiation gun, which was the essence of the machine. I recall that it was a steel pipe about 2 inches in diameter and about 10 inches long. Holes were bored in it and semiprecious stones, or jewels representing a different wave band were set in the pipe. The jewels had to be imperfect (see item 6 of the inventor's own summary coming up), so we heated them in an autoclave up to 5,500 degrees F to cause imperfections."

According to the Nemes papers, U.S. Patent #2,850,661 covers the first unit of the "short and long wave radiation system," that he had devised. The inventor summarized the principles of his Nemescope in August of 1956, and submitted an amendment to his patent application, which had been filed in July 1955.

The summary will be first printed verbatim, then his comments, unfortunately without accompanying drawings, will also be verbatim.

1. The first unit is a cold cathode tube (lamp) (U.S. Patent 2850661) with multiple filaments directly but separately charged. The filaments preheat the platinum, gold, germanium and tungsten targets. The function of this invention is explained in "Additional Claims on Lamps, Cold Cathode Tube, Reissued to United States Patent Office to Patent 2850661." The cathode gun acts as the primary source of illumination and bombarder of the specimen.

2. The second part of the instrument, which is called the long and short wave high frequency condenser, contains high frequency coils, quartz window, filters and radio-active emitters, electrostatic or electro-magnetic coils, and also quartz prisms or lenses to focus the relatively long wave rays.

3. When the specimen is bombarded with a multiple source of radiation and the proper excitation potential arranged, the organic or inorganic matter emit an ultra-spectral image in true colors. Concerning the molecular structure, diffusion, cohesion and wave length of the examining matter, the rays can be arranged so that the primary source of radiation, by adjusting the condenser by wave length or potential, will induce the appearance of the true image.

4. The radio-active emitter or gun maintains a radium filament with individual filters for Alpha, Beta and Gamma rays. Also we could use, if so desired, **isotopes such as carbon 14, cessium and cobalt.** The Gamma ray could be emitted also by interchangeable extra tubes. The radium crystals and other isotopes also can be melted into the quartz condensor lens. Furthermore, shields of very thin plates of gold, aluminum or platinum can be used to control the radiation.

5. The specimen is under a quartz cover slide, or in the cases of gases or liquids, **is in capillary attachment, emmission attachment** or between mica plates or other transparent usable material. The specimen also could be examined by the capillary system across high voltage and the temperature changes could be measured indirectly concerning the examined specimen.

6. Pick-up unit. Fine grain fluorescent screen is incorporated to a system of optically corrected quartz lenses, thereby the invisible radiation can be picked up and transferred to longer rays. The lens could be coated with evaporated metallic silicate, aluminum, magnesium, boron, etc., with the mixture of the impure sphalerite single crystals, activated phosphides of zinc sulphide, zinc cadmium sulphide, etc. If the pick-up quartz or diamonds have impurities such as single micro-crystals of metallic silicate, phosphides of zinc sulphate or zinc cadmium sulphate, these impurities **act as fine grain fluorescent material.** In that case the resulving power could be increased by such fluorescent impurities that the single crystals or particles act not only as a fine grain screen but as individual 360° degree emitters and resolution is theoretically unlimited and the magnification increases in proportion. Therefore a single molecule can be picked up individually and reproduced by spectrum and lines and structure. The single image is directed by focusing plates or prisms to the reflectors, mirrors, or single or double prism system and through this set-up **only the preferred image will be picked up by the image amplifying tube.**

7. The amplification system contains: (A) deflecting cathode, (B) deflecting prism, adjustable by axis. In the amplification system the amplifying units contain concave shaped cathodes and plates, silver or rhodium coated, where not only amplification but further magnification can be obtained. The plates relative to the cathode are more positively charged. The amplification units can be individually separated by perforated mica sheets (See drawings) and further correction of the image can be maintained with secondary and tertiary correcting screens. The final image is directed to the prism and reflecting system.

8. Additional interchangeable filters can be incorporated to filter out undesirable rays. Skiatron or equivalent color sensitive projecting tube is indirectly energized. Additional lenses can be added for different types of projection. The previously mentioned amplification unit, if further magnification or amplification is desired, can be repeated. Technically and theoretically, by this system, resolution depends on the wave length of the selected short wave radiation sources and the ultra-microscopic size single crystal-screen. Magnification of such is unlimited and the instrument is able to maintain images in full color and spectrum.

Following that summary, Dr. Nemes wrote of his "additional claims on lamps and the cold cathode tube." His comments may serve to further our understanding of the technology.

(A) *Multiple illuminator filed with the U.S. Patent Office in 1955. (Docket No. 2470 in 1955 by Harris, Kiech, Foster, Etc., Patent Attorneys Ser. No. 540, 740 Oct. 17, 1955 Illuminator Mailed Aug. 9, 1956.)* Claiming that the continuous flow of energy can be maintained by creating an ion differential between two poles of different materials (metals, gases and some other elements) which exhibit the K factor, as Boron, Magnesium, Tungsten, Titanium, Wolfram, Beryllium, Krypton, Hard Carbon, Zirconium, Gold, Platinum, Nickel, Aluminum-Sulphate, etc.

As stated in the Work Book, page 47, (between July 11 and October 10, 1955) a chain reaction takes place and maintains a continuous electron flow or shorter ray flow after preheating the cathode with an electric current. The two elements involved have different behavior and charge. (Ref. page 42; Merk index: listed 55 different elements, possessing the K factor, as possible sources of continuous energy production plus a second element, Magnesium, Aluminum Sulphate, etc., and maintain the flow without any further charge.)

On page 50 of the same Work Book, the inventor shows a drawing of **a Magnesium coated Platinum cathode,** energized by a Zirconium arc. A continuous flow of energy was produced even after the electric current was cut off. This setup was tested in October 26, 1955. The enclosed picture from the next page shows schematically the principle of the cold cathode tube.

The drawing under M 2599, October 26, 1955 explains the working of the principle by using a set of multiple cathodes and anodes that can be adjusted to different distances of the emitters. Therefore, a chain reaction, which can be adjusted to various frequencies, takes place without further use of external energy. Drawing No. 13351, Fig. 1 and 2 show the construction of the instrument.

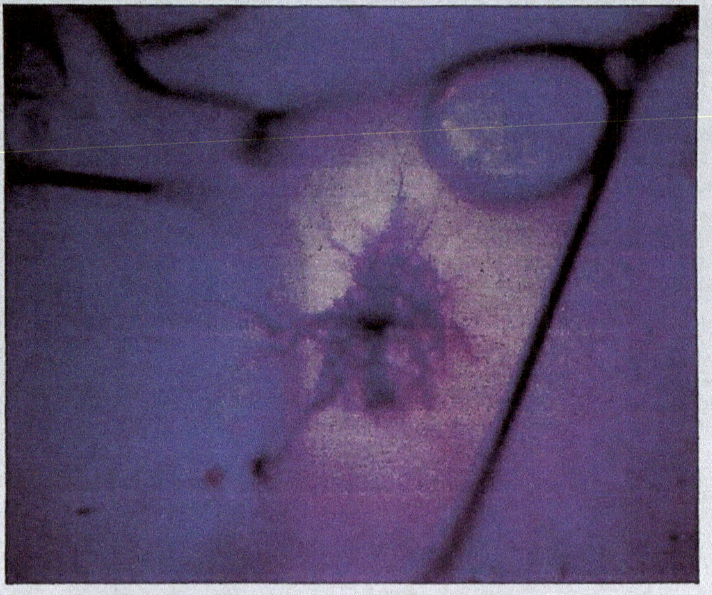

A cancer virus! Dr. Nemes, being a medical doctor, was primarily interested in pathology and had planned many valuable uses for his invention.

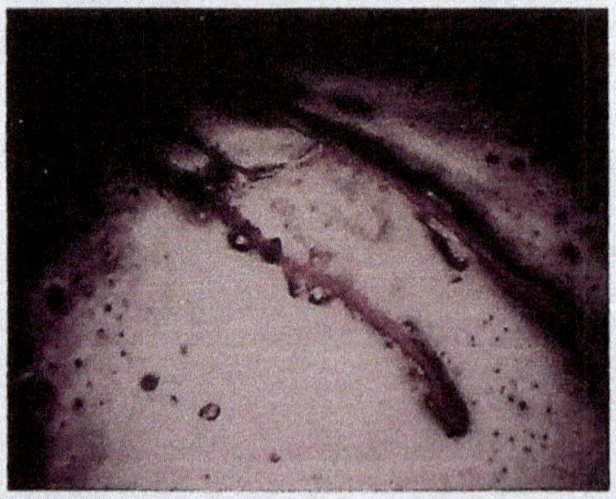

A healthy living cell showing the strings of nucleic acids forming in the nucleus, with strong membrane.

8

The photo above is part of an exhibit at a 1950's Worlds Fair. The Upjohn Company designed the exhibit from a monograph made of the cytoplasm of a cell. Below, the Nemescope version of the same cytoplasm "sticks." Nemes said his Nemescope provided a "true view of the structure with geometric pattern and nucleic radiations of helium" making the splashes of illumination on the picture.

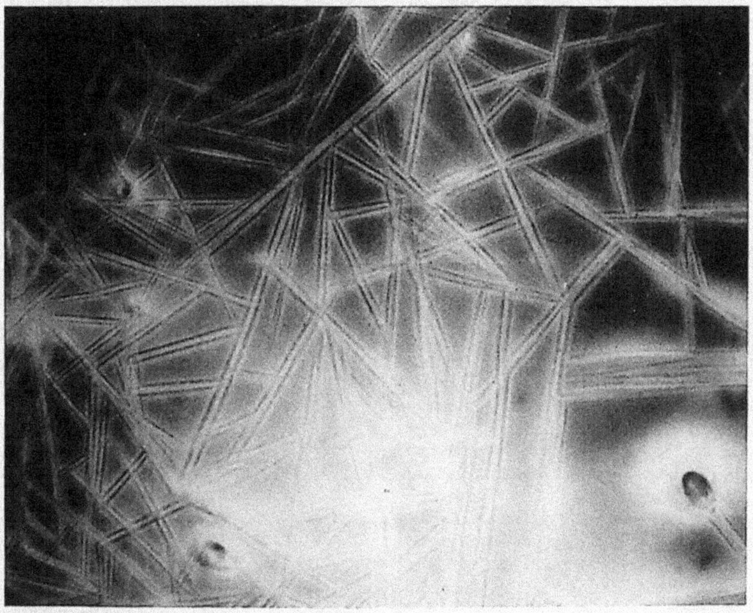

Said patent application mentions also a gas inlet to the chamber through which various gases could be injected as Argon, Helium, Nitrogen, Xenon, Hydrogen or combinations of such. These could create the same effect as the various coatings of Magnesium, Boron, Aluminum, Sulphate, Etc.

(B) In the construction of the Nemescope the incandescent energy source was used further only to create a broader spectrum since the cold cathode radiation was tested as to its efficiency without the combination of the primary charge. The presence and maintenance of the chain reaction was proven as existing between cathode, anode, and grid without the primary energy source.

The cooling coil as reported in the cold cathode tube served the purpose of prolonging the life of the filaments in the tube. Our setup with the special arrangement of the targets proved to be capable of keeping the temperature slightly above room temperature, whereas, otherwise the temperature would rise to 100°C or higher.

NEMESCOPE ADDITIONAL CLAIMS

In Patent 2850661, Paragraph 39: "It is preferred that the target be made of platinum or other material having the property of absorbing oxygen as its temperature increases and giving off oxygen as its temperature decreases. The absorption of oxygen by the platinum when the platinum is heating up produces a cooling action in the surrounding atmosphere and materially reduces the operating temperature of the filaments of the lamp." An essential factor in the cooling process was therefore achieved through the basic nature of the targets and their arrangement.

In the Nemescope the principle of the cold cathode tube has existed for several years and has been called "black body energy." The targets (cathode) energized through indirect heating by the Zirconium arc, consisted of gold and platinum, tungsten, germanium, etc., and were different in weight (ratio 1.5; 1.01). The Grid consisted of 2 antennae and one rhodium coated concave mirror in an electromagnetic field, directed the cathode rays to the center of the beam going through the axis of the specimen.

In the patent of the cold cathode tube No. 2850661 is also demonstrated a rhodium coated concave mirror behind the target and the filaments arrangement which serve a double purpose: (1) to focus the visible ultraviolet rays, etc., to the center of the spectrum and (2) act as a focusing grid for the cathode rays.

Finally, in 1959, two years after the prototype unit had been stolen, Dr. Nemes was encouraged by Betty Lee and his other partners to write a "construction guide" for his Nemescope. We now reprint the complete document for the first time:

The multiple frequency source called, "Cold Cathode Tube or Lamp," (A) contains a radium S_H and platinum plates S'_L & S_L. The wave lengths of the gun become ineffective long before they reach the specimen, but they do modulate the carrier frequencies composed of shorter wave lengths of light radiations. The low frequency light is obtained from filaments H_1 H_2 H_3 heated to incandescence by 110 VAC. The heat produced by this incandescence is used to indirectly heat the gold and platinum which starts a reaction between each other. This is self-sustaining, once started.

These gold and platinum sources must be adjustable. It is suggested, that they be mounted on screw-mounts, the heads of which have a 90° arm with magnetic tips, to be turned magnetically through the glass envelope of the cold cathode tube. To reflect most of the radiation of the chain reaction between the gold and platinum plates, a coated concave mirror M_{foc} is placed behind the filaments. The focal length of this mirror is to be such as to focus correctly to the suspended quartz lenses F_{L1} in the condenser. This mirror may be compared to the cathode in the somewhat similar cathode ray tube, hereinafter referred to as CRT. Therefore it is to be negatively charged or at 0 reference potential. The subsequent elements are the intensity control G_1 and the focusing grids or anodes.

At the radiating end of the cold cathode tube a window of quartz maintains the low vacuum within the cold cathode tube. The function of subsequent quartz windows Q_ZW_1 through Q_ZW_5 is similar. The presence of the following gases is suggested: helium, Argon, nitrogen, Xenon or a mixture thereof. The radium gun, opposit the cathode reflector C_{REF} emanates Alpha, Beta and Gamma radiations, comprising the higher frequencies.

The structure of the cathode is as follows: if the structural metal of the cathode is tungsten, molybdenum, platinum, gold, a plating of rhodium, magnesium, aluminum or beryllium is suggested; the object being to make the sum total molecular weight of the structural and coated metal as high as possible, keeping the ratio of molecular weight as low as possible with the coating having the lower molecular weight.

The focusing coil L_{foc} and the deflecting plates of gold and platinum A_{def1} and A_{def2} help insure focus. The mass of the deflecting plates is not altogether critical, but the ratio of masses is critical in that it must be a ratio of 1.01 pf gold to 1.5 of platinum.

Between the cold cathode and the next component, the condenser "B", a slot must be left open to allow the insertion of interchangeable filters. These consist of four different types. First, a gold and silver leaf (a thickness of 1/10,000th of an inch), transparent filters; third, an infra-red filter which can be constructed of carborundum, or any other suitable material; fourth, a blue filter. It is advised that these be structurally supported by quartz on both sides, and that these be mounted on a motor-driven circle which has one position open for a neutral filter, composed of either nothing or black carbon.

Since it is desirable to obtain variable resolutions and since resolution is directly governed by the wave length of the radiation passing through the specimen, it is necessary to vary the wave length. This can be most easily done by modulating the constant wave length radiations of the cold cathode tube with a wave length from an electronic oscillator. For this purpose a coil M_{mod} has been constructed 90° to the radiation beam. There are plates appropriately connected to this coil which seem to act as deflecting plates for the shorter wave length radiations.

There are also focusing lenses mounted adjustably to focus the radiations. All optical components **must** be optically corrected. If these lenses are **radium** impregnated, the radium guns would no longer be necessary.

The coating of the lens or the gun can be of any suitable radio-active material or isotope which emits Alpha, Beta and Gamma radiations. These are otherwise necessary because the effective range of Alpha, Beta and Gamma rays is

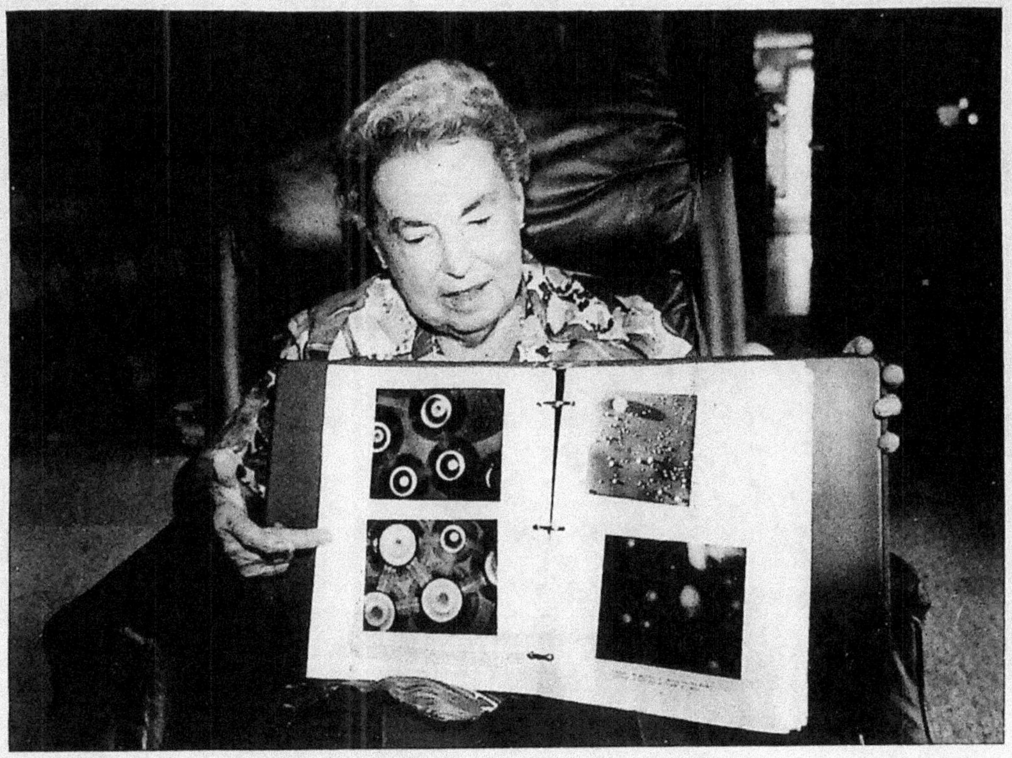

Berry Lee Morales, in her Topanga Canyon home, holds her Nemes experiment photobook open to illustrate one of the many wonders of the early research. The top photo on the left hand page near Betty Lee's finger shows nucleates of iron after the "life" had departed from the specimen, which was juice from a Jade plant. The bottom photo, shows clearly the "energy emissions" as they vibrate between the nucleates at a time when the juice was still filled with "living energy."

only 3.9c. if unaccelerated artificially. Around the assembly of the cold cathode tube and condensers must be constructed a radiation shield of lead approximately 1/8" in thickness.

After the shield, the sample slide can be inserted. This slide must be of quartz glass, or some other material more pervious to short wave length. Here are also mounted two high frequency parabolic antennae to radiate the electromagnetic frequencies from the oscillator. These antennae are encompassed radially (only) by focusing coils.

Close to the axial center of the radiation beam, yet outside the beam itself, should be mounted one or two small (1/4 watt) fluorescent bulbs I_{f1}. The output of these is not critical, for through the amplification of three x 10^6 their wave lengths become strong enough to project the image to almost any distance.

The next unit called image amplifier, "C", contains first some gold and platinum deflection plates A_{def3} and A_{def4} and then a quartz prism P_1 unto which the beam is focused by the focusing lenses F_{L2}.

The optical system components can be made of either quartz or commercial diamond. The quartz must be coated with metallic silicates, phosphides, etc. The commercial diamond must be electrostatically charged so as to procure current amplification due to the inherent impurities in commercial diamonds. This electrostatic charge has to be in sequential order of positive-going electrodes in reference to ground; to avoid repelling the radiation beam. The reverse side of prisms P_1 and P_2 are to be mirror coated with conventional materials. The focusing coil L_{foc} in the vicinity of prism P_1 should be adjustable as well as all other focusing coils; that is they are to be constructed so as to permit axial movement.

The dynodes D_1 to D_9, inclusive, are the amplifying electrodes between which a voltage of not less than 18 VDC is to be maintained. The curvature of the dynodes is to decrease successively from Dynode 1 to 9.

The correcting screens R_{s1} and R_{s2} are to be constructed of mica or quartz which is to be perforated by electro-static breakdown of the mica, across a spark-gap. The holes on the

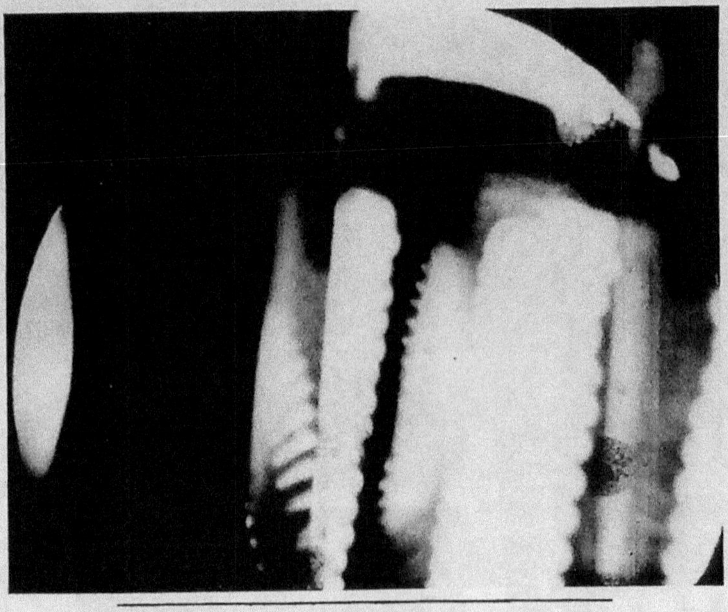

This is a Nemescope screening of an experiment to demonstrate magnetic flux. A permanent magnet 1/2 inch thick is glowing at the left. The magnet, either ceramic or alnico, it is not known which, was placed in the path of the light-like Nemescope emission. At the right are two parallel screws and a screwdriver tip. The Nemescope did not operate upon focal distance, but through the emission of extremely short wave radiations where particles of the bombarded specimen may be reconstructed. Through tertiary emission, the image of any specimen was produced and projected onto a screen in color. As the bombarding wavelength was shortened during this experiment, the structure and spectrums of the screws and the screwdriver were reproduced on the screen, while the actual lines of force were reproduced as a continuity of particles. This is the only "picture" of a flux field ever captured to our knowledge. "Until the Nemescope," the inventor wrote, "no available method was able to demonstrate the actual lines of the magnetic flux, although by empirical methods the directional lines of the flux had been established."

two screens are to be located so that the beam which passes through a hole on screen R_{sl} does not pass through a hole of R_{s2}. The screens are to be coated with suitable phosphorescent material, then activated by a radio-active source prior to installation.

The screen R_{sl} is to be positioned so that the beam will first strike the mica and then the coating. This screen is also to be located at a 90° angle to the beam, half way between dynode D_2 and D_3. This screen is also to be located in the magnetic field of the second focusing coil in the vicinity of dynode D_3.

The screen R_{s2} is to be so located as to present the coating first. Prism P_2 is to refract the beam from Dynode 9 through quartz window Q_zW_5 and quartz filter Q_zFIL which is interchangeable much like the before mentioned quartz filter. The lens projecting system F_{L3} is to project the amplified image onto the screen.

For further amplification, repeated stages of amplifying tubes can be used, the only limitation being the supply of voltage. After sufficient amplification, the image can be photographed from the screen, or directly from the instrument. For television closed circuitry, a camera need only be directed towards the image end of the image amplifying tube and either color or monochromatic television can be projected.

It is suggested that no orthodox color tube be used for projection, but that one be used which has been modified with a radium gun directed toward the cathode of said tube; thusly the heater of said tube can be eliminated after having heated the cathode sufficiently. This is to achieve scatter resolution finer than that perceptible by the naked eye.

Continued on Page 28

Continued

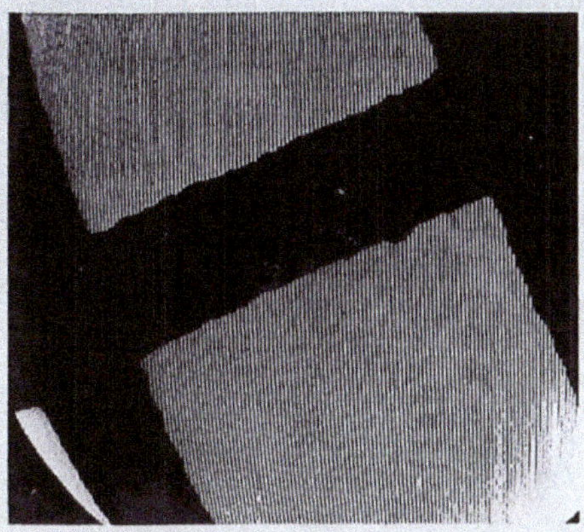

Comparing an electron microscope reproduction (18,000X) with a Nemescope reproduction of the same material. In the top photo the grid, which is impregnated with uranium, shows only black and white straight lines. The Nemescope projected not only the lines, but the spectrum of uranium and structure and shadows of impurities, due to the method of preparation of the uranium screen itself. The inventor wrote: "Revealing the contamination demonstrates the extreme fidelity of the Nemescope."

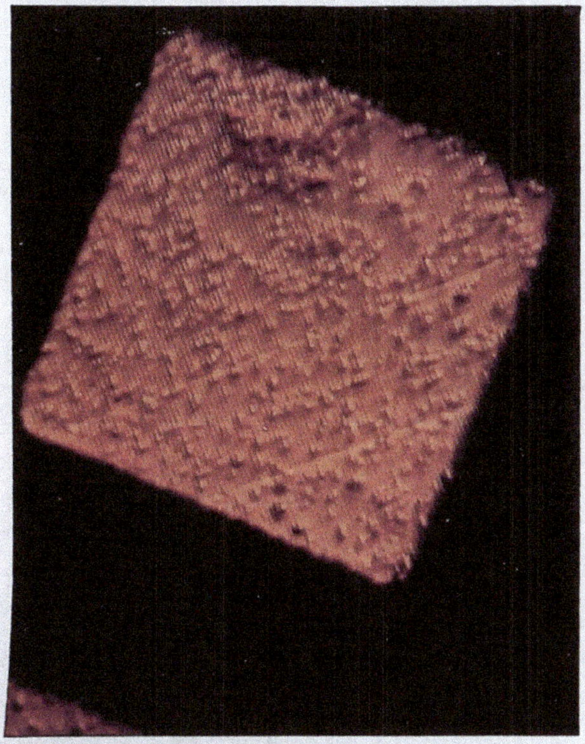

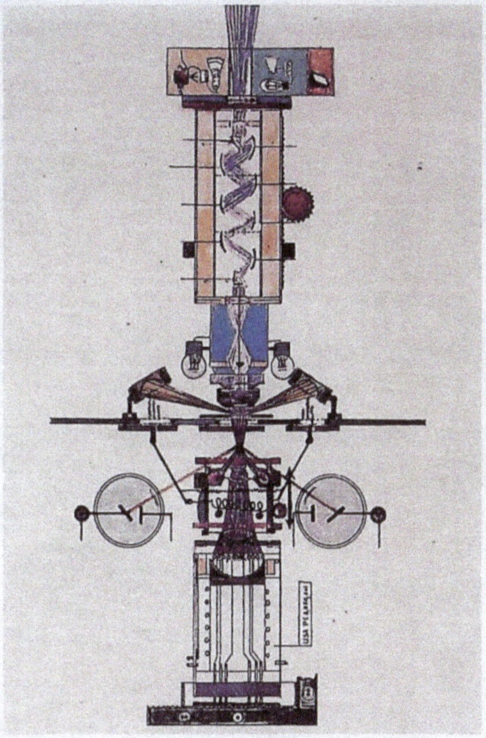

A Color Rendering of the Nemescope was produced on a canvas by the inventor. It's all that remains to work with as far as drawings go. Compare this drawing with the detailed explanations in the feature article.

It is in the interest of science and technology that **MAGNETS** has presented this feature. Should the Nemescope, or a comparable device be forthcoming because of this information, our ability to understand the universe around us will be considerably enhanced. Perhaps we might even learn to focus and analyze variations in magnetic fields, thereby expanding our knowledge considerably.

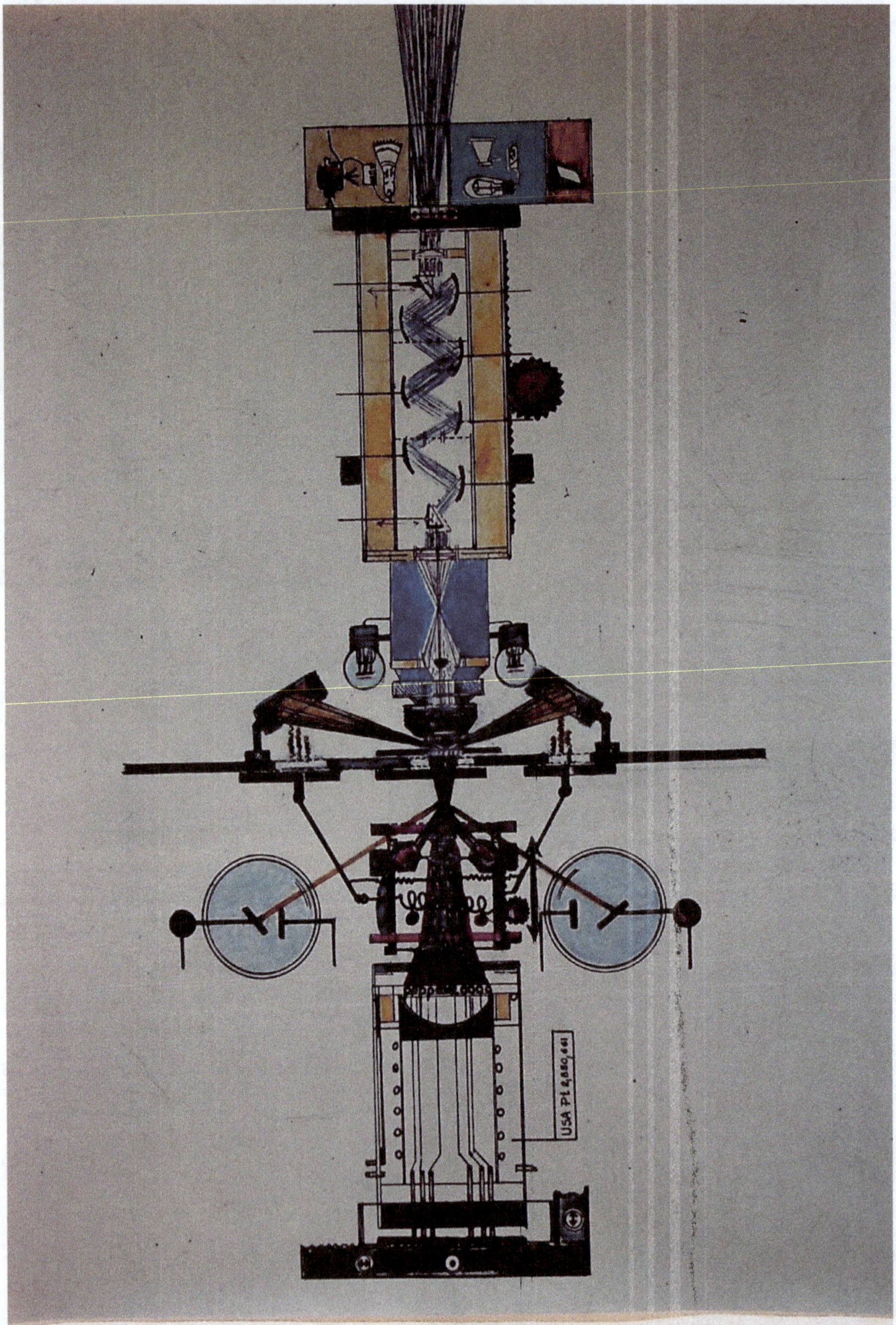

NEMESCOPE

Original Photographs Taken Through the Nemescope

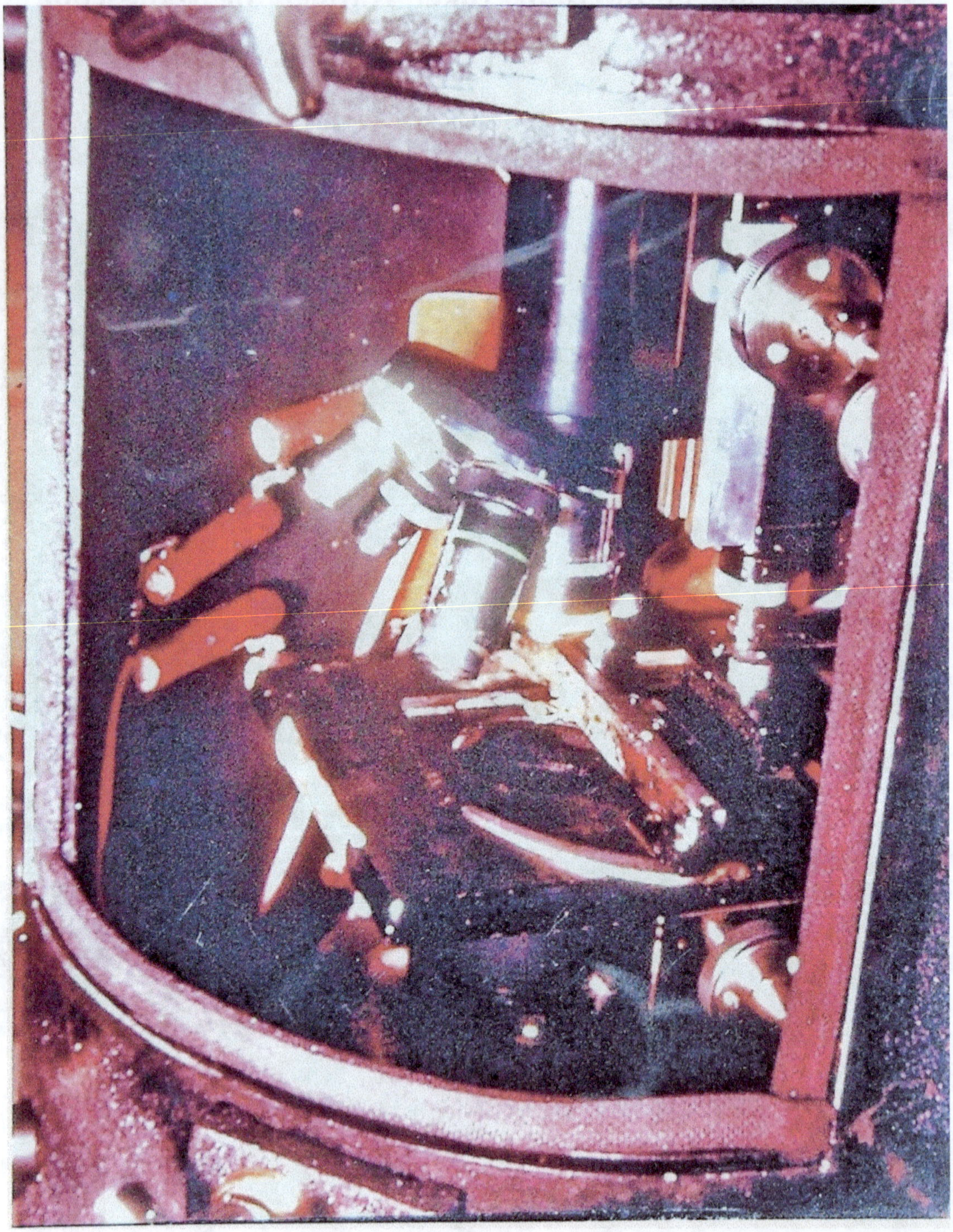

IRON NUCLEATE: By shorter wave length, more magnification and resolution, showing the basic atomic and molecular groupings, representing not only more emitted spectral lines from the iron nucleate atom, but "energy lines," revealed by magnification of structure and internal resolution, towards the nucleus of the atom.

HONEY; Shows the unstable atomic structure with large dilated nuclei and interrupted and invaginated membrane particles in the plasma.

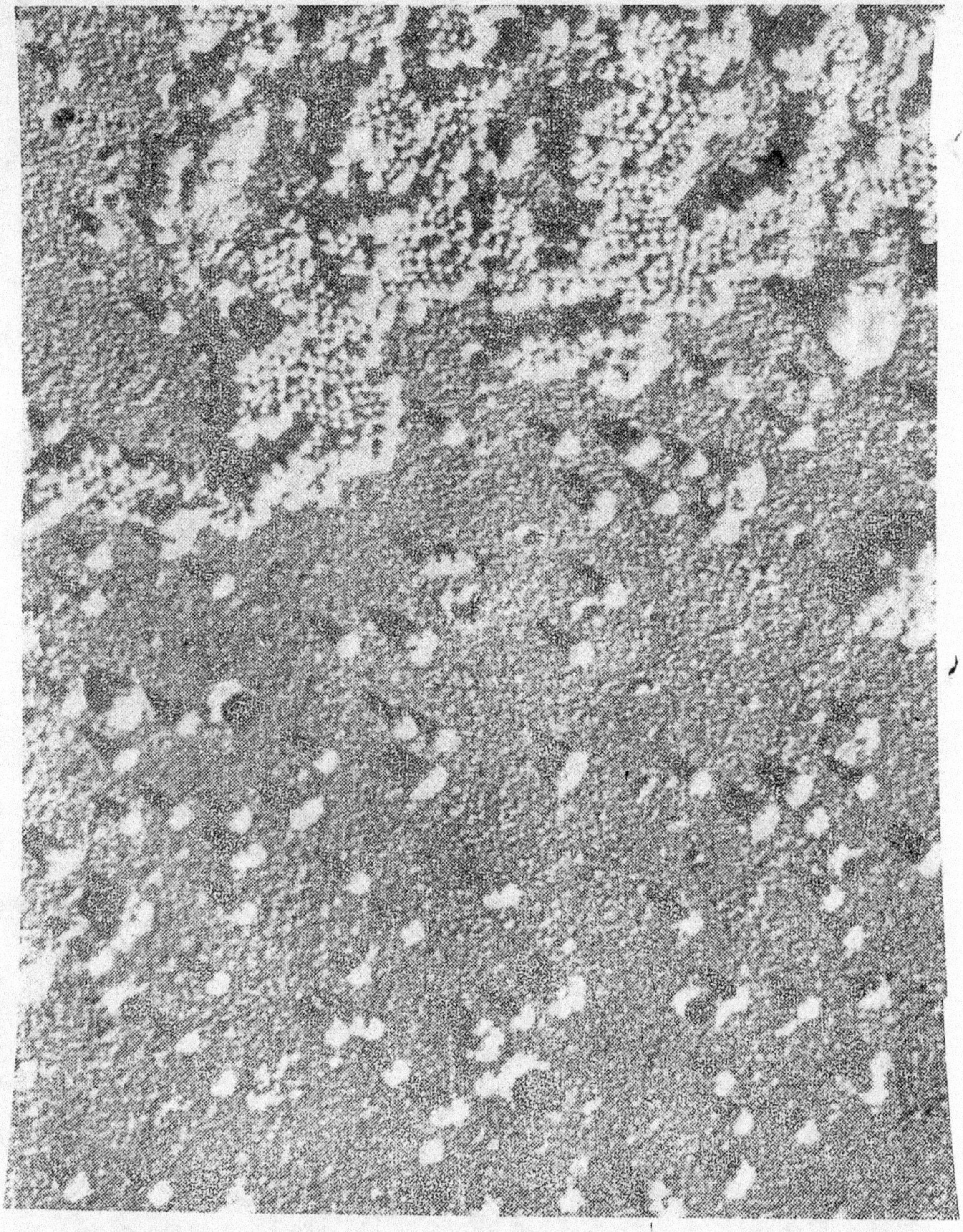

POLIO VIRUS: 63,000 X by Electron Microscope (Black & White) no internal structure of the virus; only angulated particles and masses, without characteristic resolution

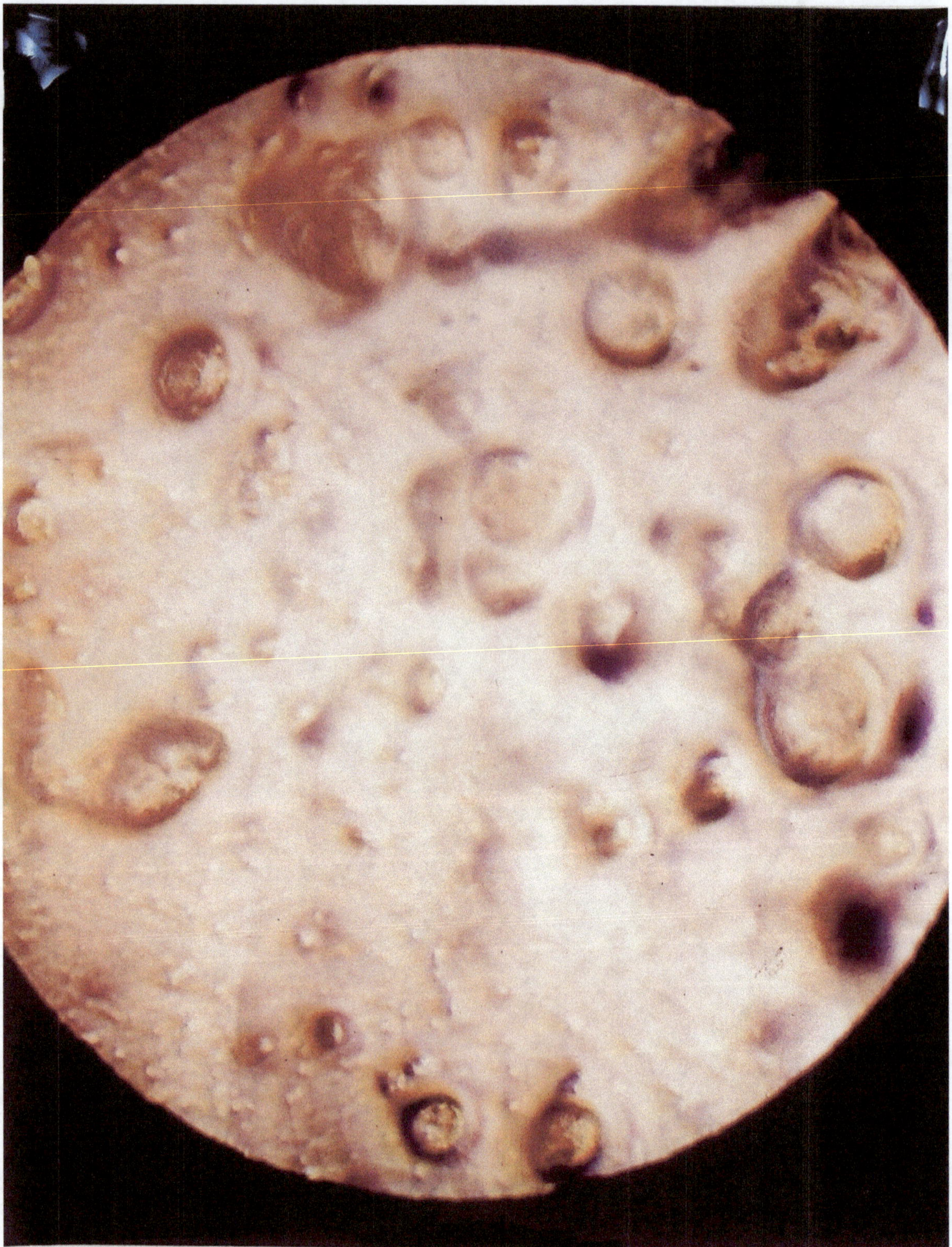

POLIO VIRUS: By Nemescope, field of polio viruses, the spectrum suggesting further internal structure, which can be resolved.

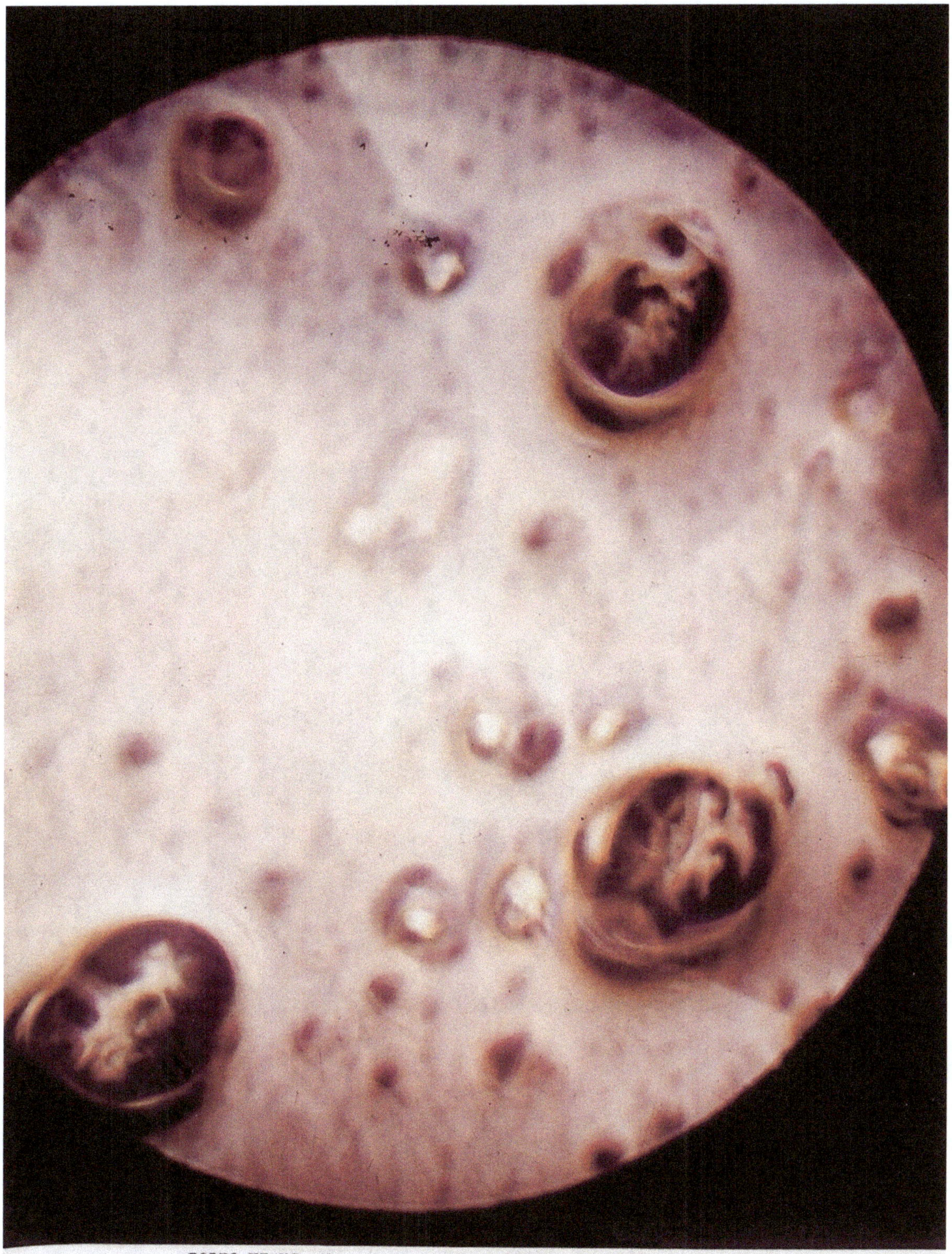

POLIO VIRUS: Nemescope photo, showing specific internal structure of polio virus, with definite spectrum.

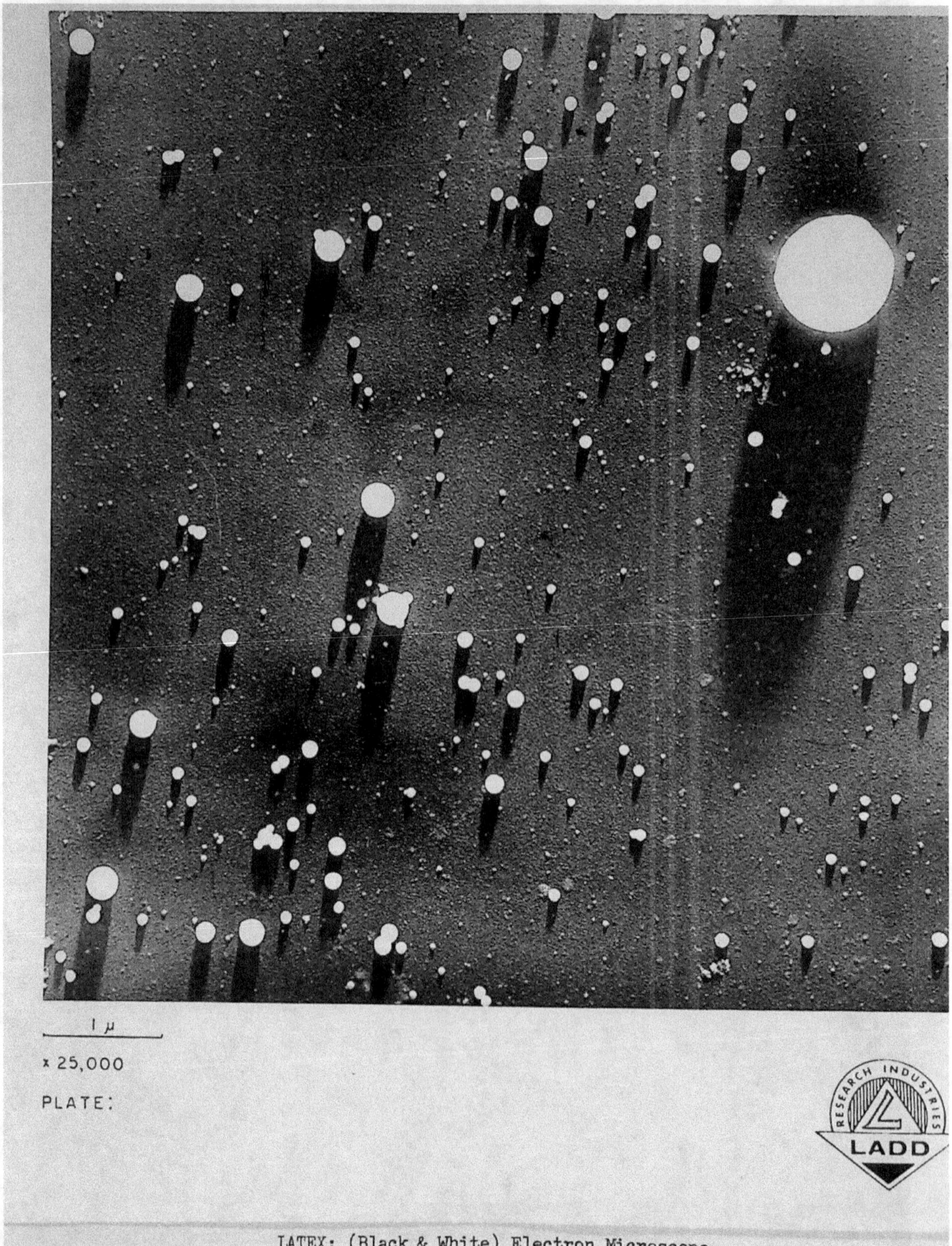

LATEX: (Black & White) Electron Microscope.

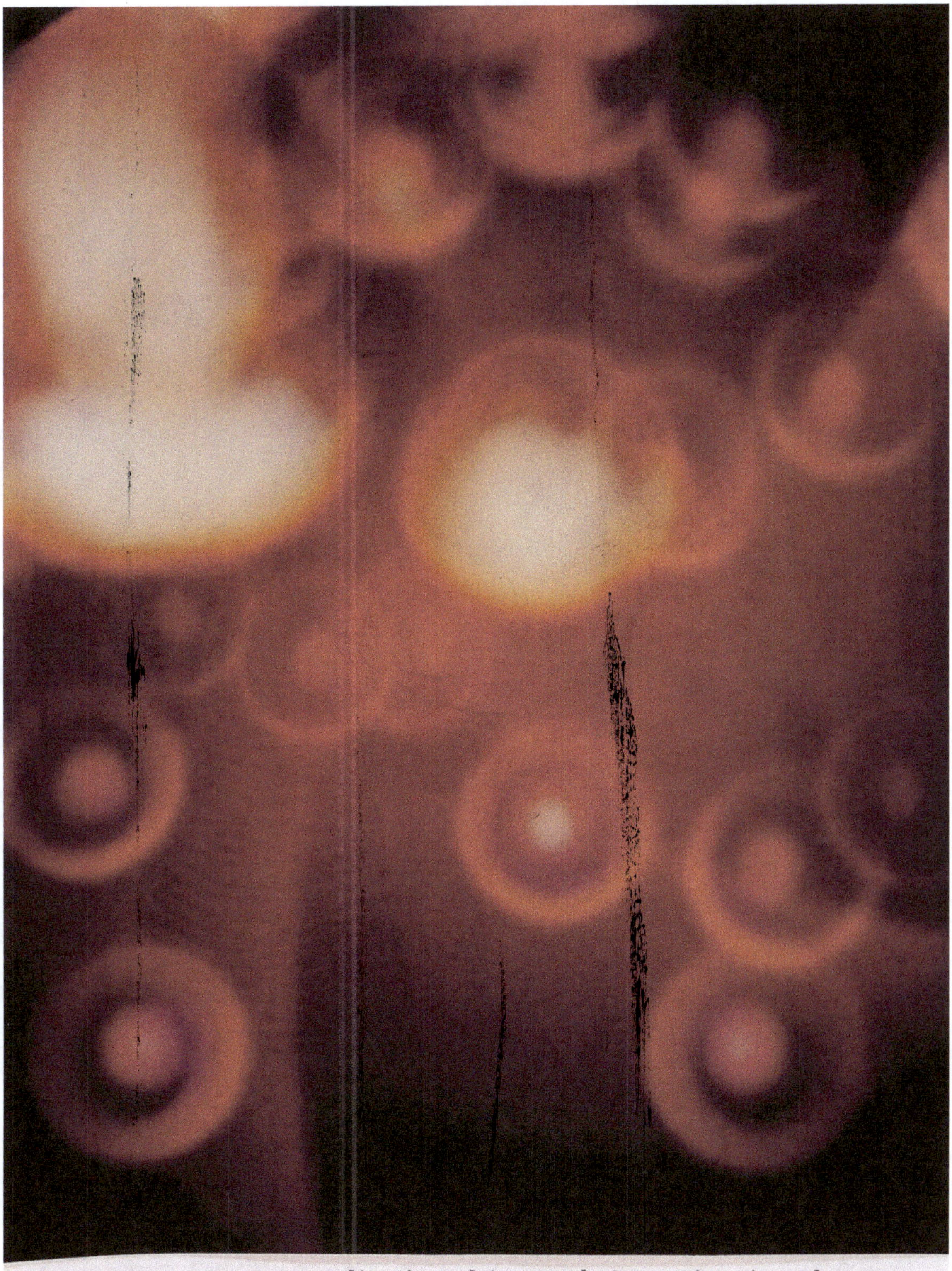

LATEX: By Nemescope, revealing the nuclei, several rings, and spectrum of same.

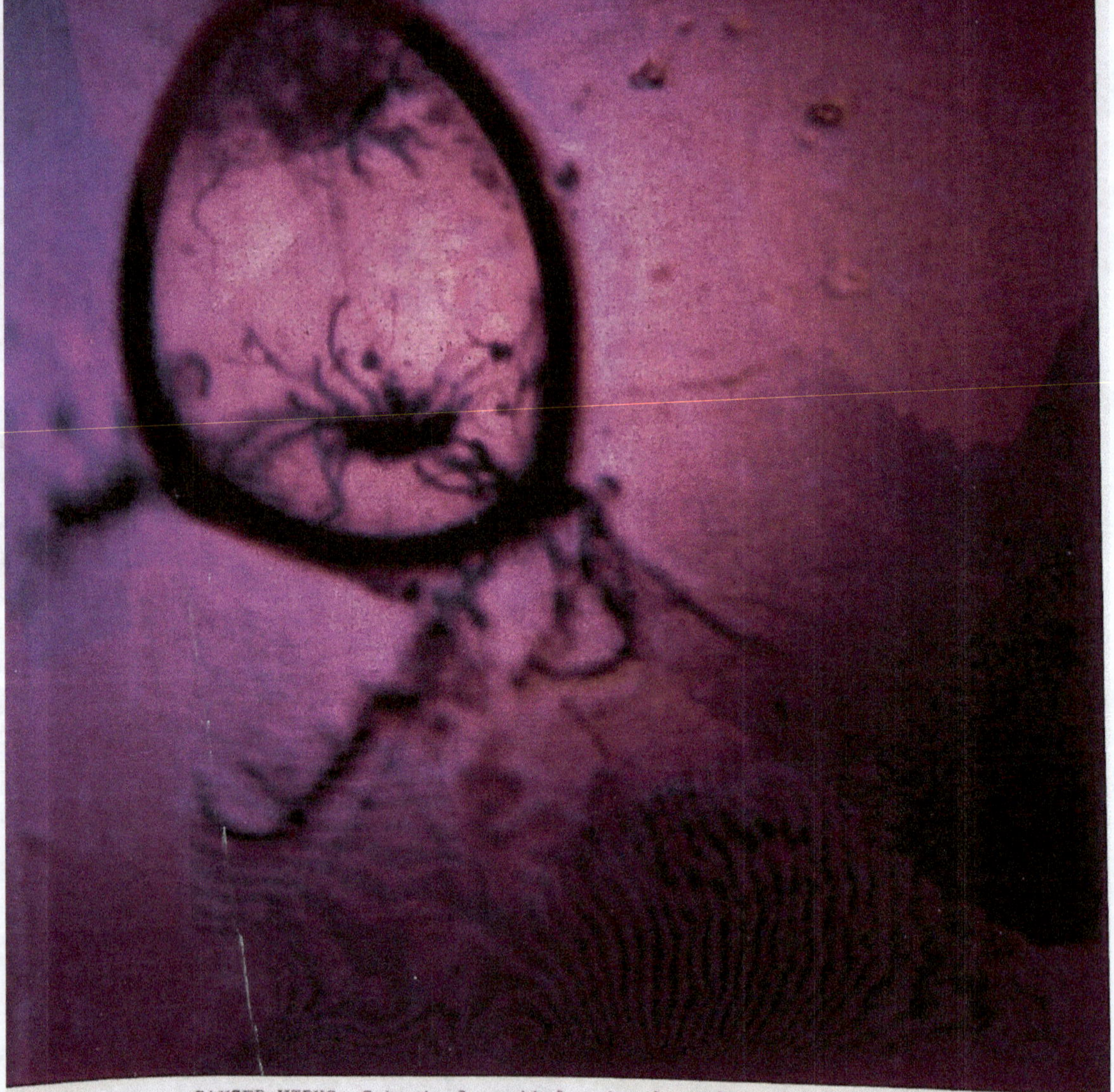

CANCER VIRUS: Spherical particles in the urine of a known cancer victim, showing intra-particle morphology.

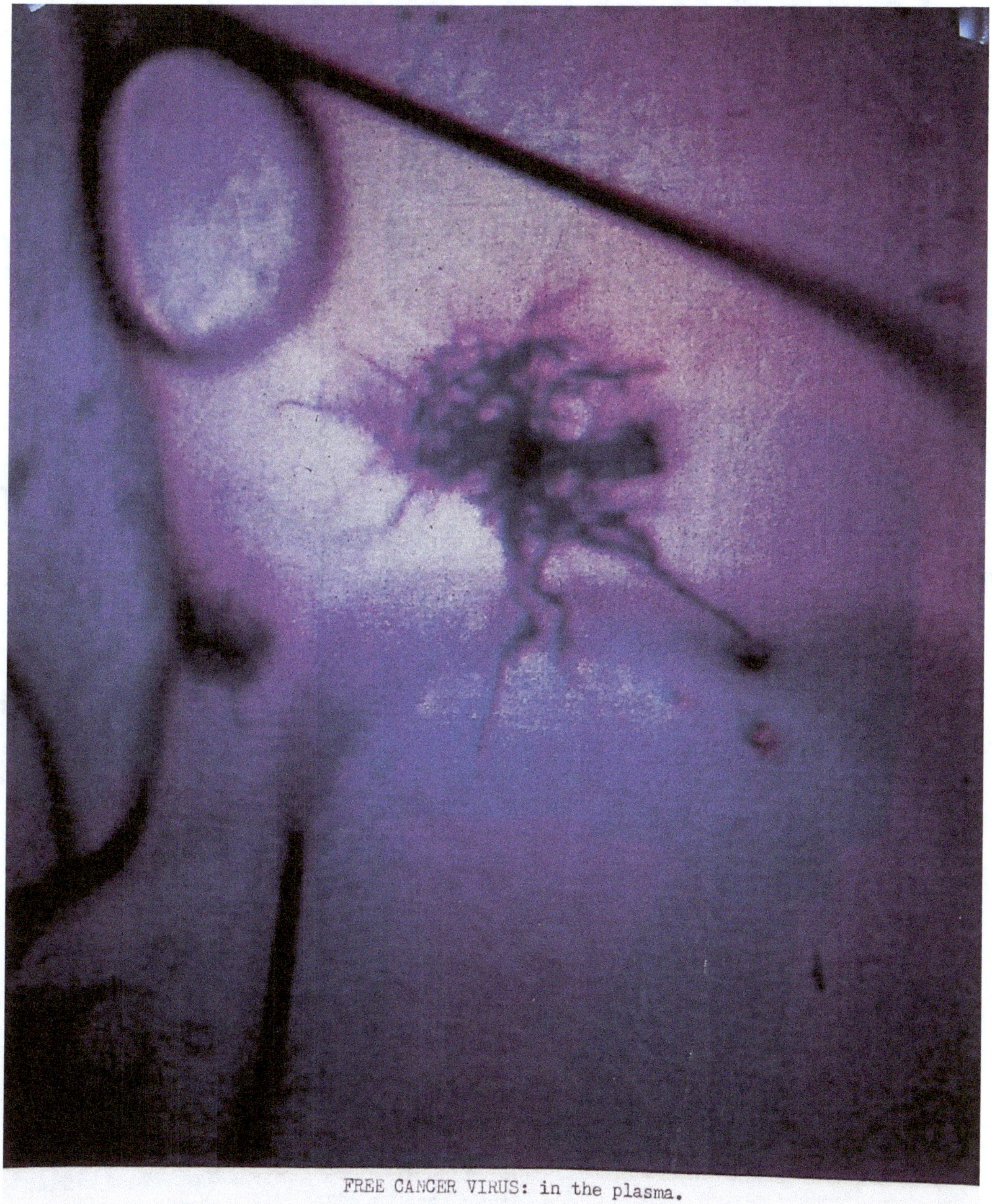

FREE CANCER VIRUS: in the plasma.

MAGNETIC FLUX: The defined lines of the magnetic flux are produced and projected through tertiary emission of the Nemescope. As the wave length is shortened the resolution is increased and the spectrum more defined. Note the impurities in the molecular structure of the screwdriver.

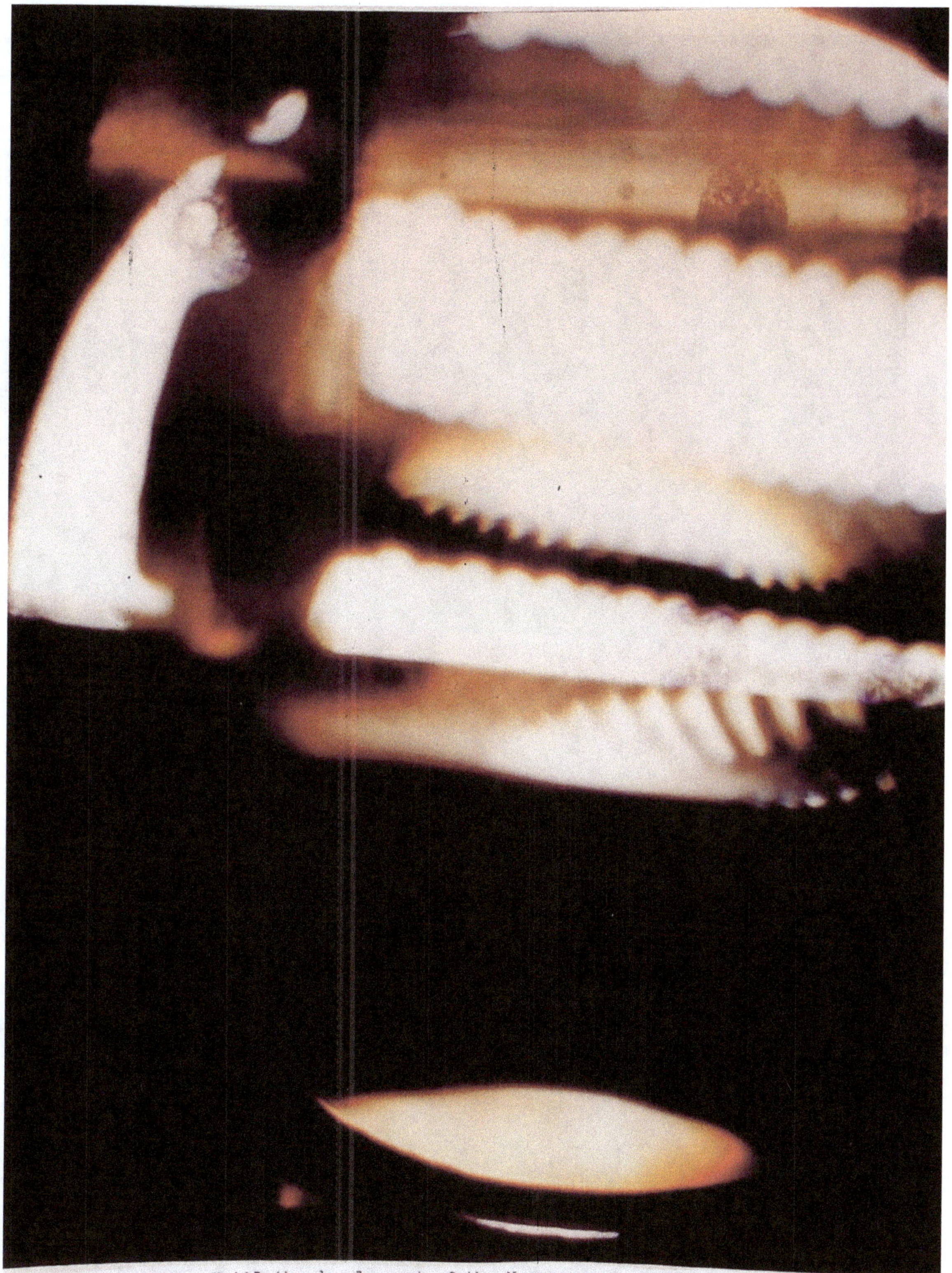

MAGNETIC FLUX: Until the development of the Nemescope no available method could reveal the actual lines of the magnetic flux, although through empirical methods the directional lines of the flux had been proved. Here a permanent magnet was placed in front of the Nemescope's light-like radiation. (Continued.)

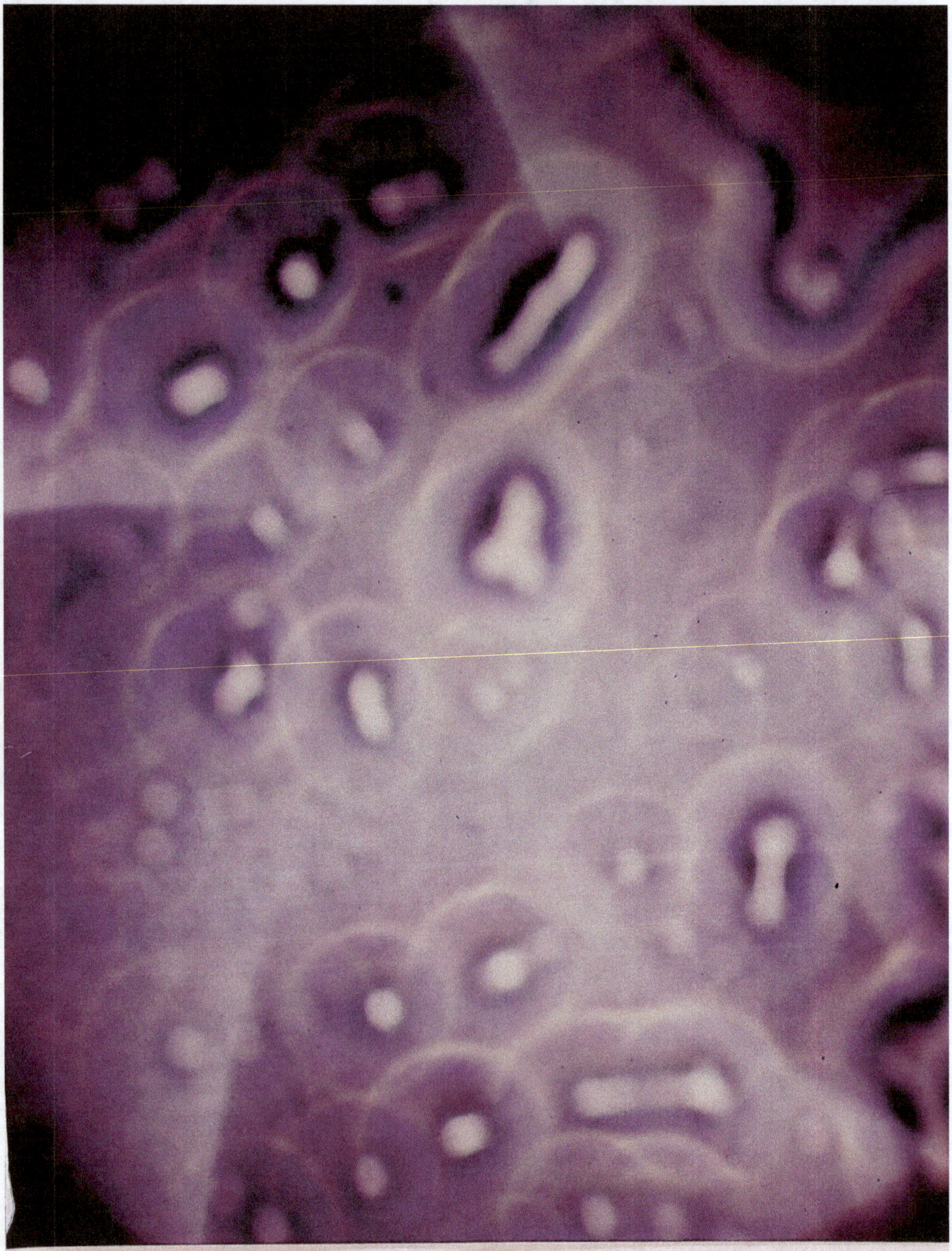

ENZYME OF HORSERADISH: With Chains. By shorter wave length, the spectral category becomes more apparent.

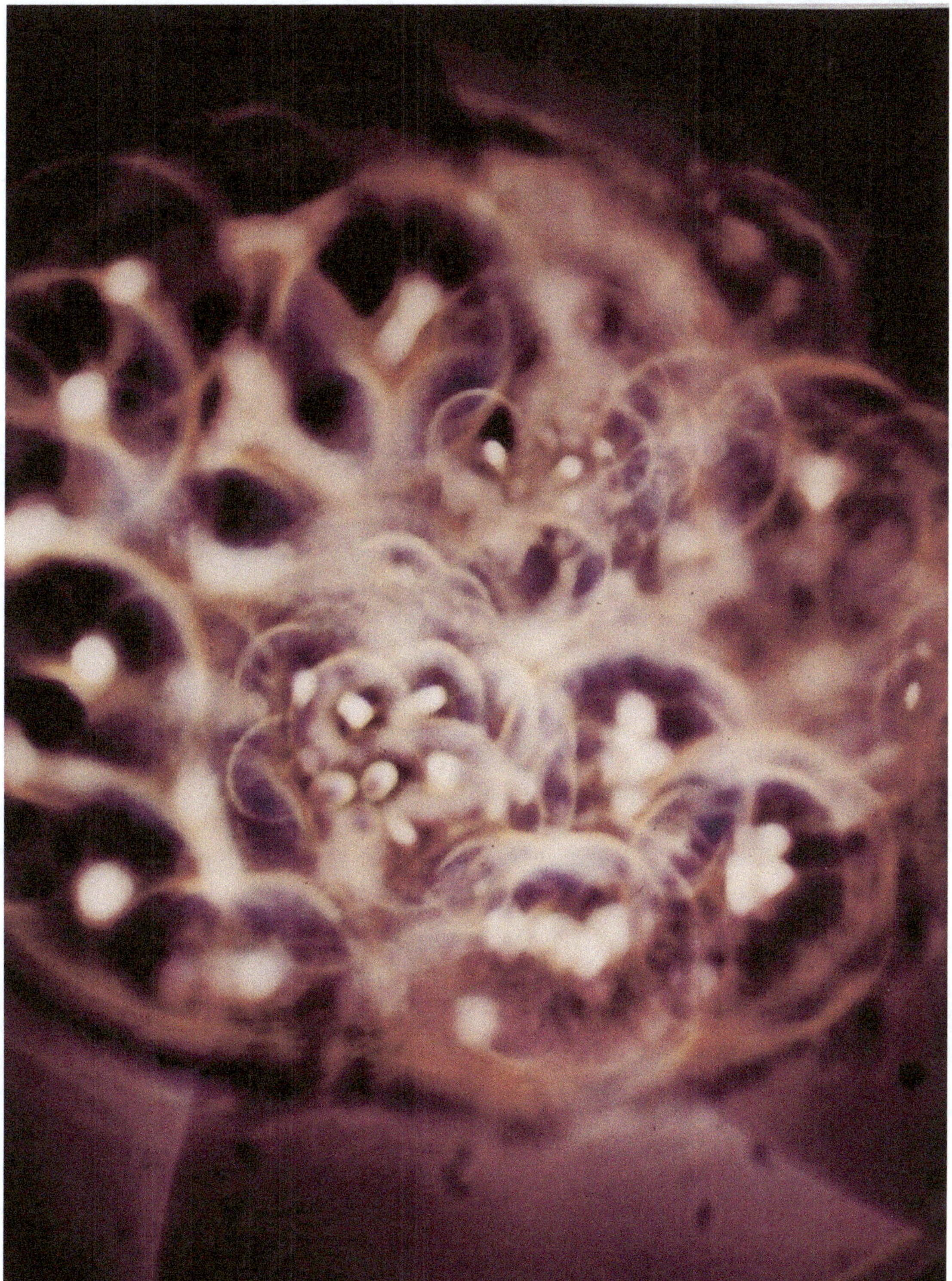

ENZYME OF IVY PLANT: This photo taken when
the enzymes were agitated and still in motion.

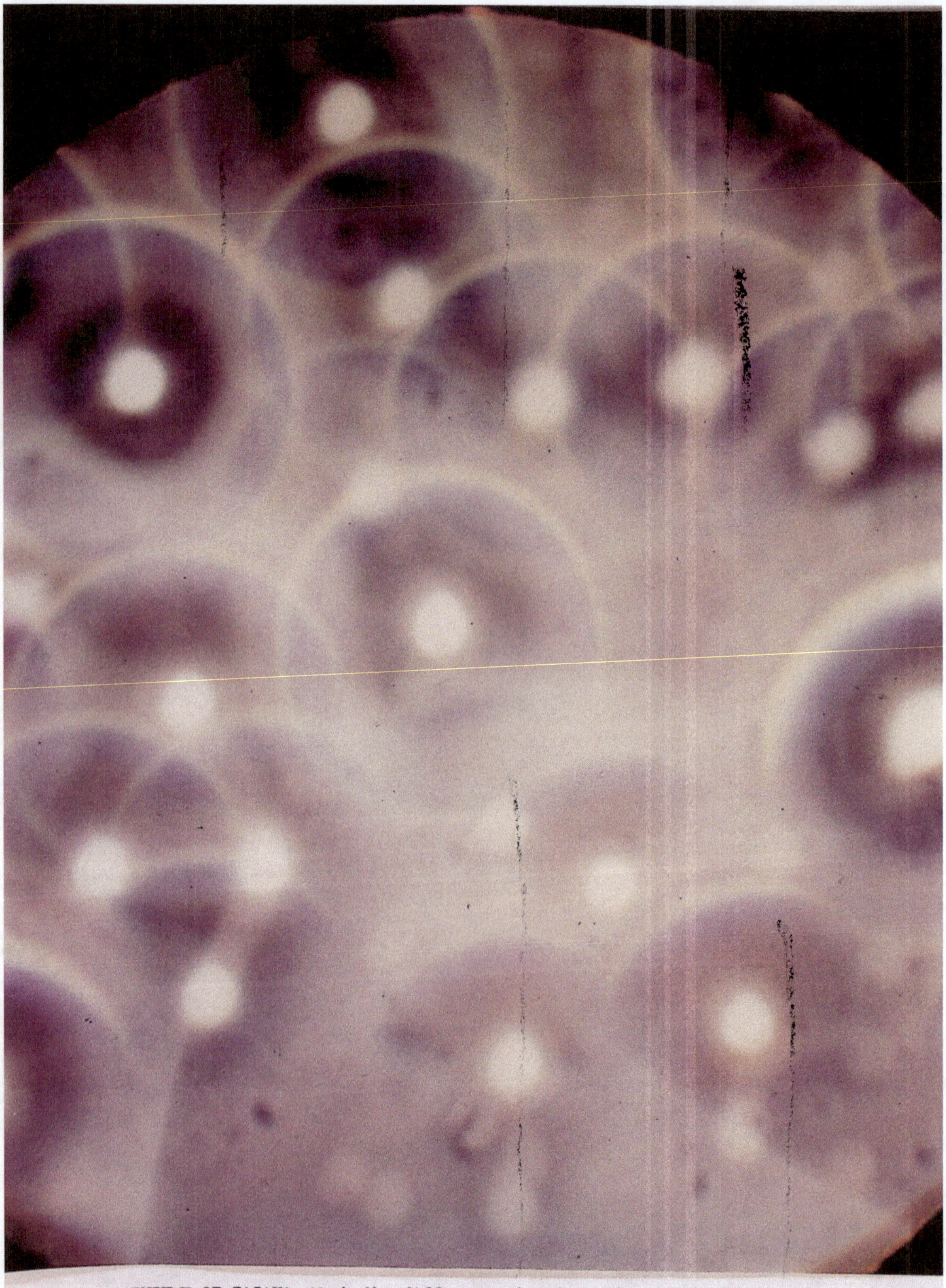

ENZYME OF PAPAYA: Mark the difference in size, the outskirt rings always overlapping the nuclei of the other enzymes.

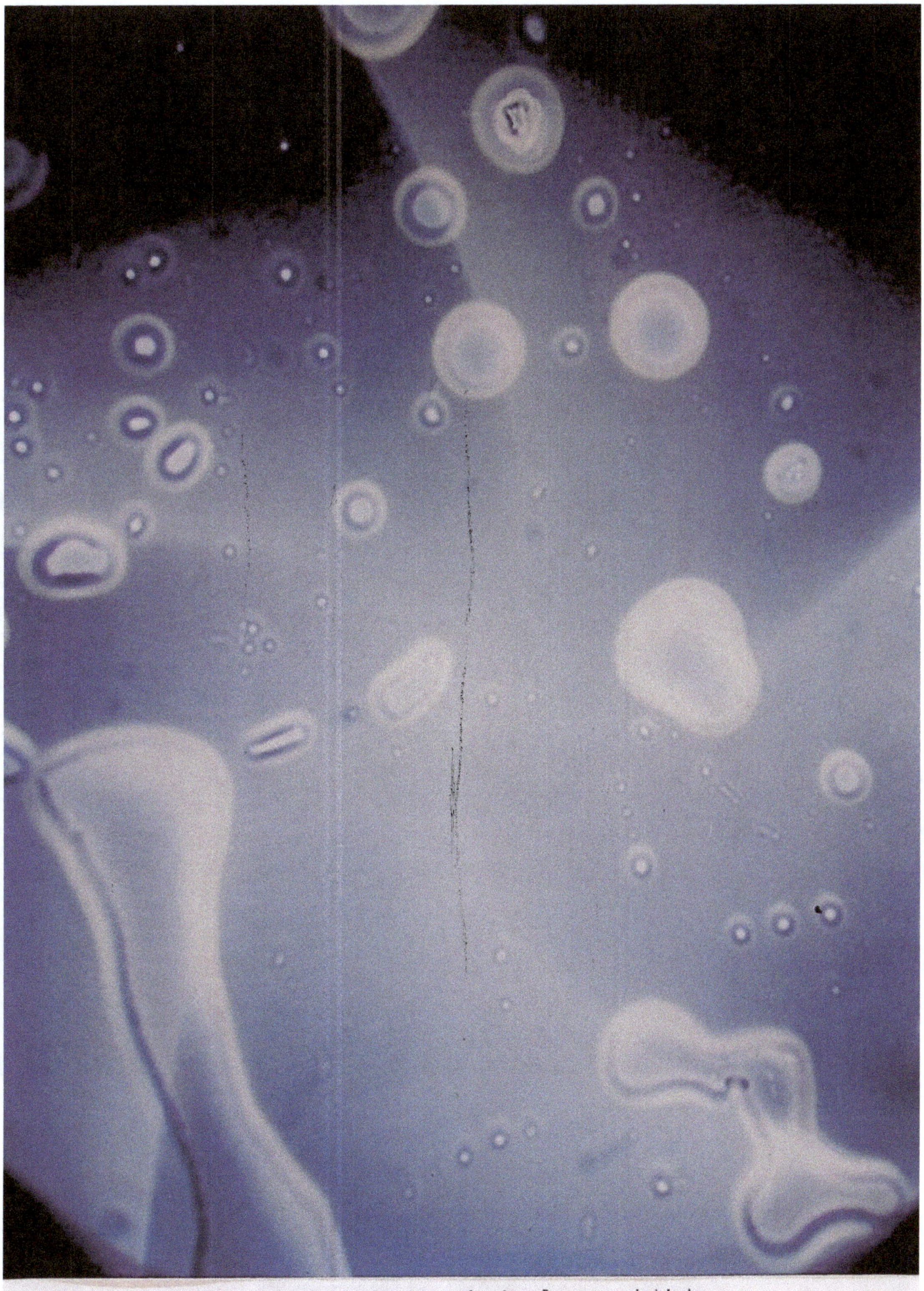

ENZYMES: of Renin, showing larger outskirts.

CYTOPLASM OF THE CELL: Model illustrates structure of the basic cell as theorized through research by The Upjohn Company. The electron microscope was employed to resolve minute cell particles (500 slices per single cell claimed). Their Monograph, The Cell, explains the structure of the life-important nucleus and nucleic acid.

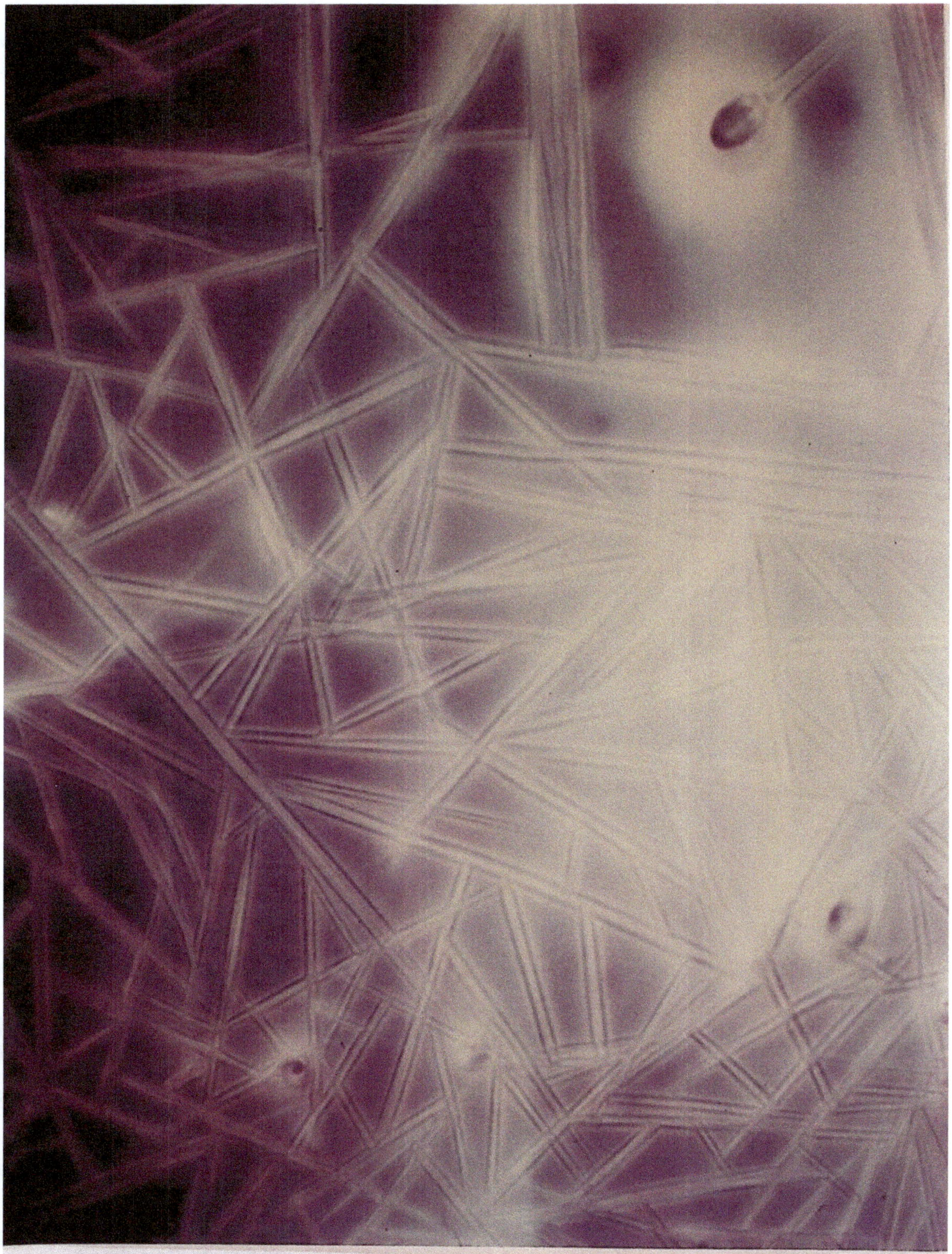

CYTOPLASM OF THE CELL: (Nemescope Photo) True structure and geometric pattern shown through nucleates in center of the nucleic acid. Active nucleus shows up as center of radiation. At base, spectrum shows nitrogen, hydrogen and helium. Nucleic radiation of helium supports primary nucleates.

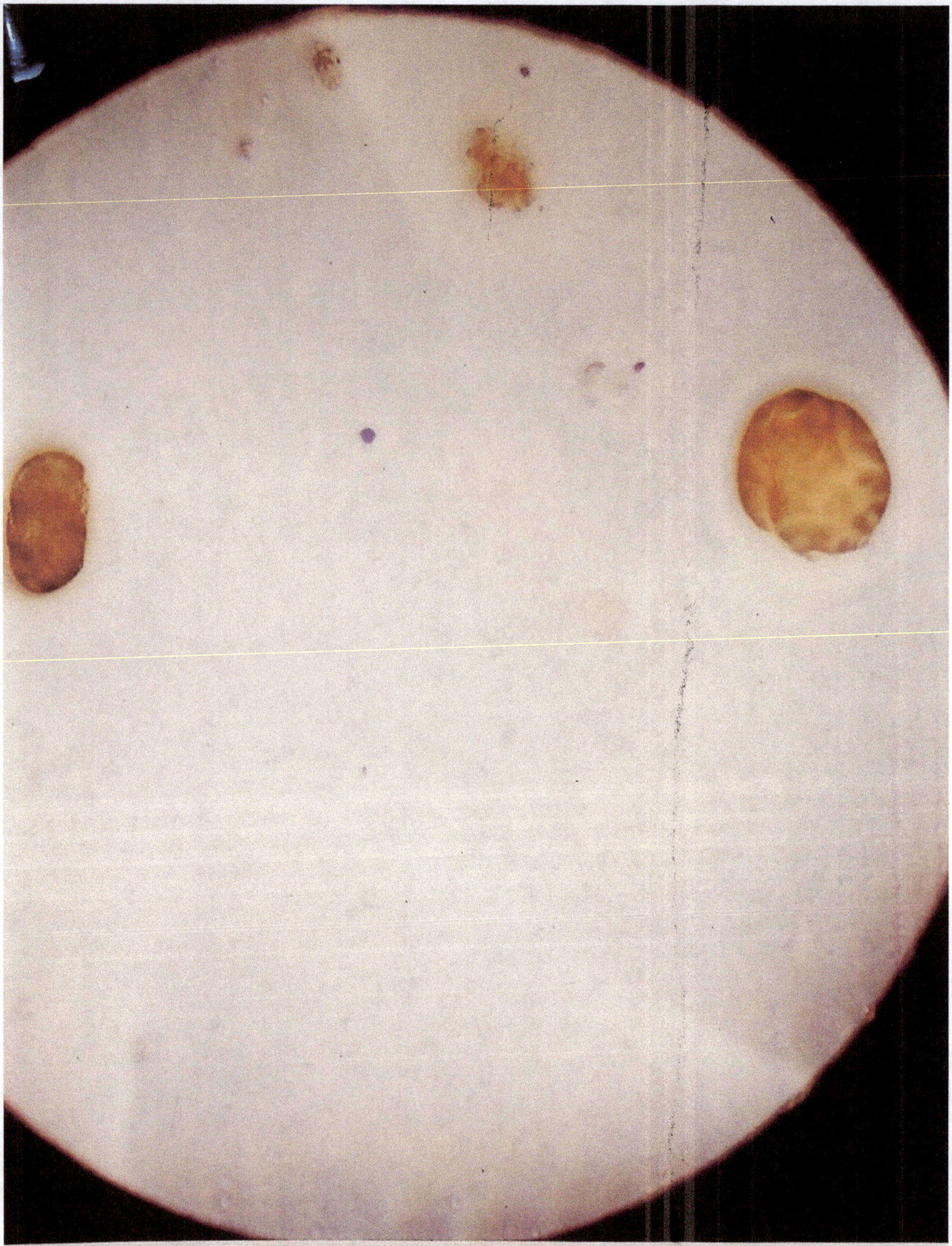

POLIO VIRUS: Nemescope photo of Salk Vacciné.

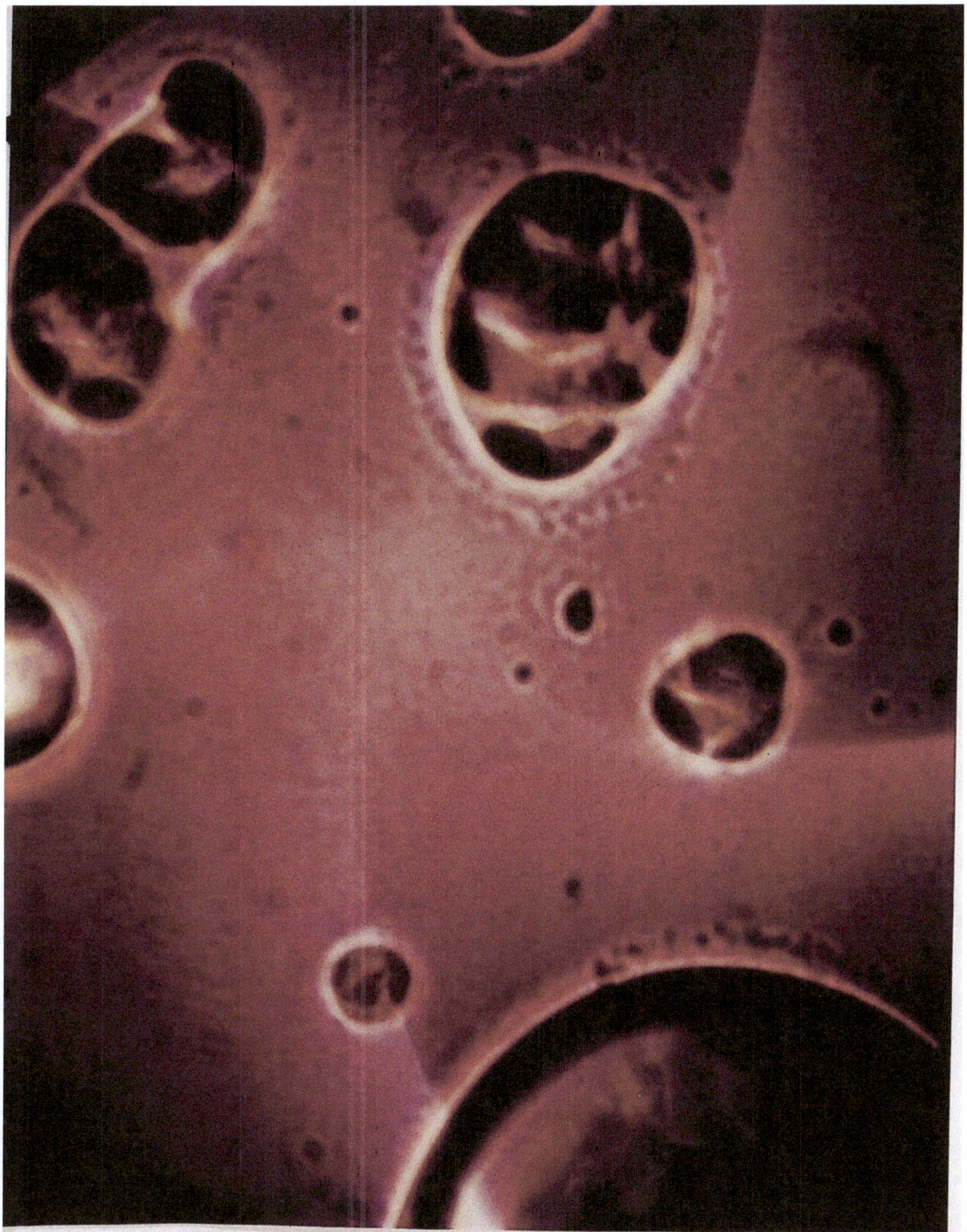

POLIO VIRUS: Same as previous picture, further resolved. The outskirt chain represents the basic toxins of the polio virus.

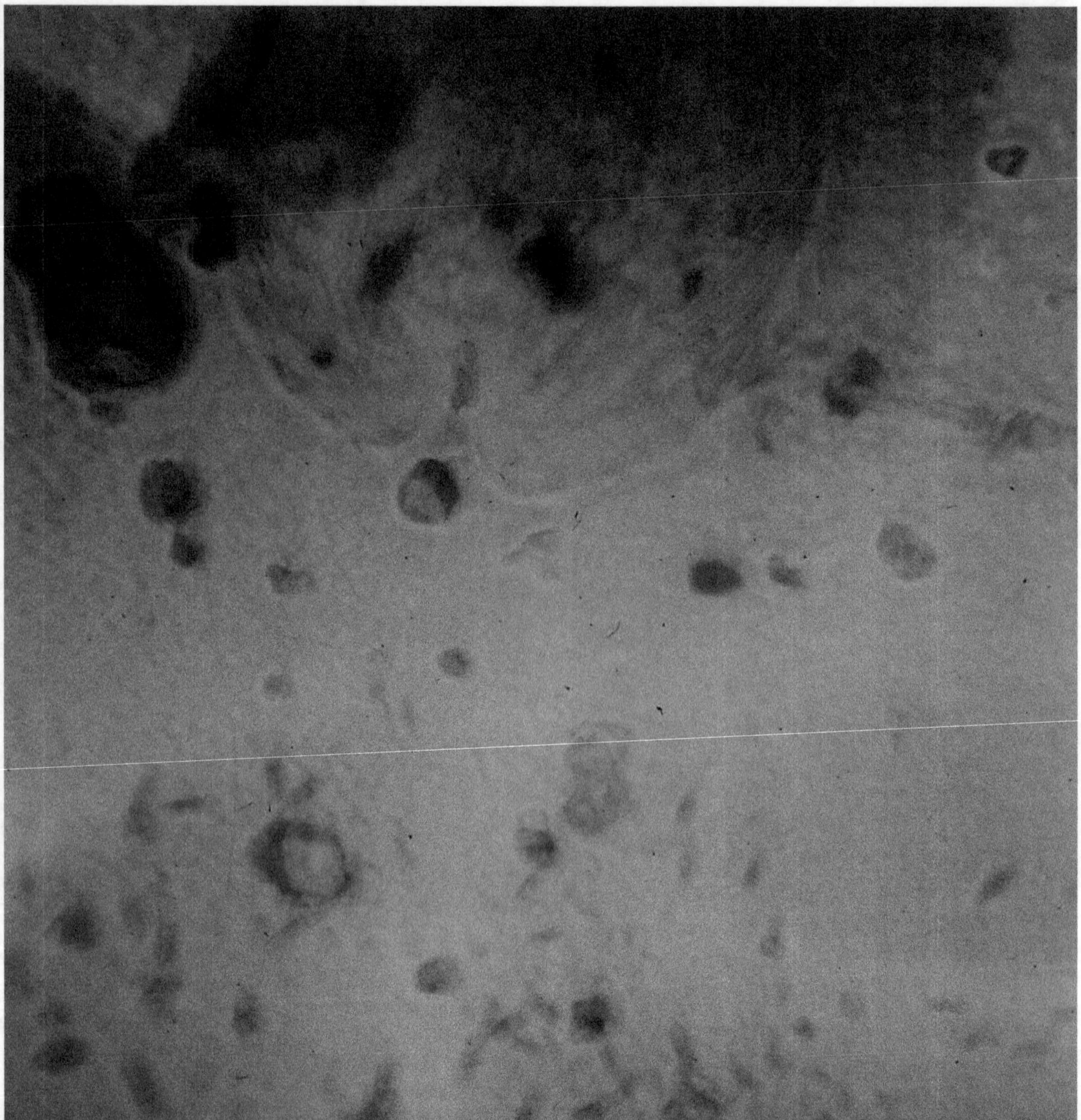

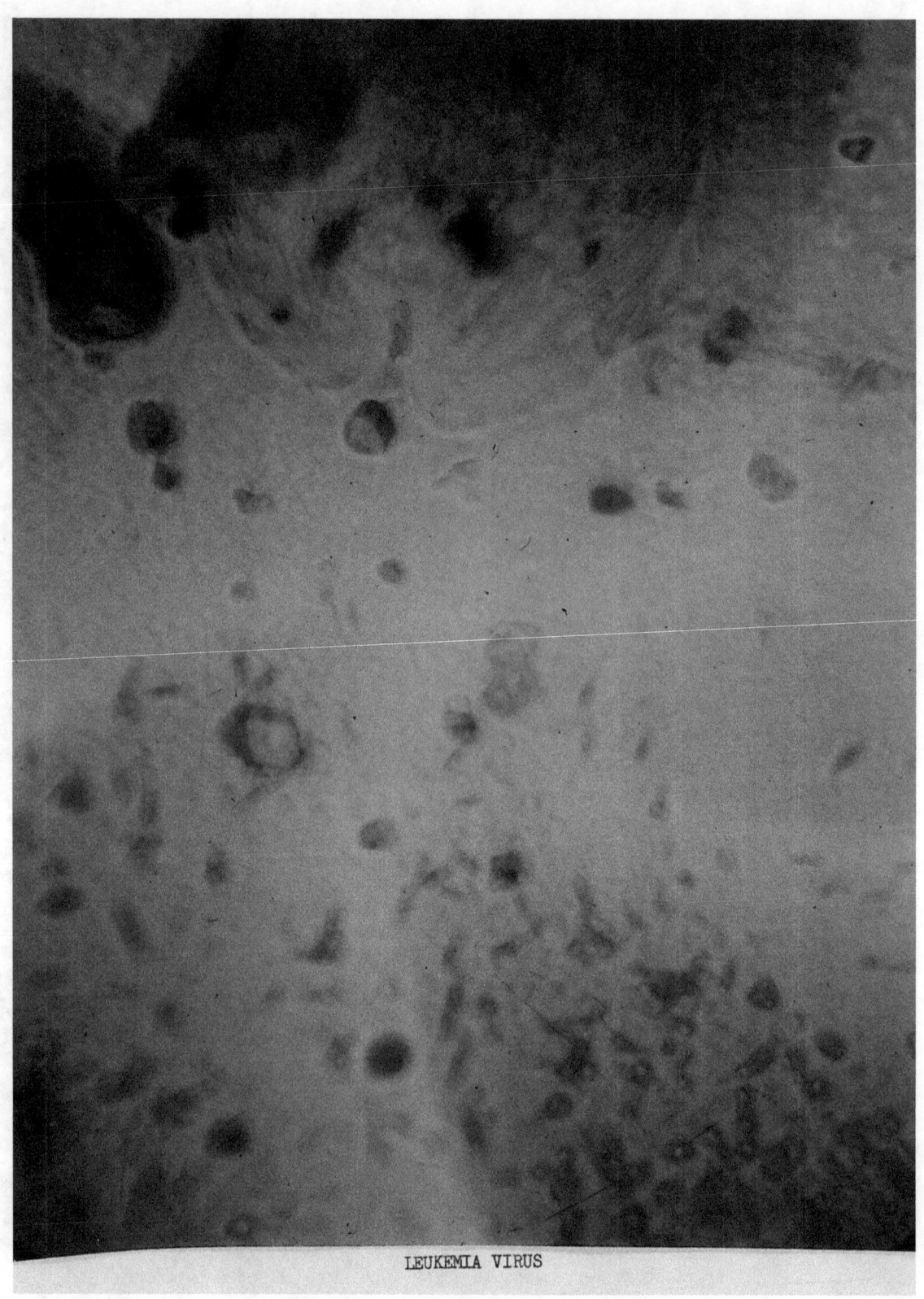

LEUKEMIA VIRUS

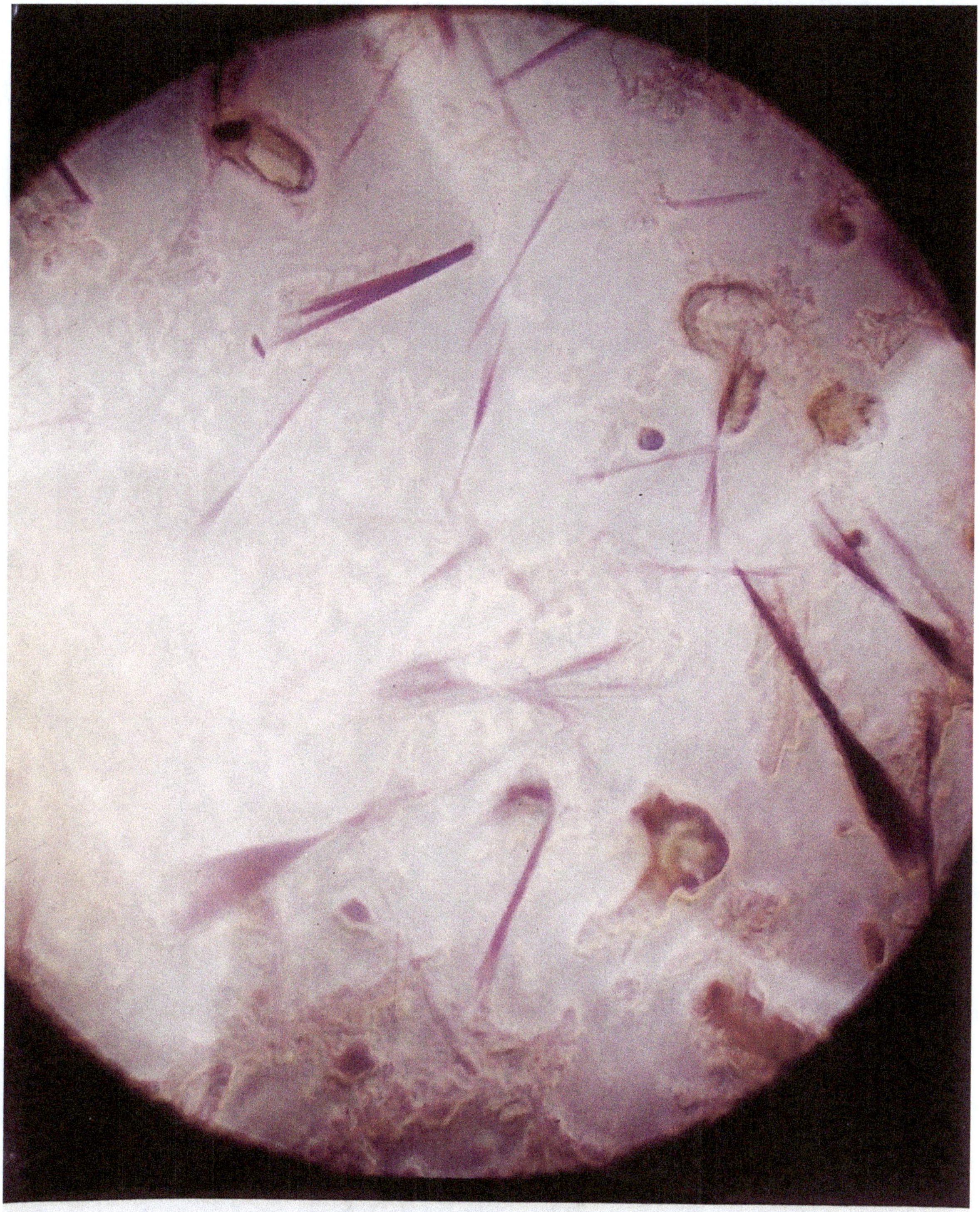

LEUKEMIA PARTICLES: 3,500,000 X resolution.

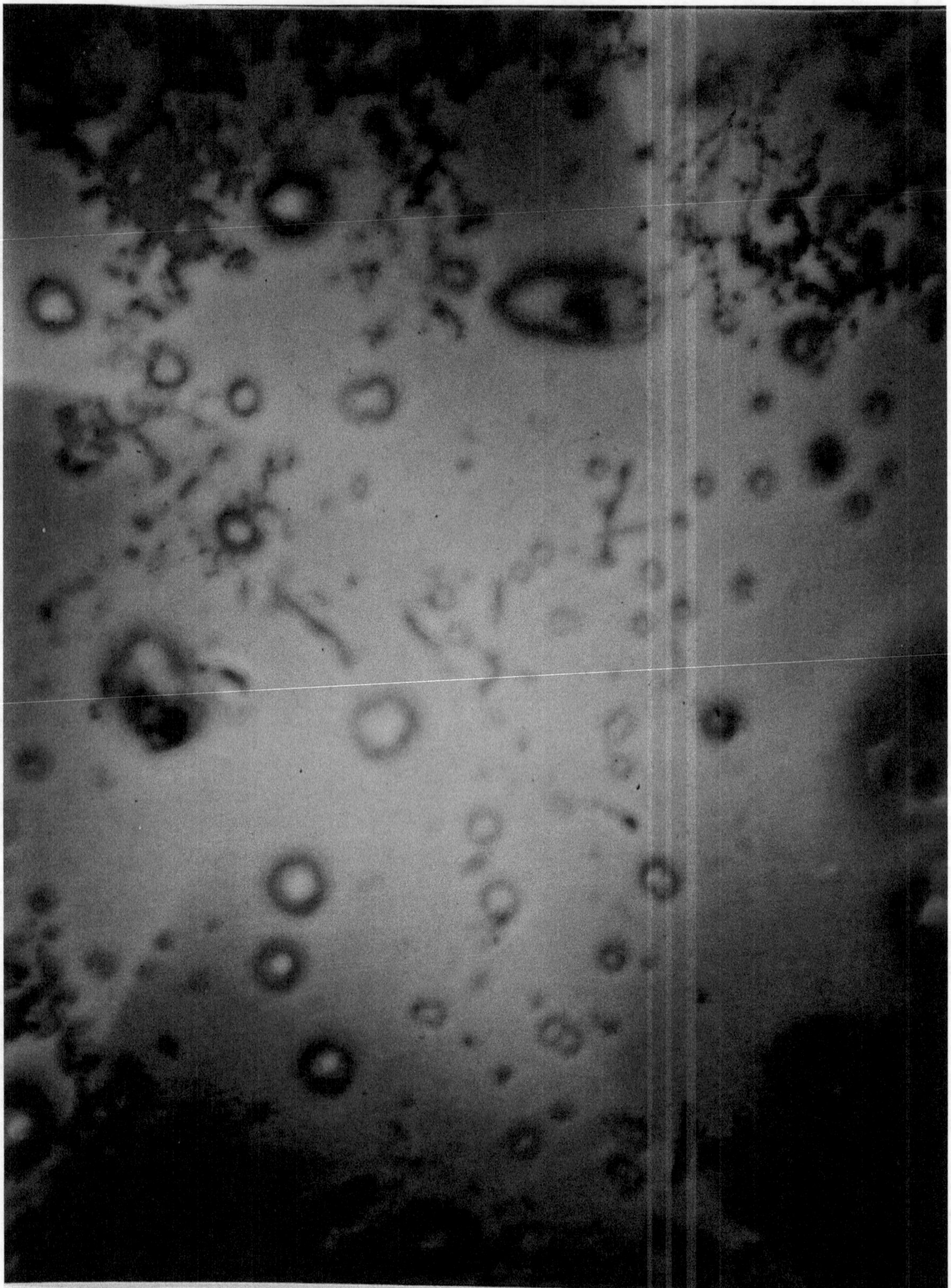

COMMON COLD VIRUS: Similar in structure to the virus first found in Brucillosis infected cow's urine (1952) through the electron microscope. Reproduction of the organisms originates from chains of nitrogen-rich atoms or granules. Before the virus expires it enlarges in size and absorbs to a specific nitrogenous ring.

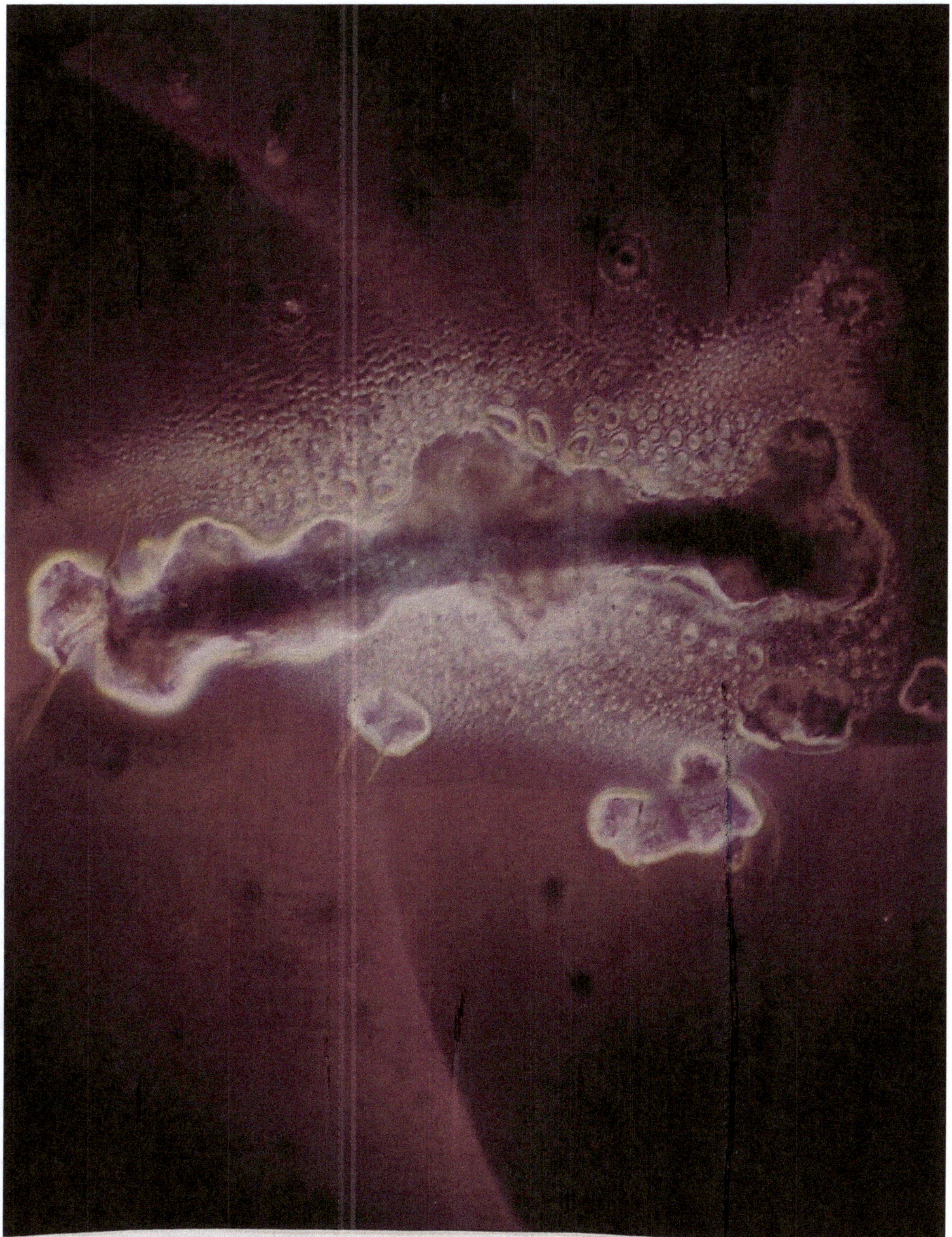

TUBERCULOSIS BACILLUS: From urine specimen of a known victim. Structure of the bacillus is indicated by the large ring of plasma and the presence of other organisms attached to the tuberculosis bacilli.

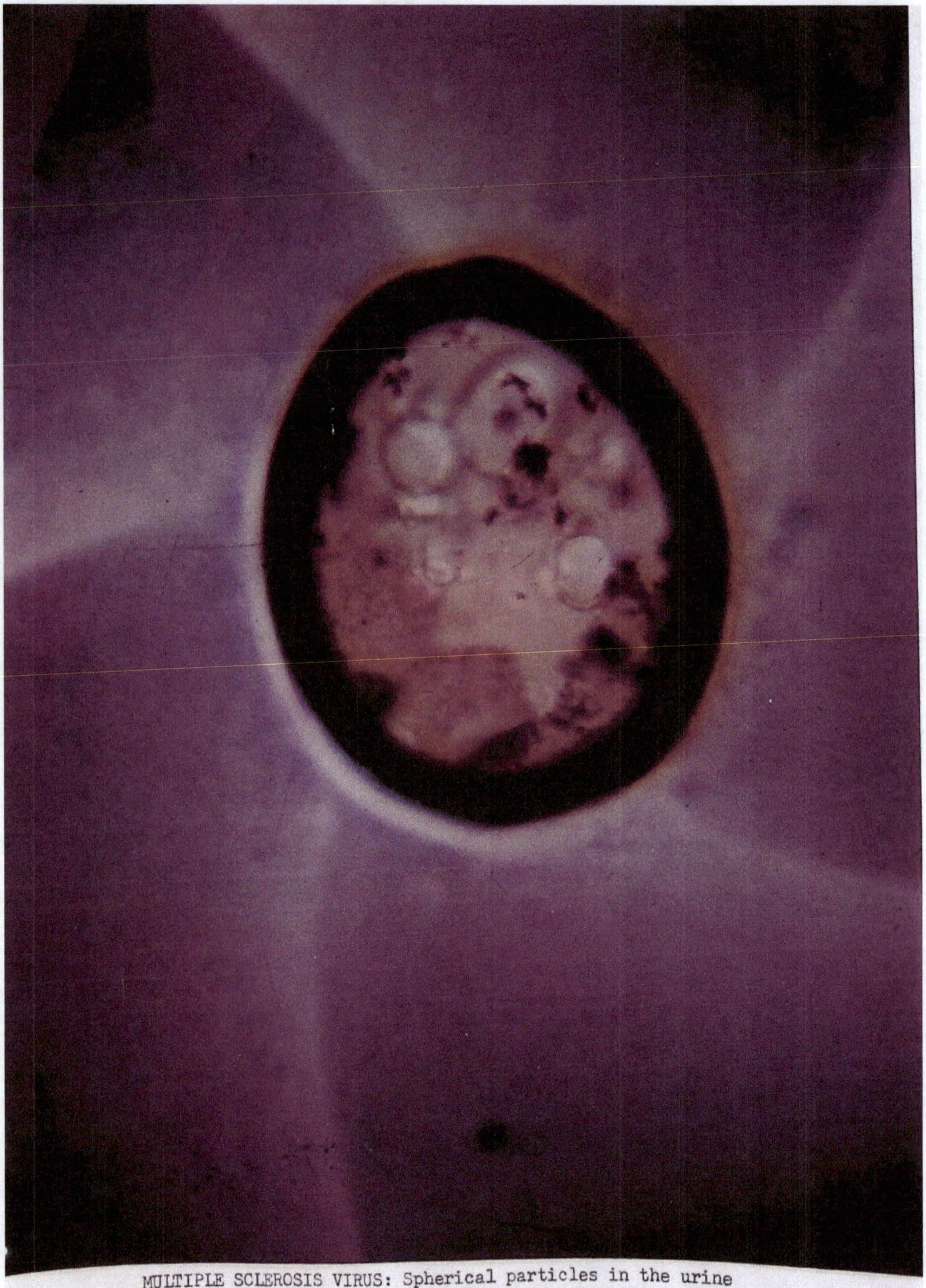

MULTIPLE SCLEROSIS VIRUS: Spherical particles in the urine specimen of a known victim, showing intra-particle morphology.

ENZYME OF THE LUNG: (cow) Complicated spectrum and lines which are created by the nature and basic function of the matter deomonstrate the importance in metabolism of the synthesis of the lung enzyme. Basic structure is shown by the emitted luminescent shadow of the enzyme, and the rings.

ENZYME OF THE LUNG: The complex nucleus, incorporating several lines, radiating toward the external ring of the gaseous base. The second ring contains basically important organic iron phosphate, etc., emitting new spectral picture and complex directional diversion of energy flows.

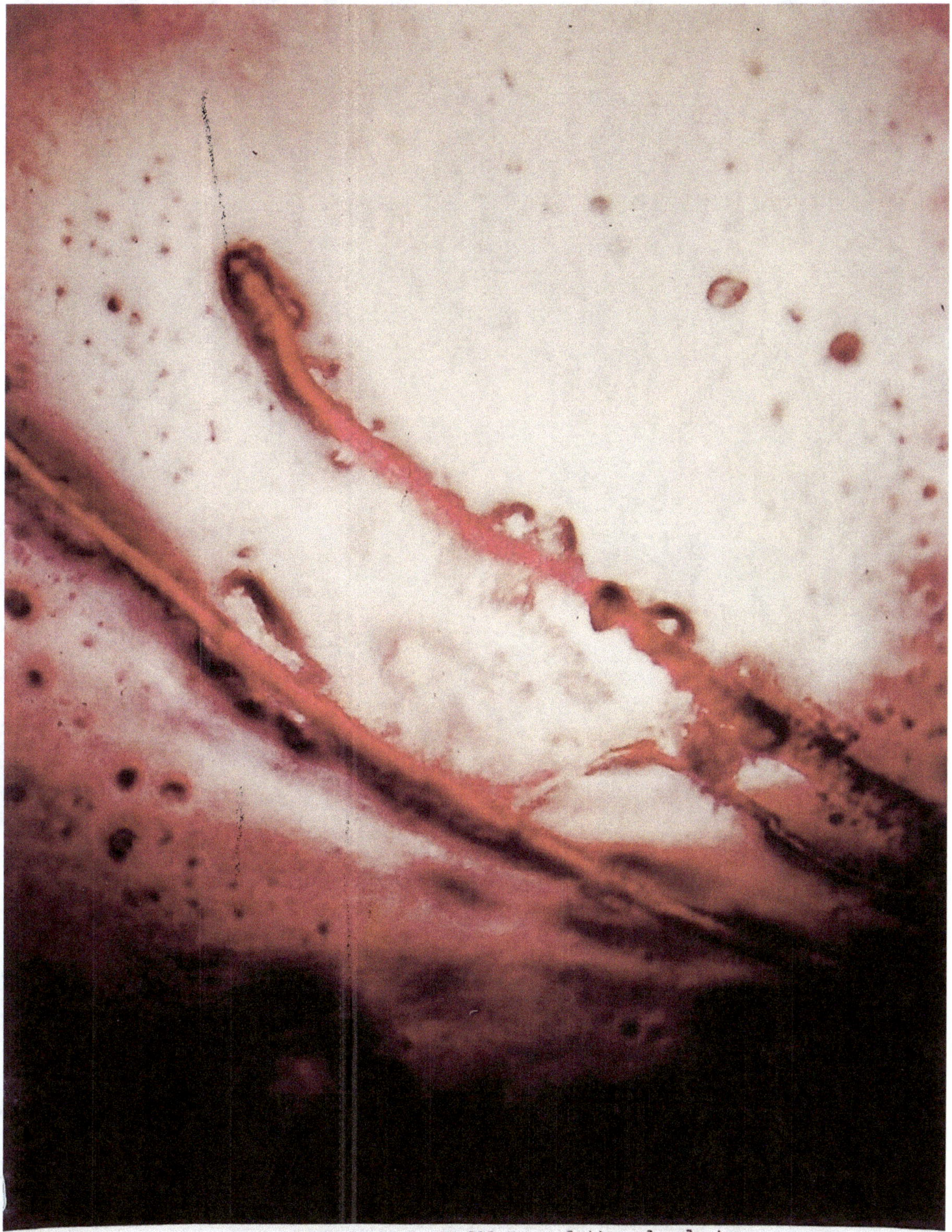

RED BLOOD CELL: 3,500,000 X resolution clearly indicates the presence of groups of nucleic acid.

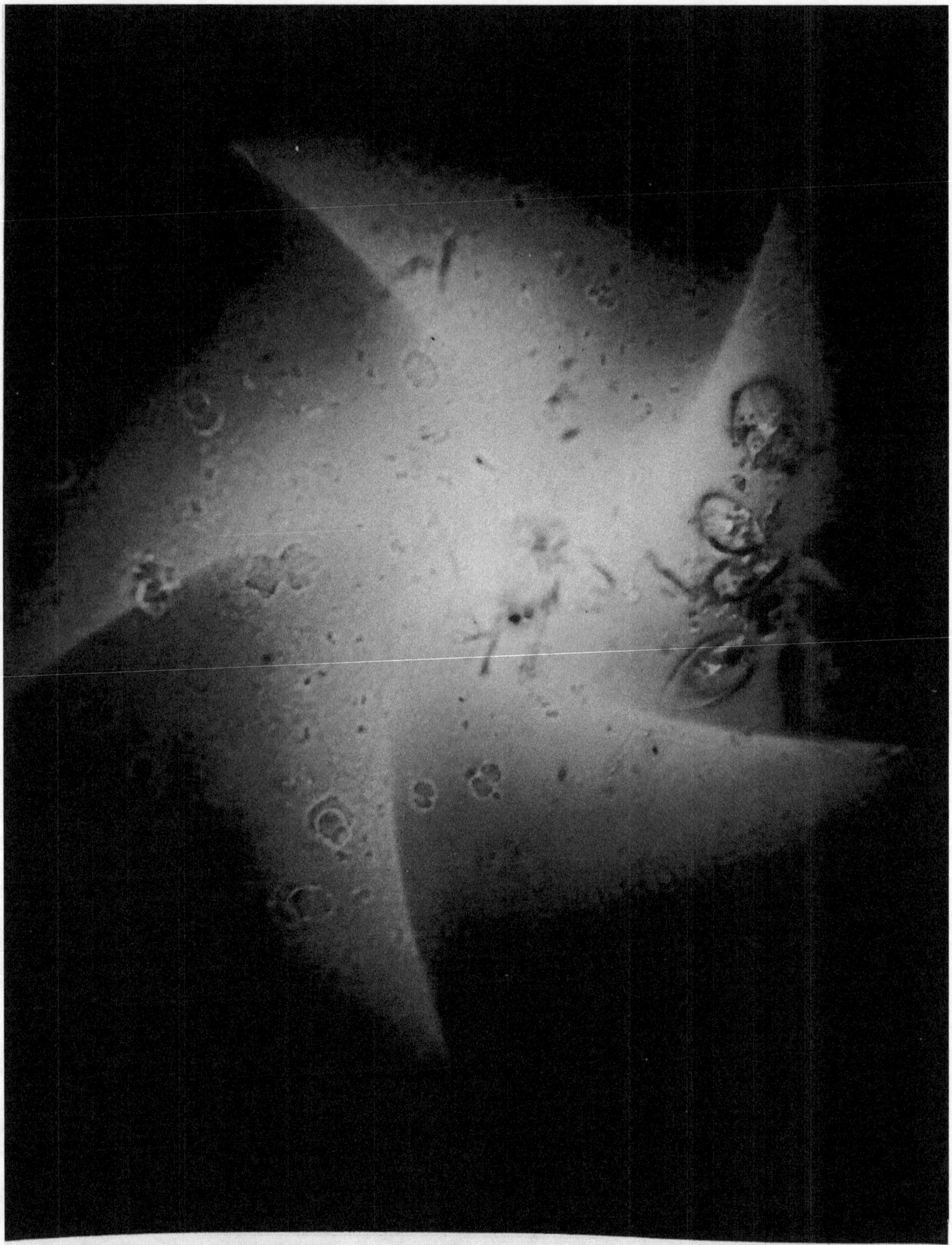

MUSCULAR DYSTROPHY VIRUS: 3,500,000 X resolution shows specific structural and spectral morphology of the muscular dystrophy-causing agent, specific to urine specimens of victims of this disease. (Discovered by Alice Jennings.)

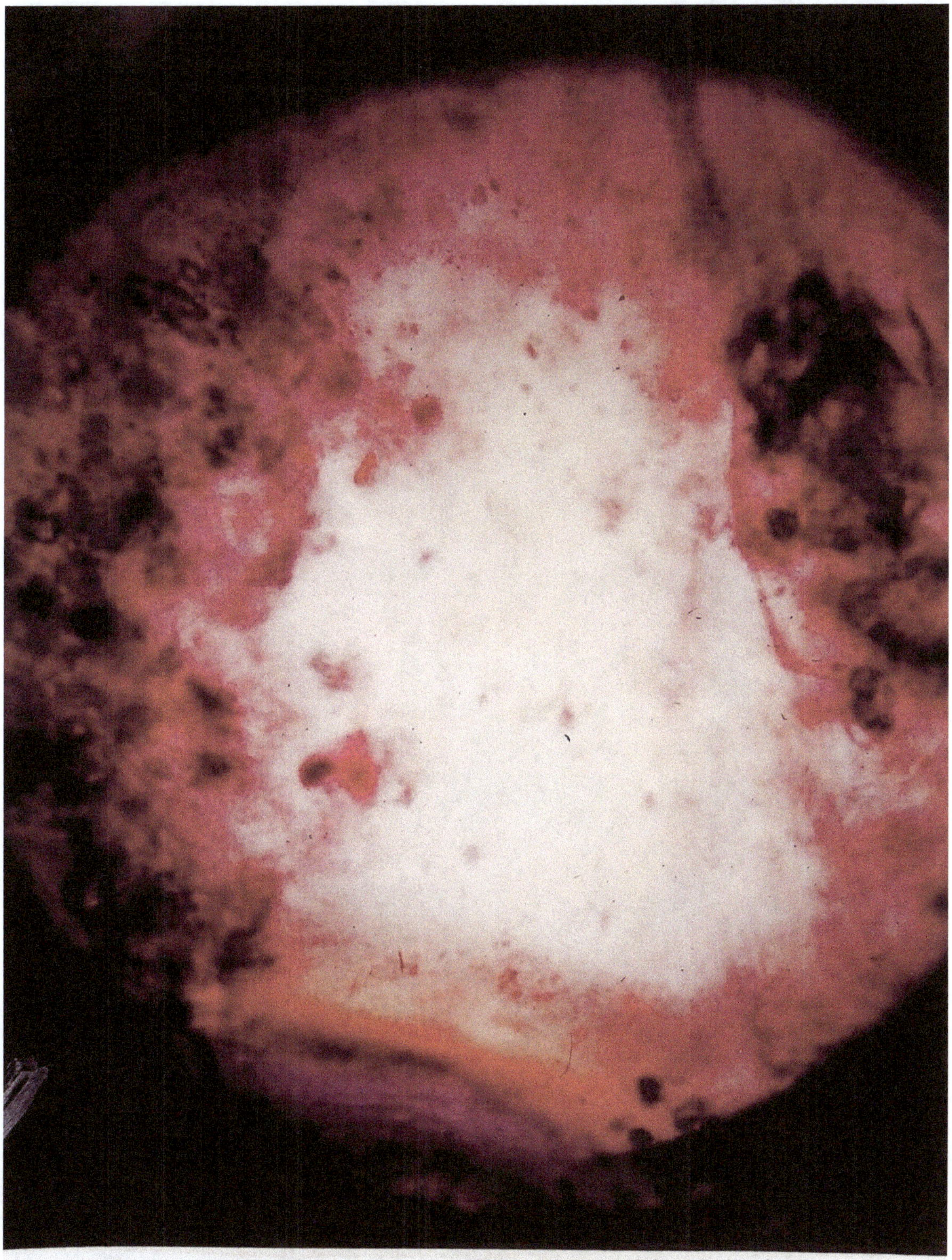

RED BLOOD CELL: Several defined nitrogen-rich structural formations and the presence of other life-important nucleates.

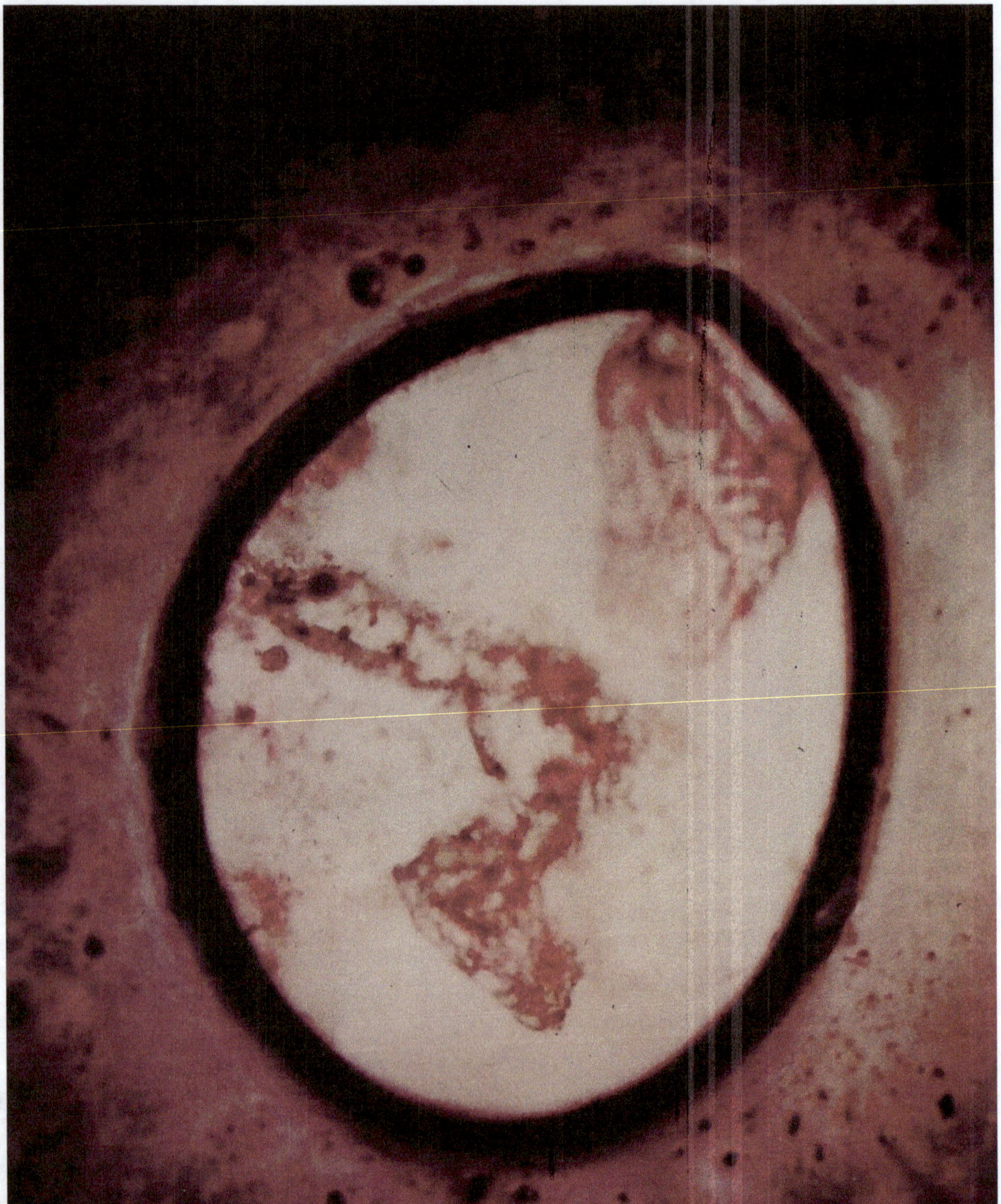

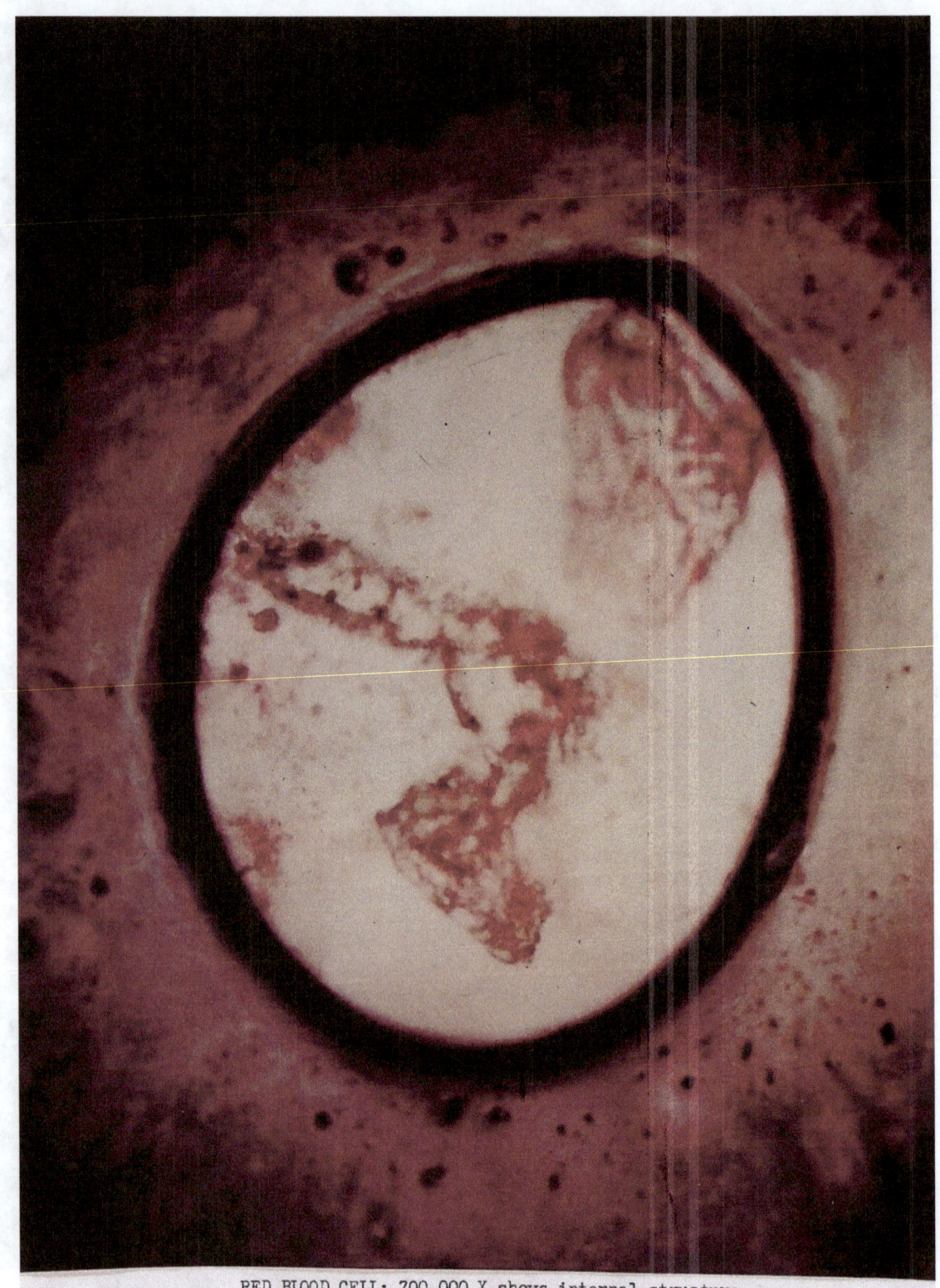

RED BLOOD CELL: 700,000 X shows internal structure
without defined adherancy, one to the other.

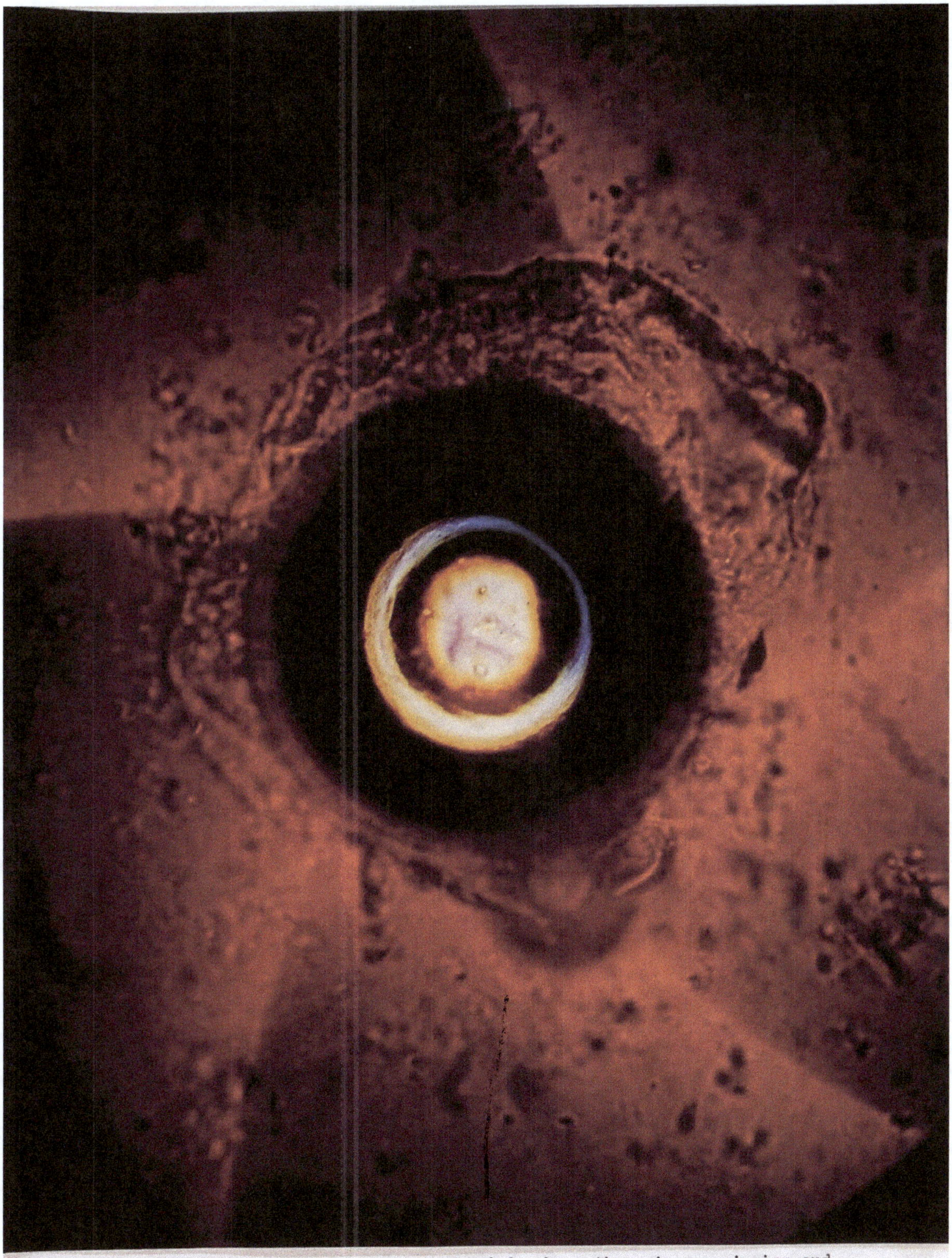

IRON NUCLEATE: Organic iron, when bombarded, shows the primary emission and spectrum of the molecules. In upper center, the spectrum of the matter is clearly visible, the connection of which is not completely resolved here.

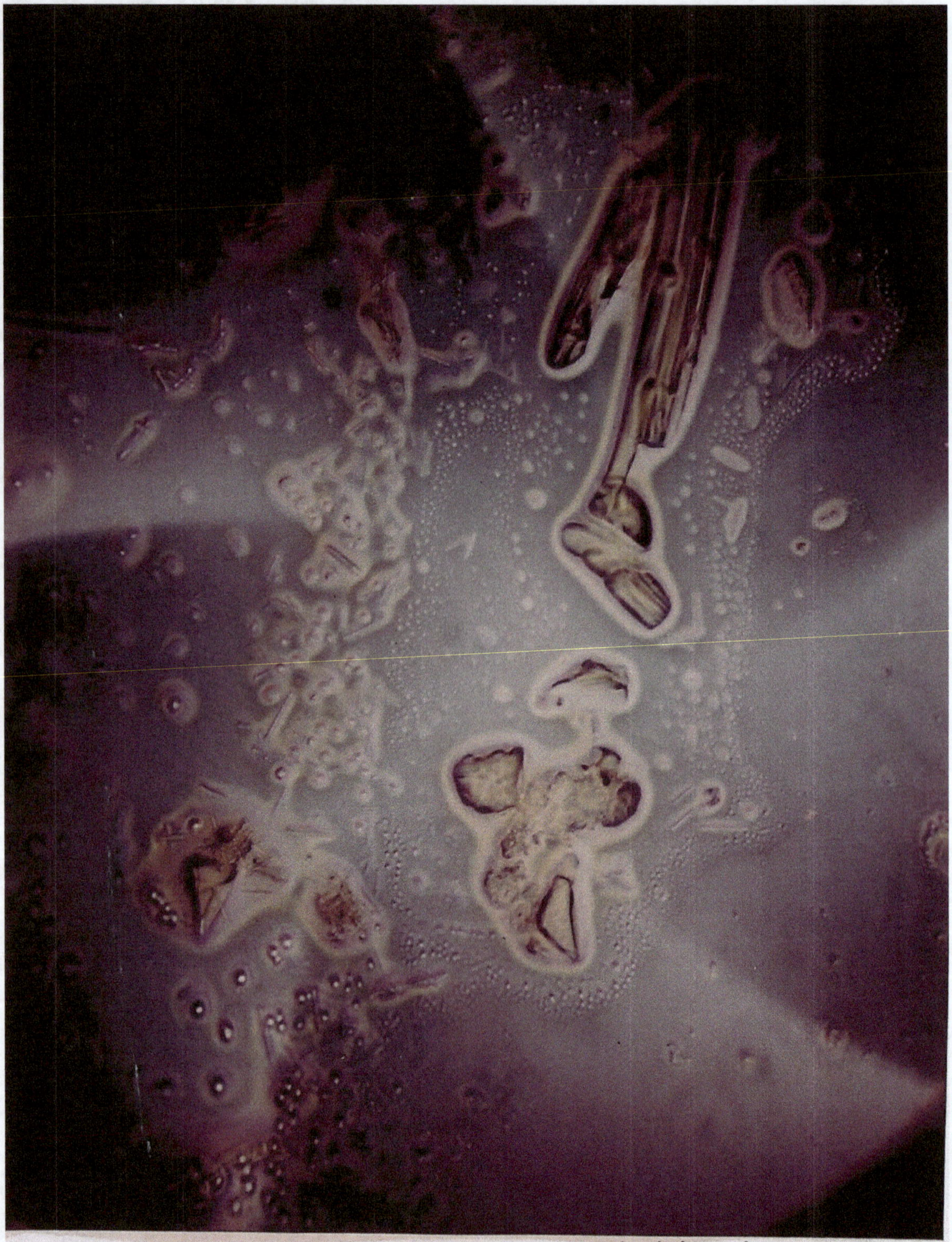

BATTERY EXPERIMENT WITH ENZYMES: The sub-atomic chains and the matter are clearly visible. Smaller enzymes in different orbit show up in still greater xx resolution.

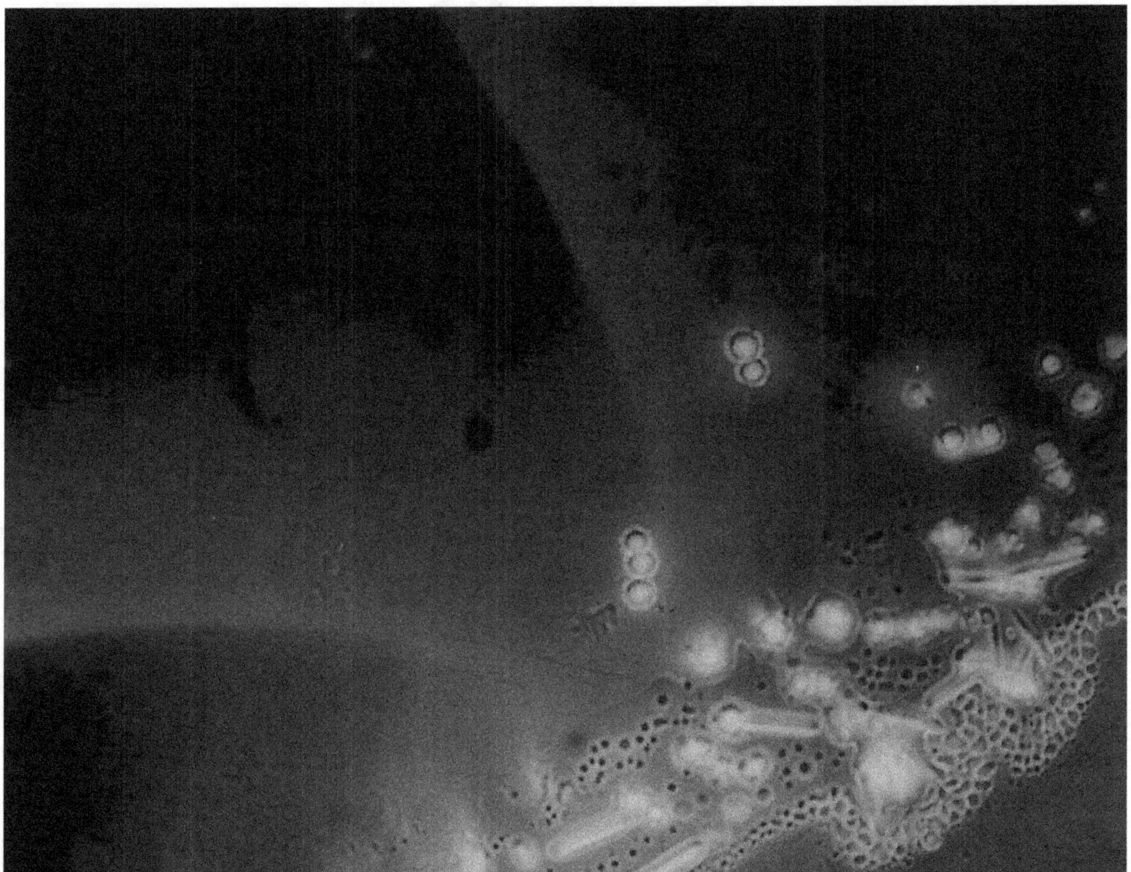

~~ENZYME RENNET~~: Completely restored atomic chains of the enzyme, with shadows. By dimension is suggested the innumerable field of the enzyme.

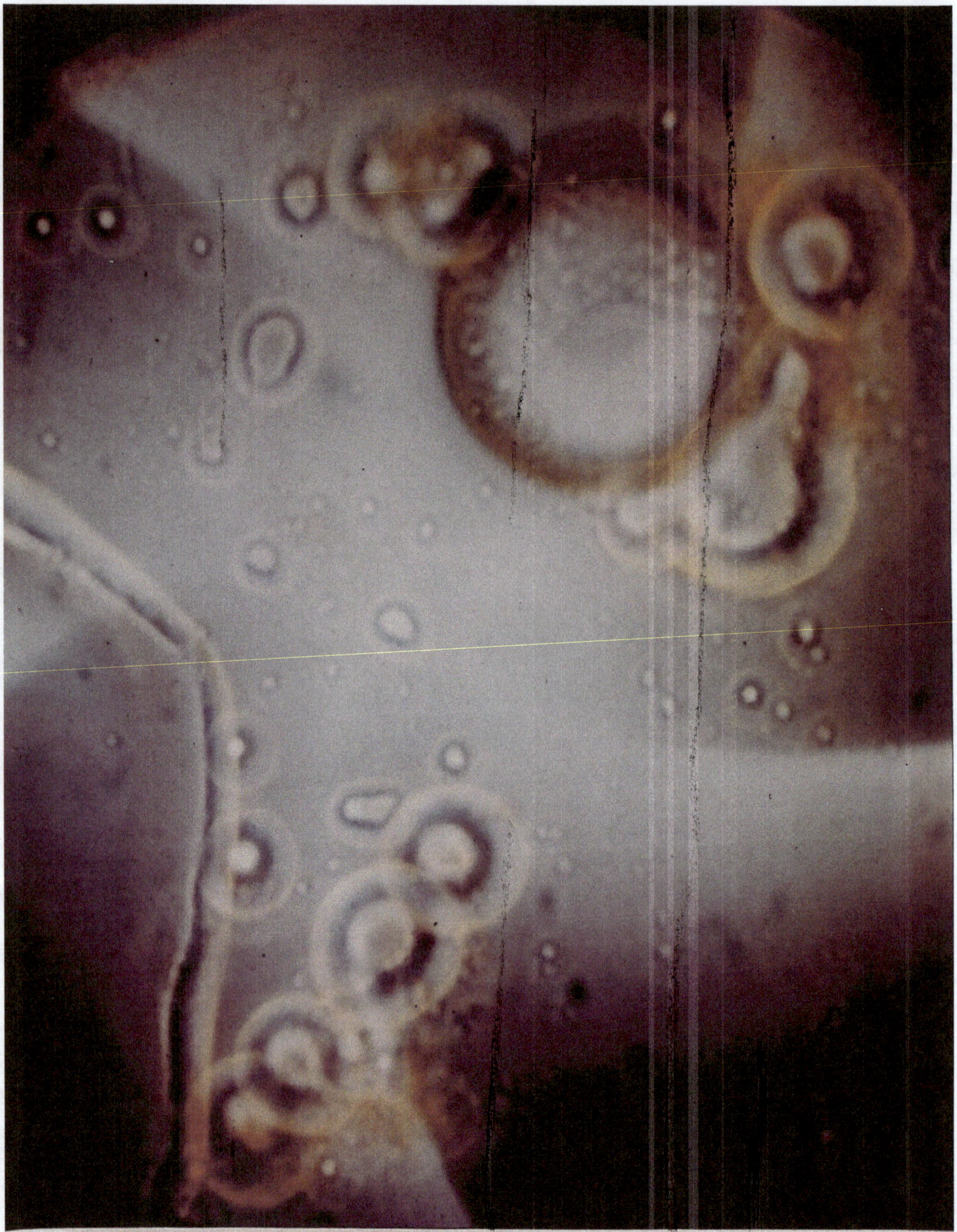

ENZYMES: of carrot juice, organically grown. The structure of t he enzyme, which appears in the plasma, clearly shows the spectrum and the chain of enzymes. The photo was taken while the enzymes were in an agitated, active stage.

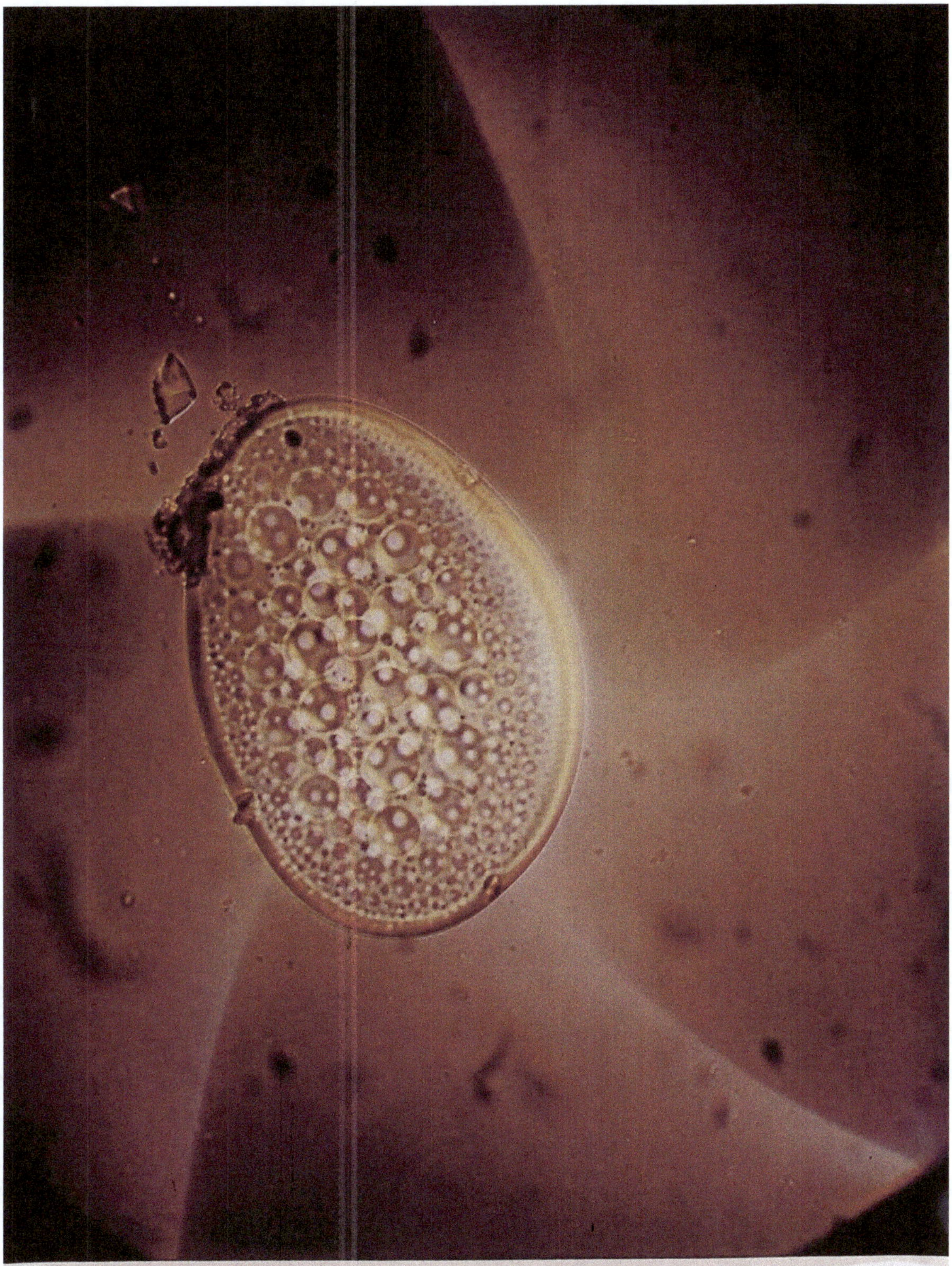

ENZYMES: of carrot juice, commercially grown with chemical fertilizers and sprays. Note how the DDT molecules present in the plasma have been surrounded and contained by the enzymes, demonstrating their tremendous catalytic activity regarding the toxic molecules.

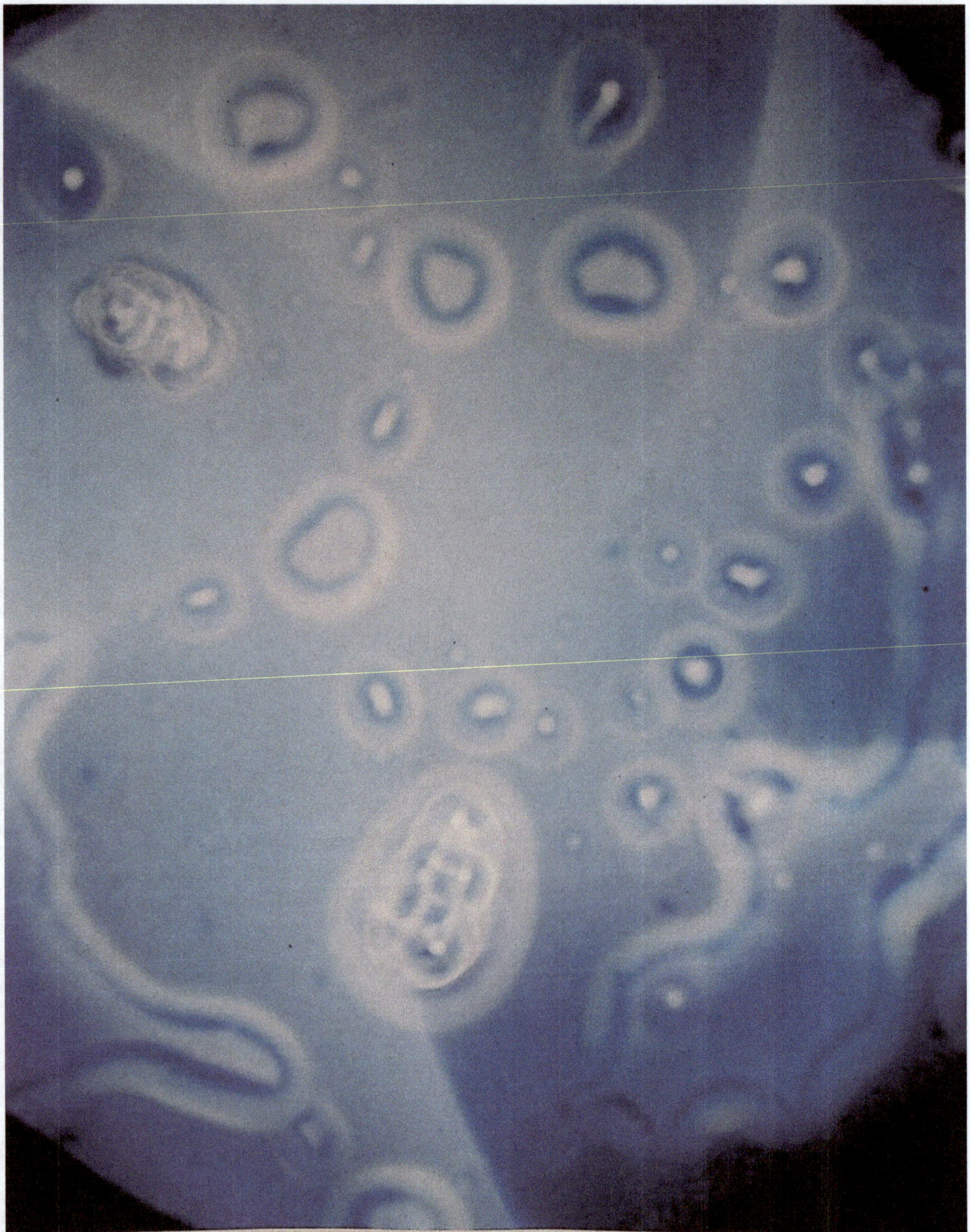

RADIATED ENZYMES: (Material furnished by Dr. Max Jacobson) Even with high radiation enzymes did not lose their activity, but through their catalytic action the radiation was controlled and only released under antagonistic metabolic effects as in illness or toxemia. Research indicates that "fallout" may be controlled through enzymatic catalysis.

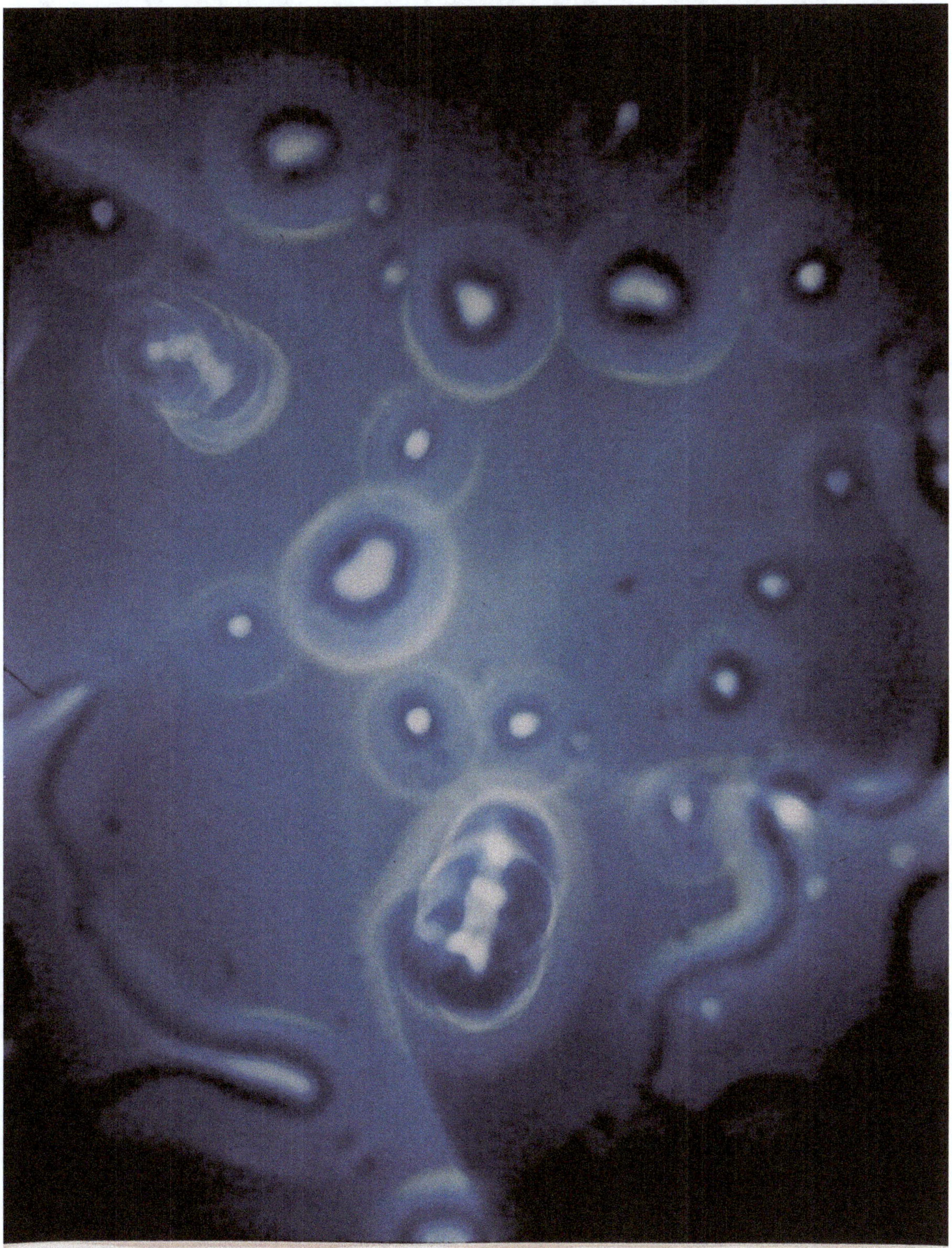

RADIATED ENZYMES: Dilated nuclei of the enzymes, showing tremendous activity.

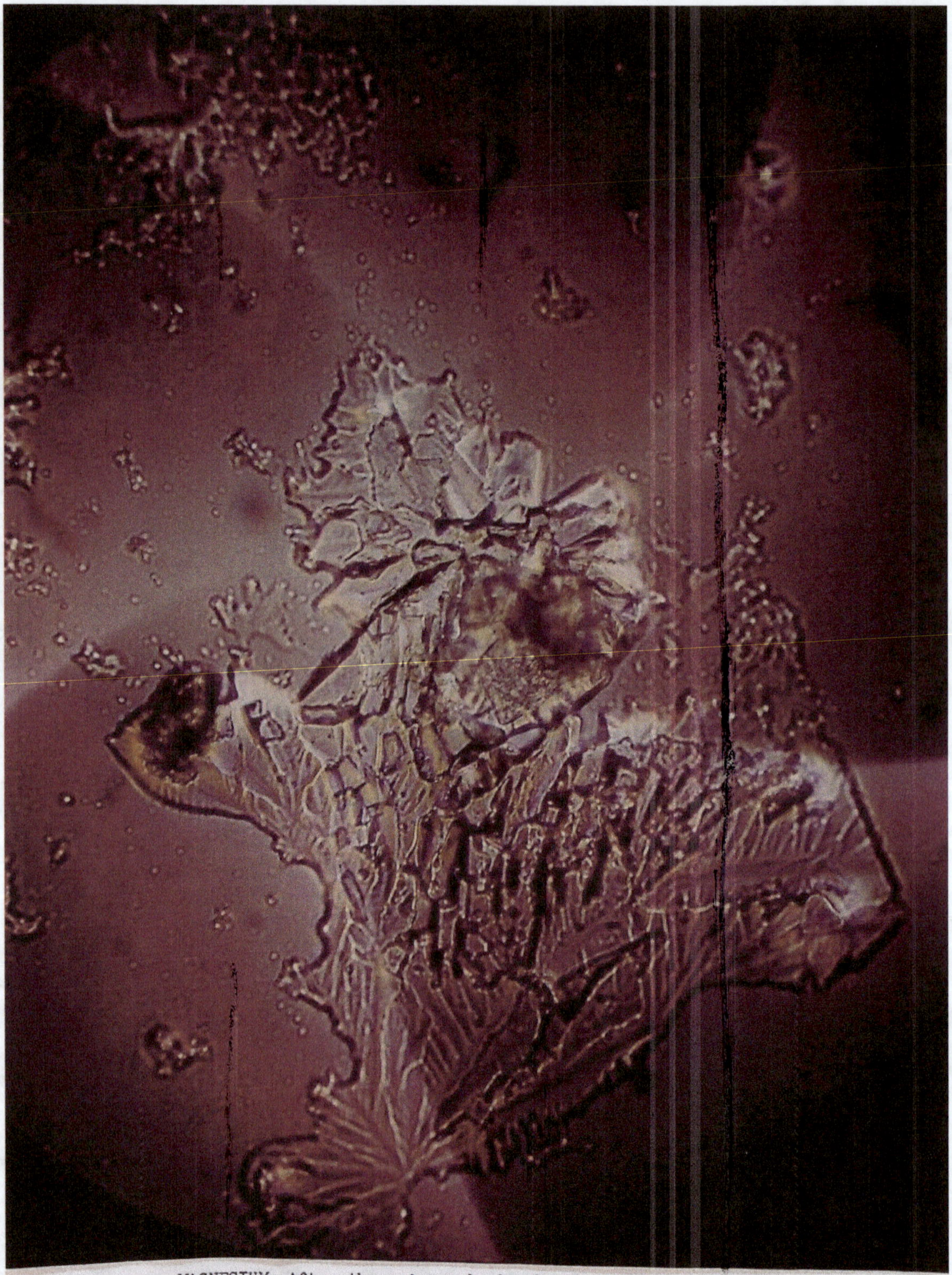

MAGNESIUM: After the primary bombardment and radiation, the atoms are clearly visible in the interrupted chains attached to the classical known formation of metalic magnesium.

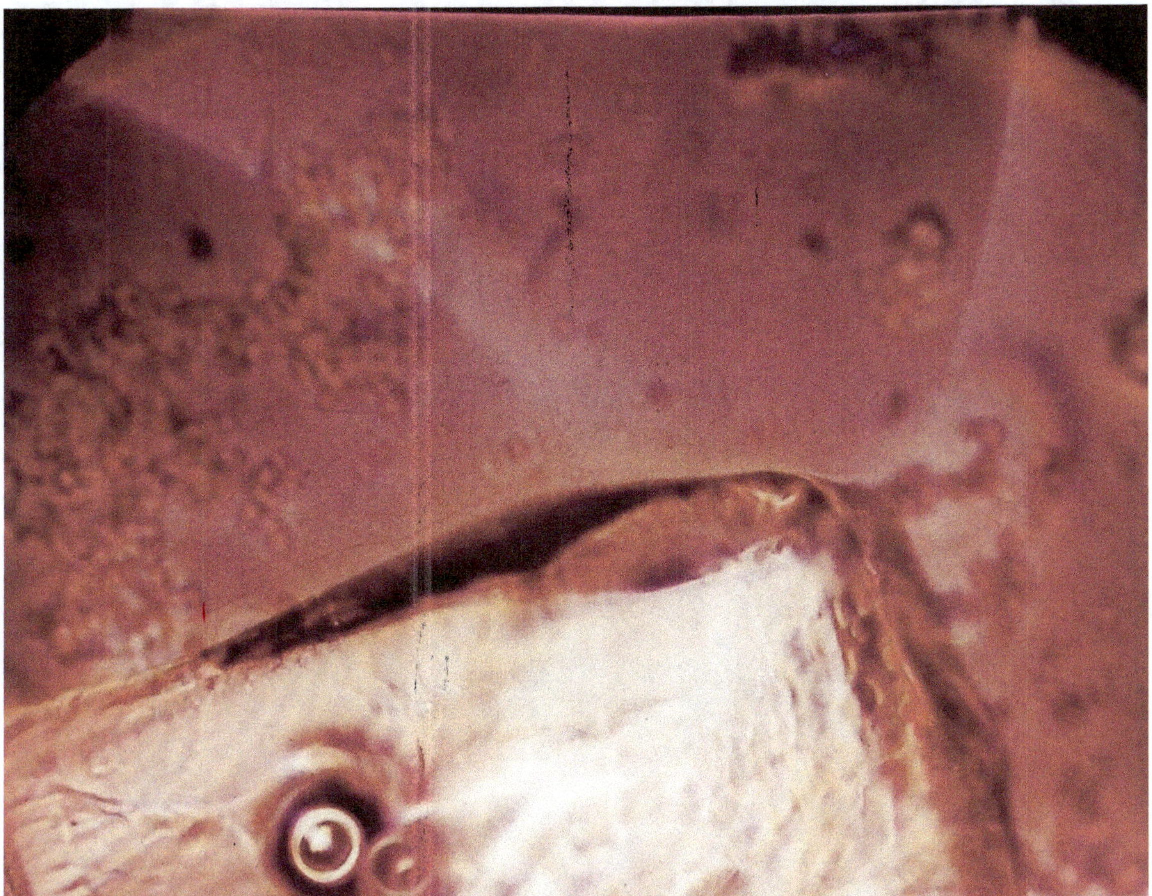

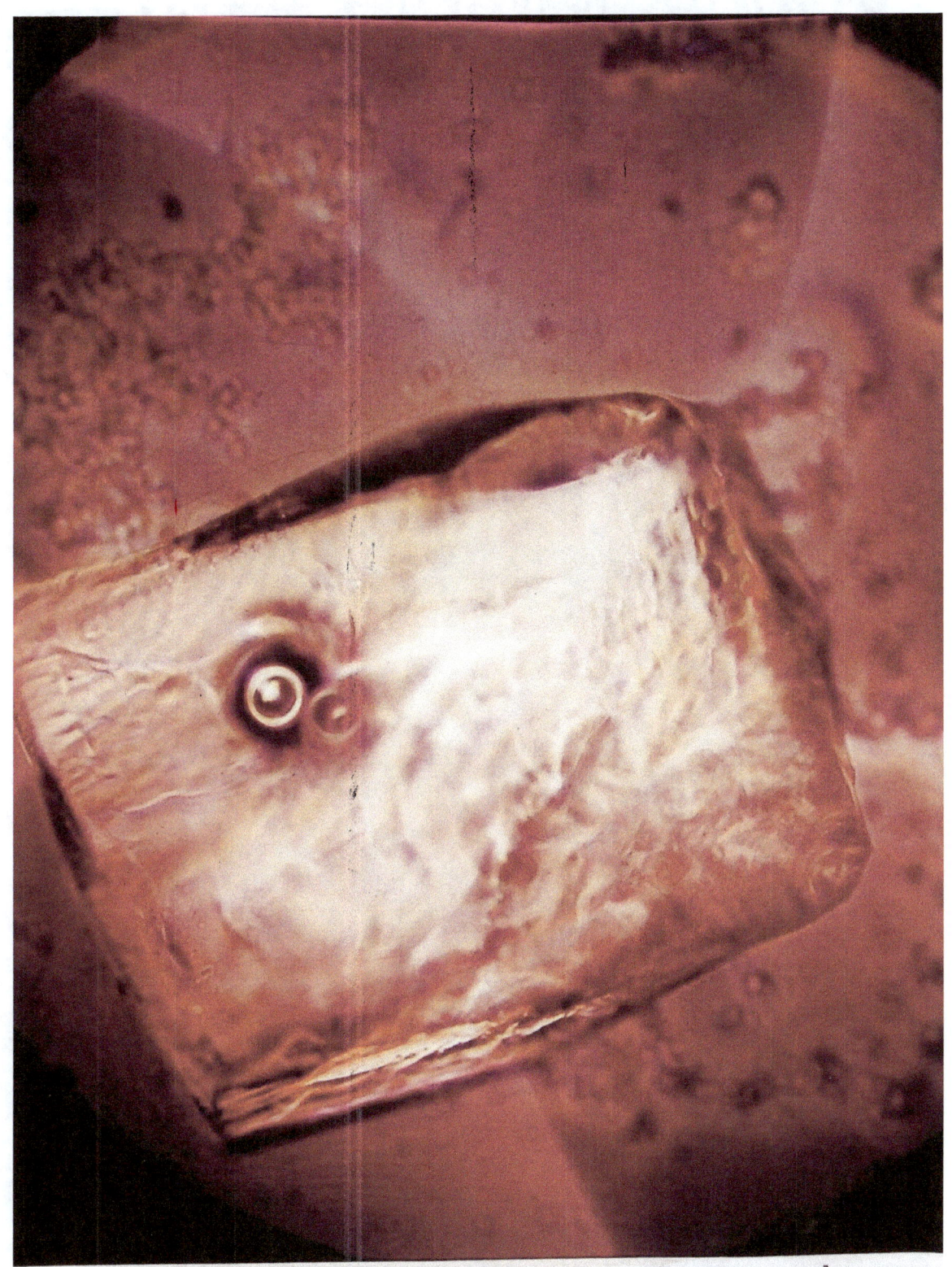

MAGNESIUM: Primary growth of single magnesium crystal, with basic nucleus.

MAGNESIUM: The base of one part of the magnesium crystal, showing the dimensional lines and the resolution of the crystal particles

MAGNESIUM: Note internal structure, revealing the almost completely closed nucleus, with atomic chains.

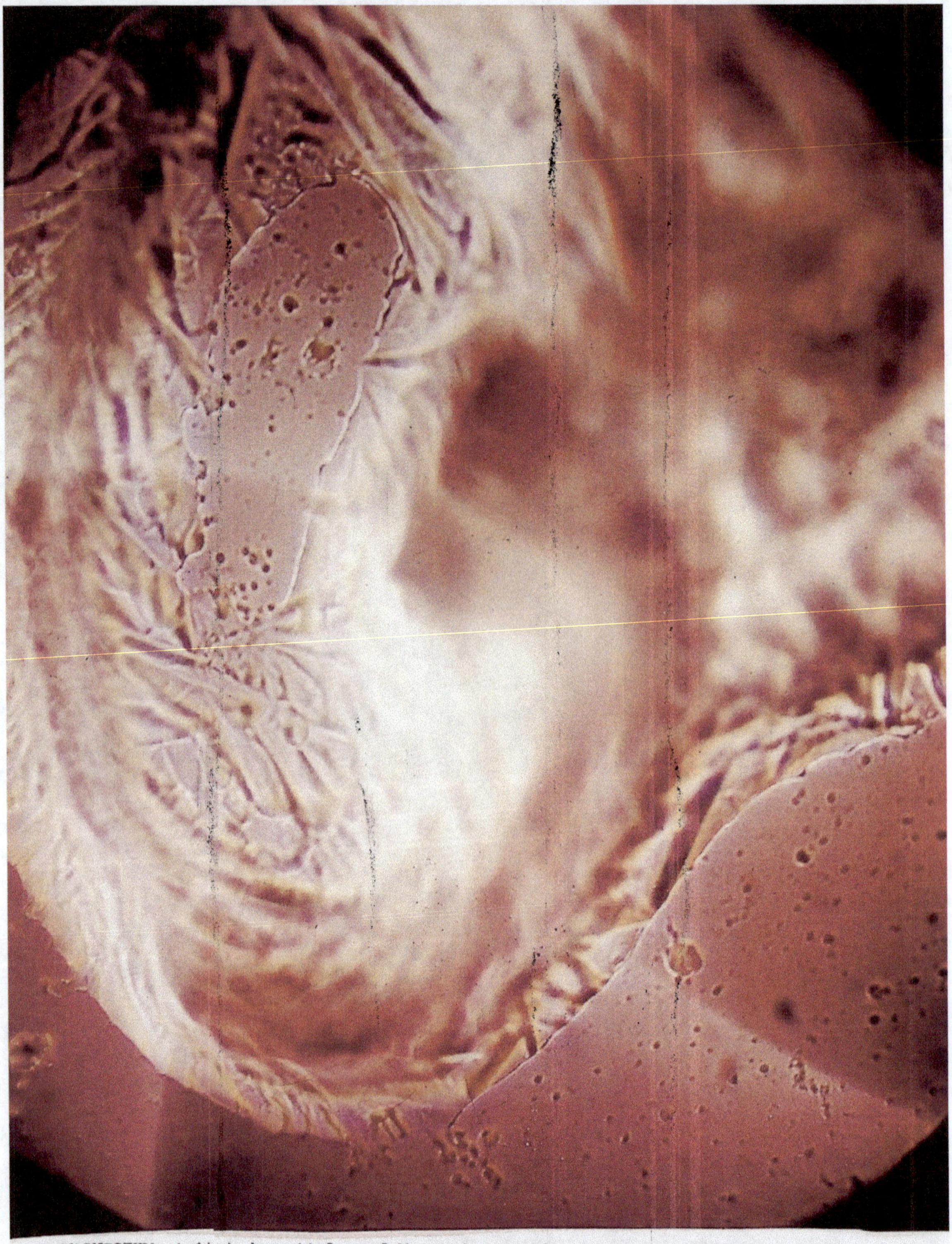

MAGNESIUM: Agitated particles of Magnesium, with primary crystalline arrangement.

GERMANIUM: Full spectrum, with molecular structure specific to Germanium.

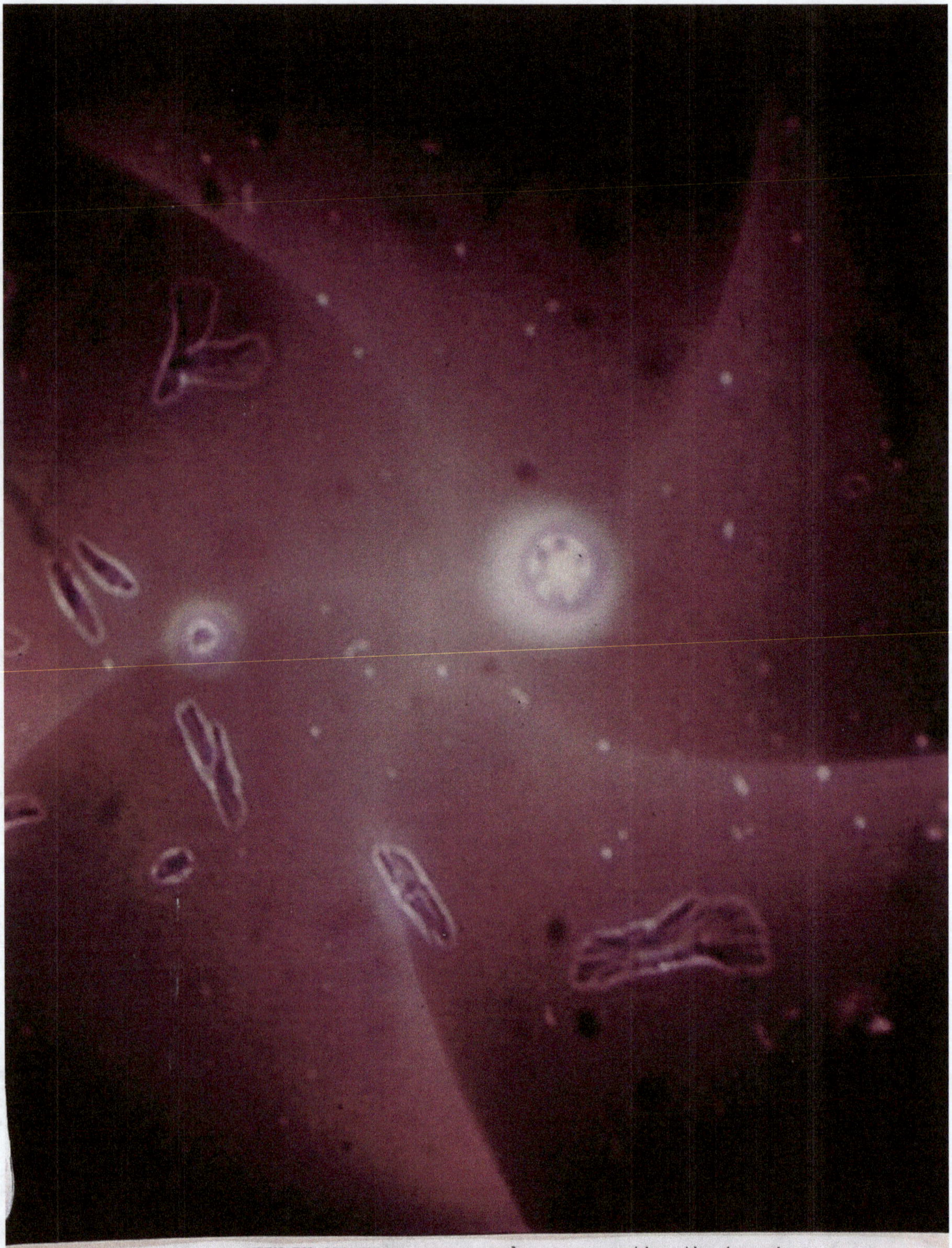

URINARY CRYSTALS: and penumbra representing the tyrosine atoms of the liver from a degenerative illness specimen.

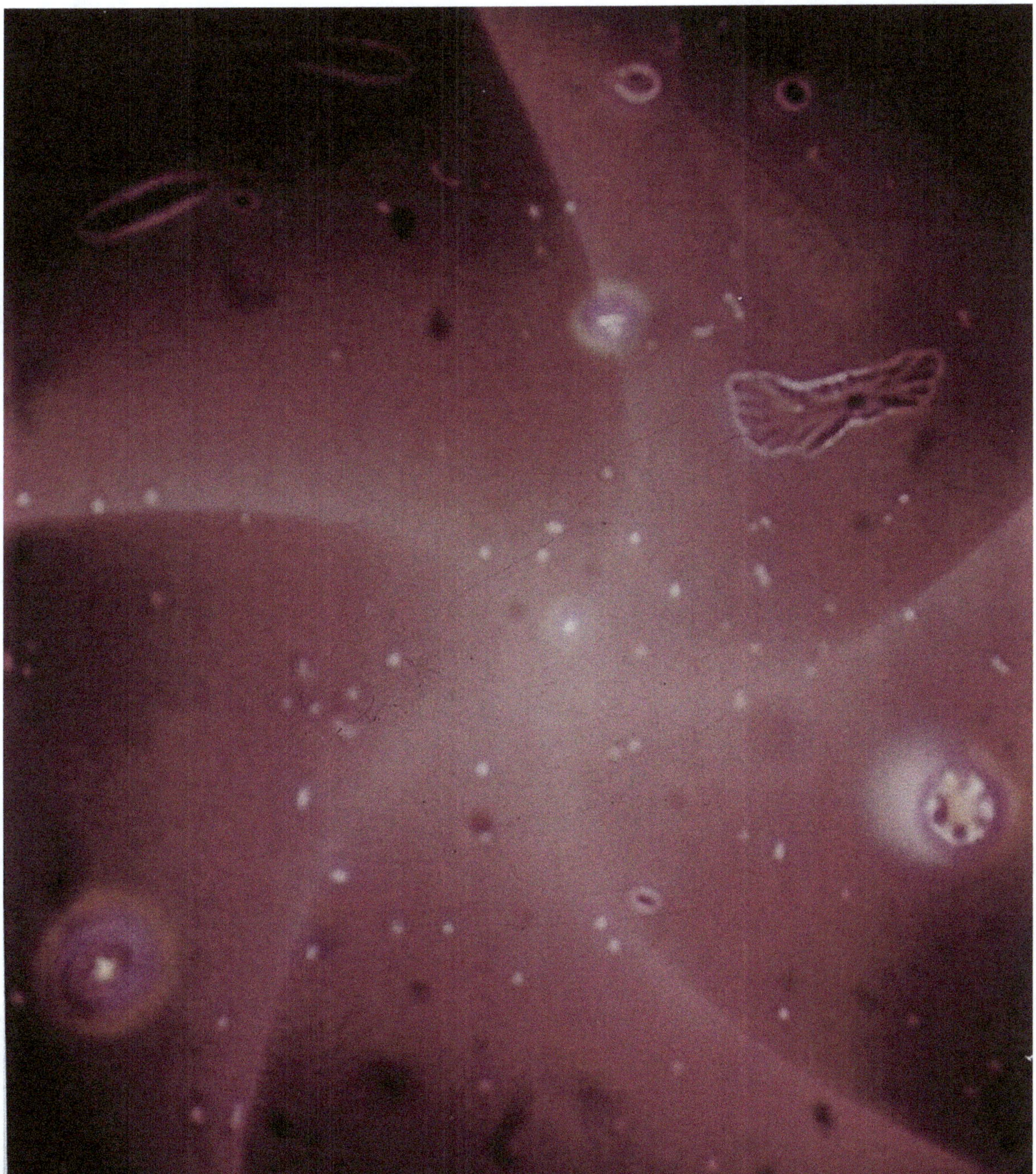

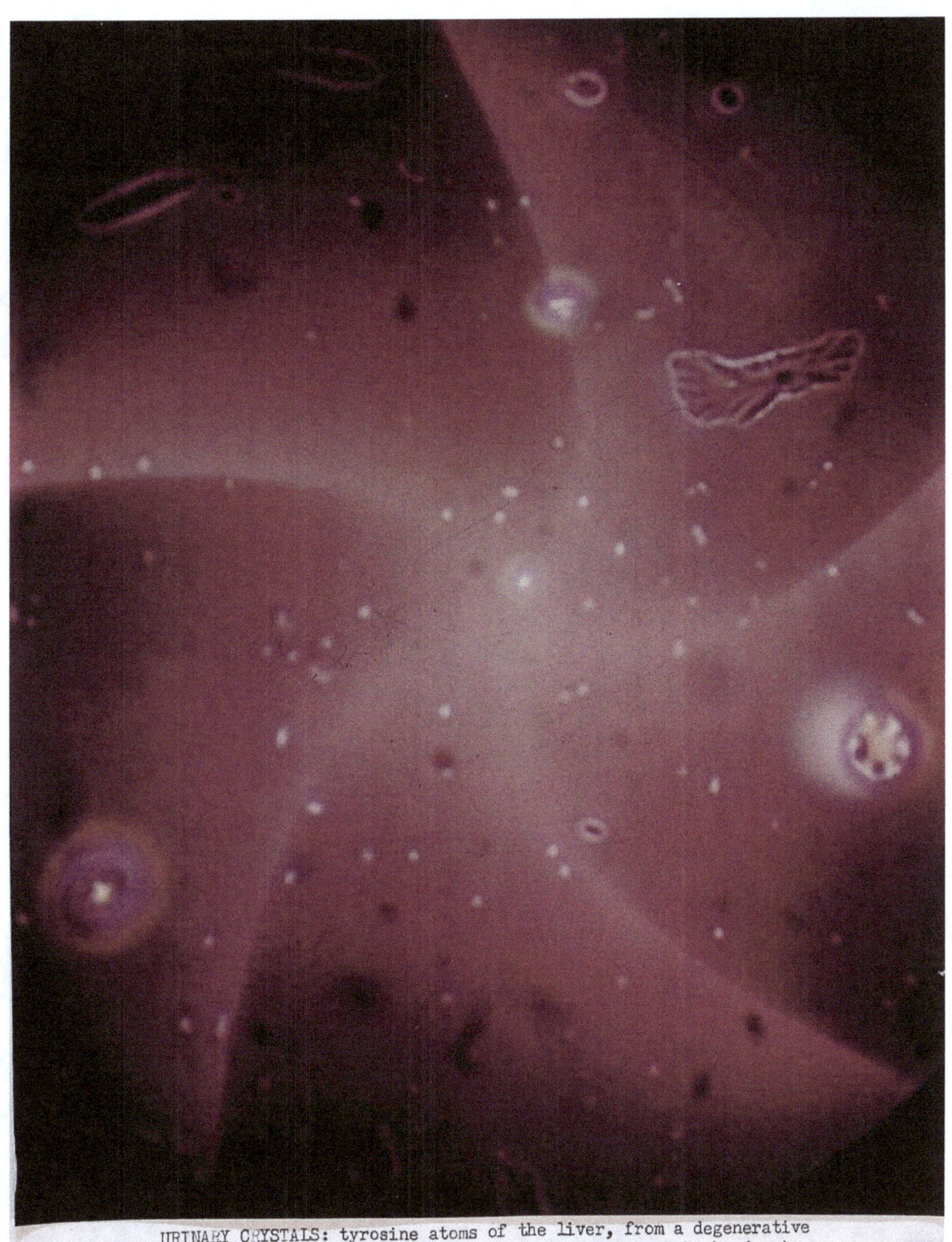

URINARY CRYSTALS: tyrosine atoms of the liver, from a degenerative illness specimen reproduced from shorter wave length bombardment.

ENZYMES: of Rennin

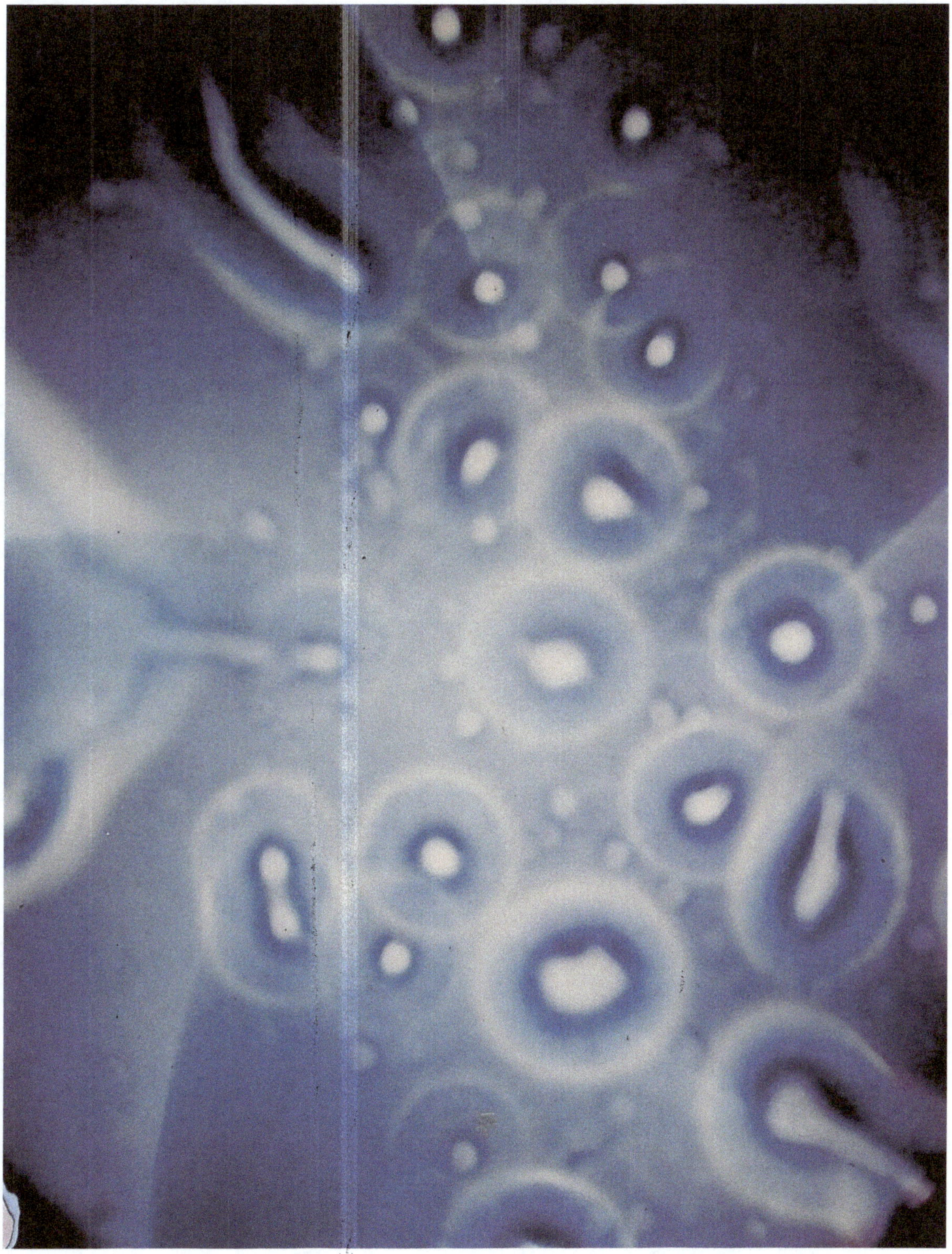

IRON NUCLEATE: Presents the dislocated nuclei of the chain, with poor resolution.

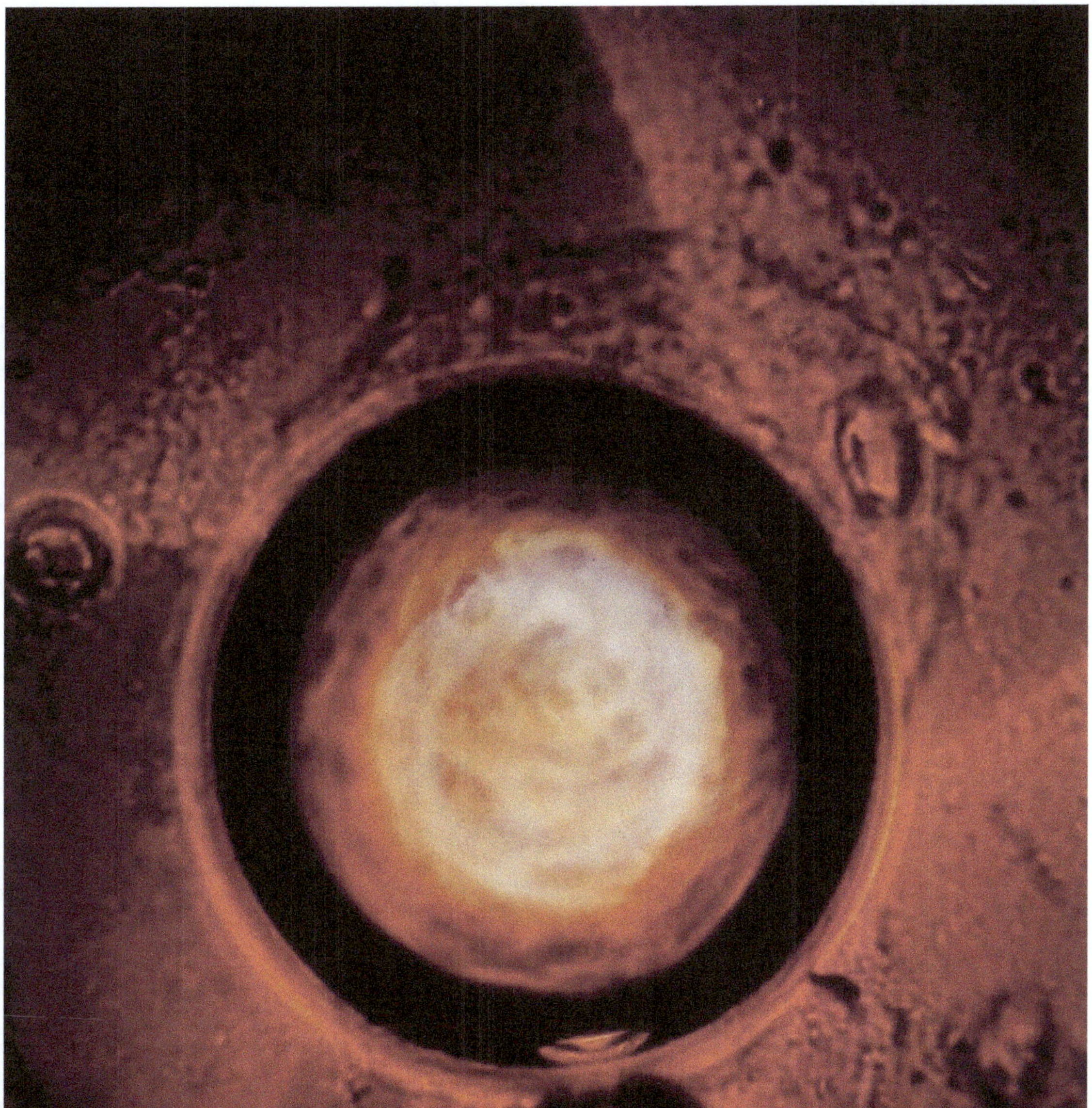

IRON NUCLEATE: Revealing the spectrum and the connection (upper center) of the other molecules, towards the basic emission.

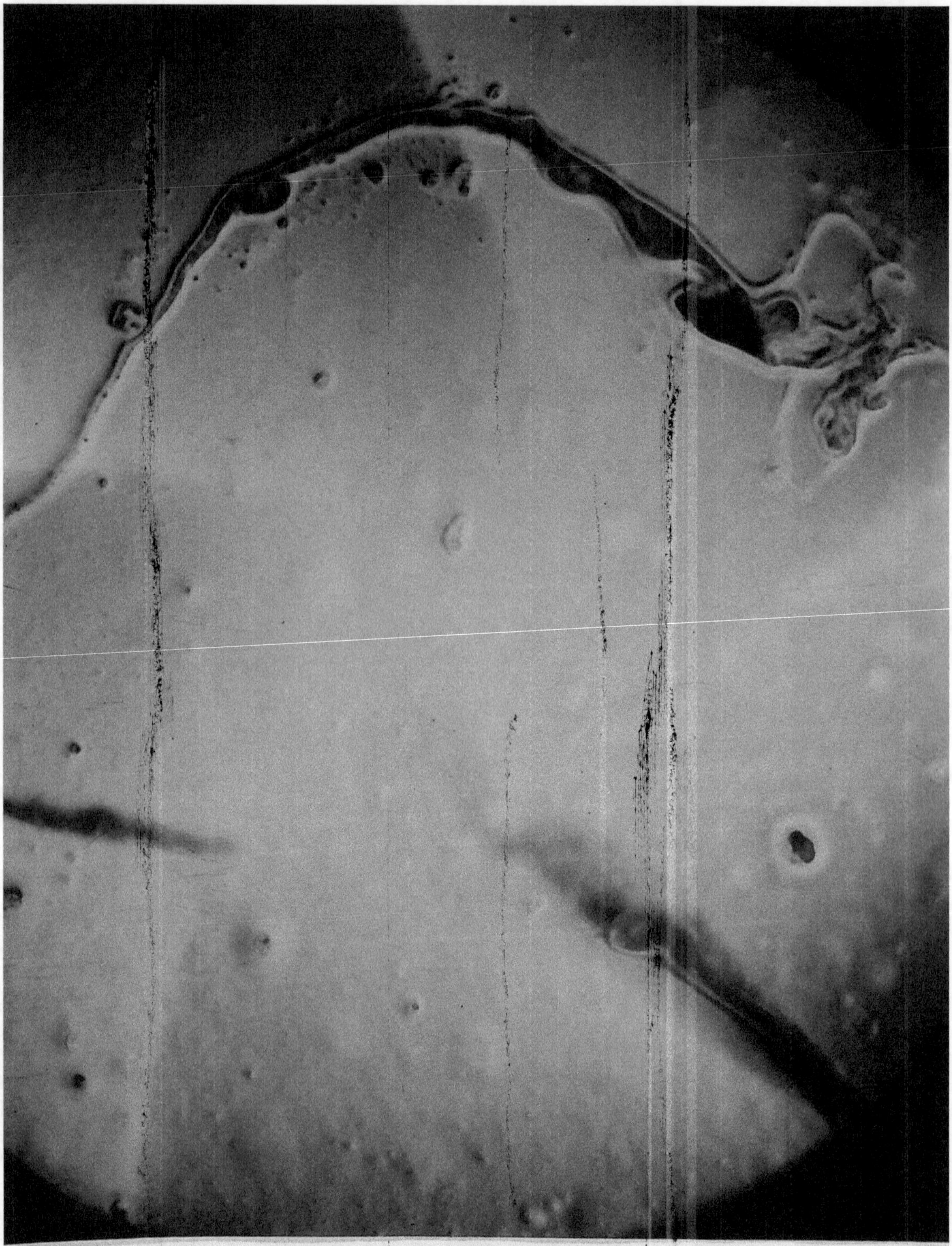

TREPONEMA PALLIDUM: Specimen in juvenile stage.

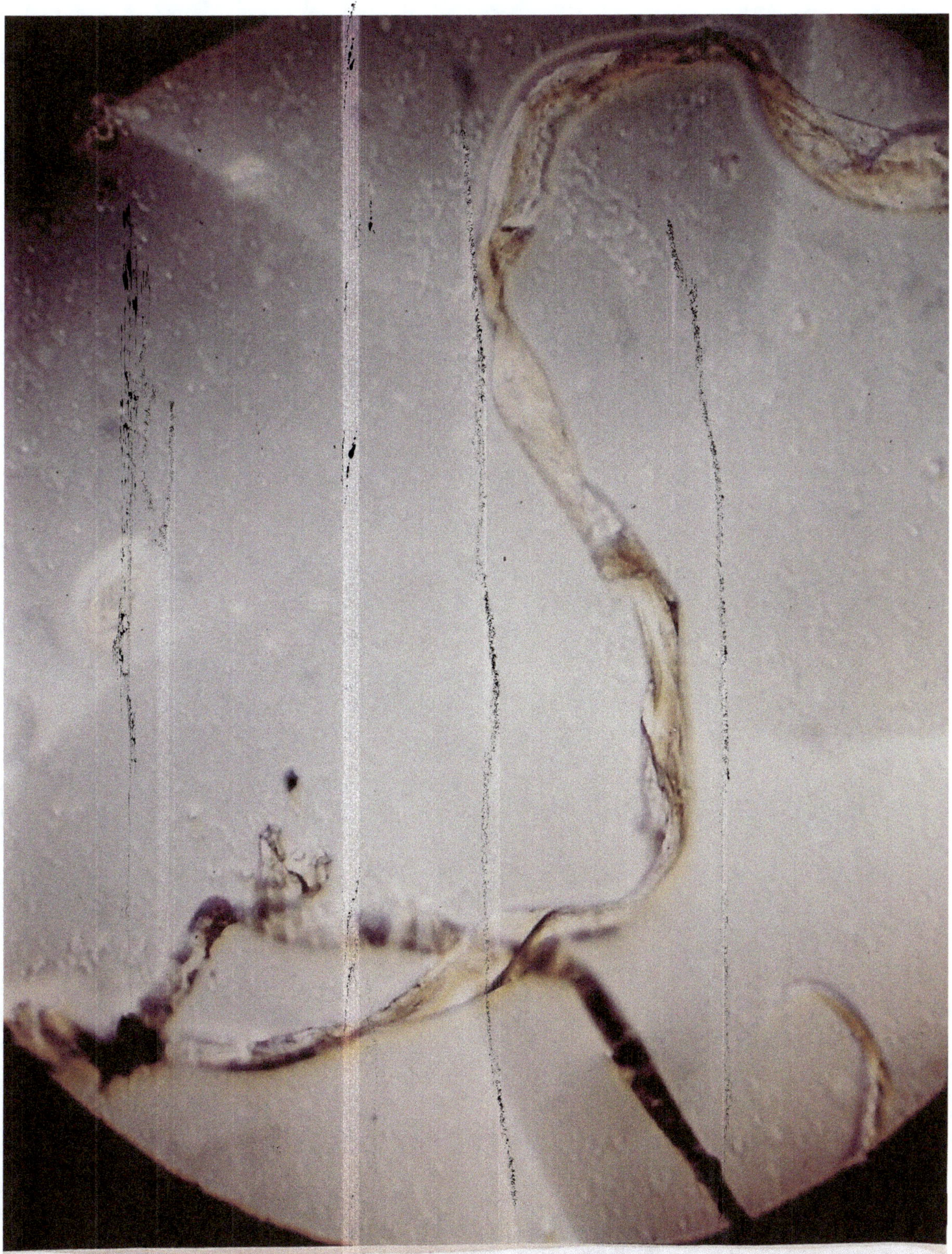

TREPONEMA PALLIDUM: The greater resolution shows the pulpus of the parasite with classical curvatures; the several spectrums indicate specimen is in the living state.

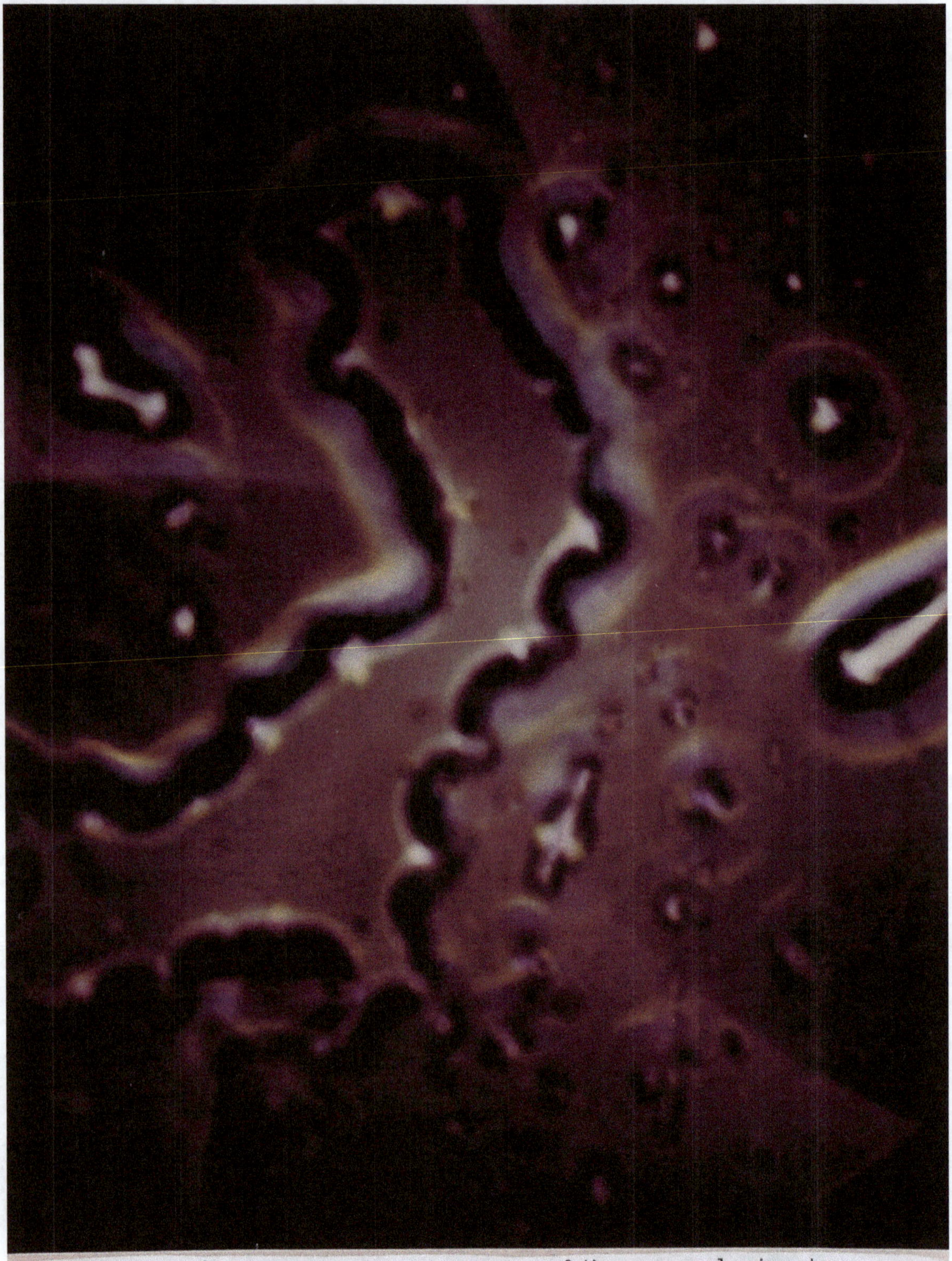

ENZYME RENNET: The visible matter shows masses of the enzyme releasing atoms.
IN

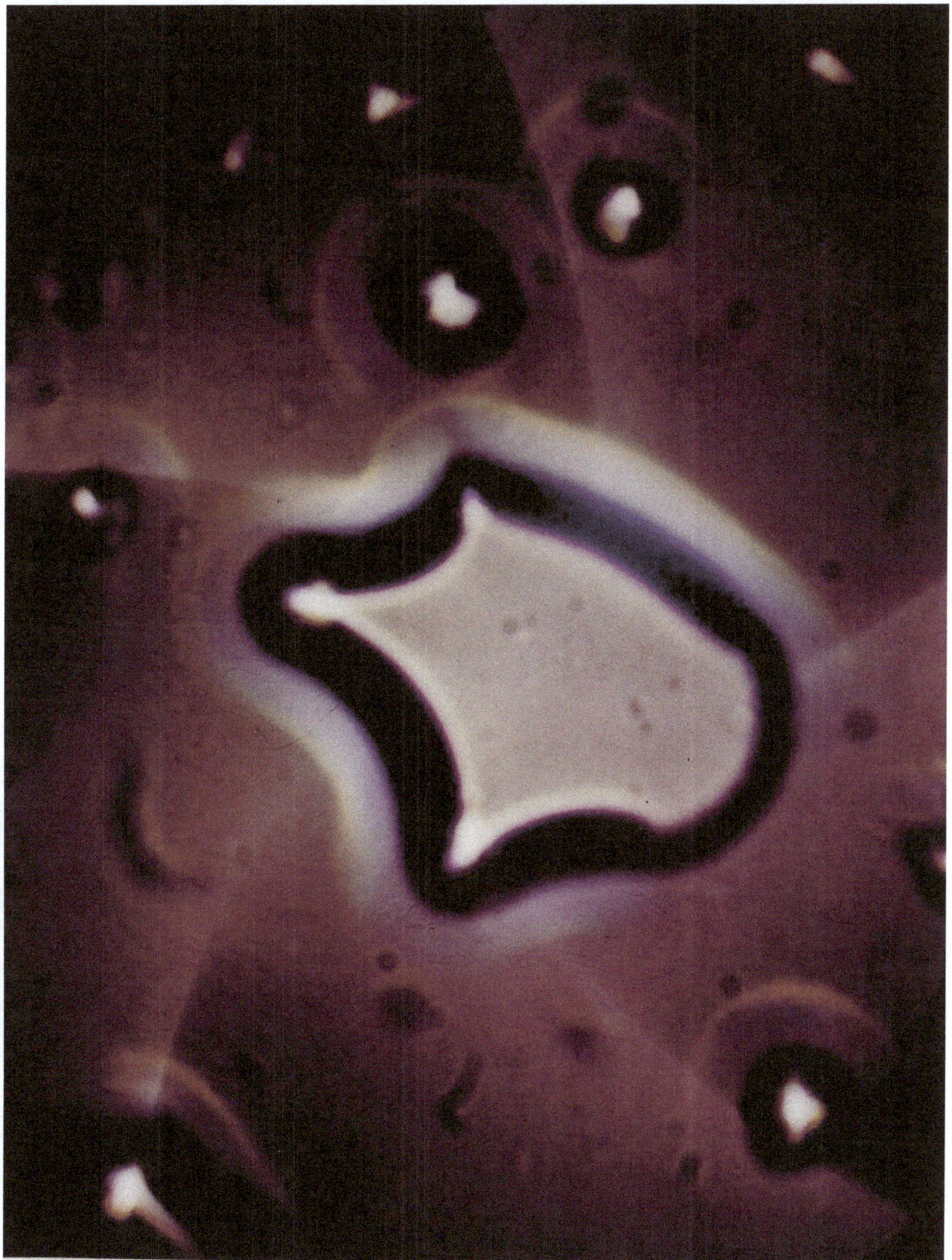

ENZYME RENNET: After bombardment the enzymes arrange in more structural position.

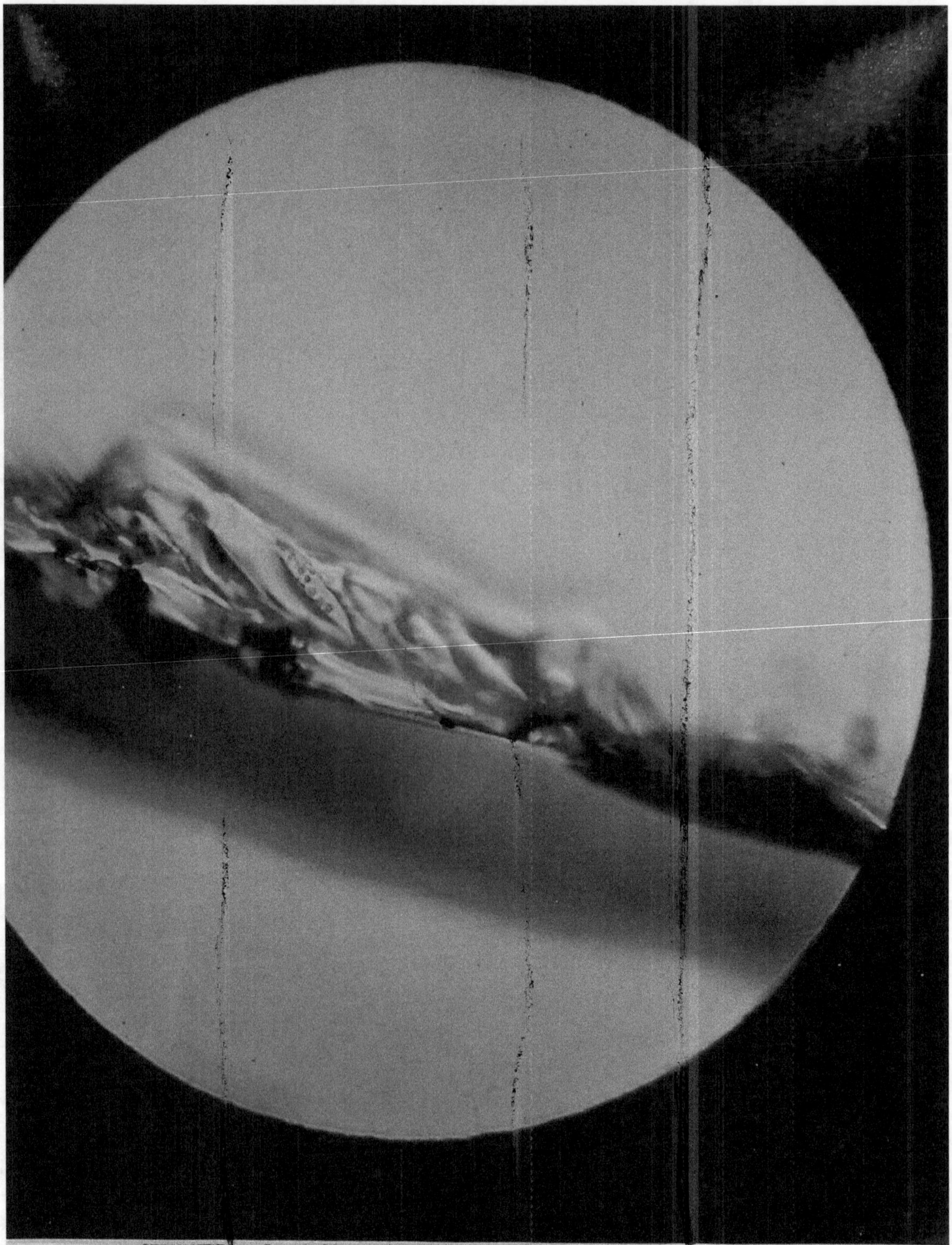

GERMANIUM: Crystalline structure and spectrum; partial structure of internal molecular structure of Germanium crystals. Photo taken while matter was still in agitation and crystals in development stage.

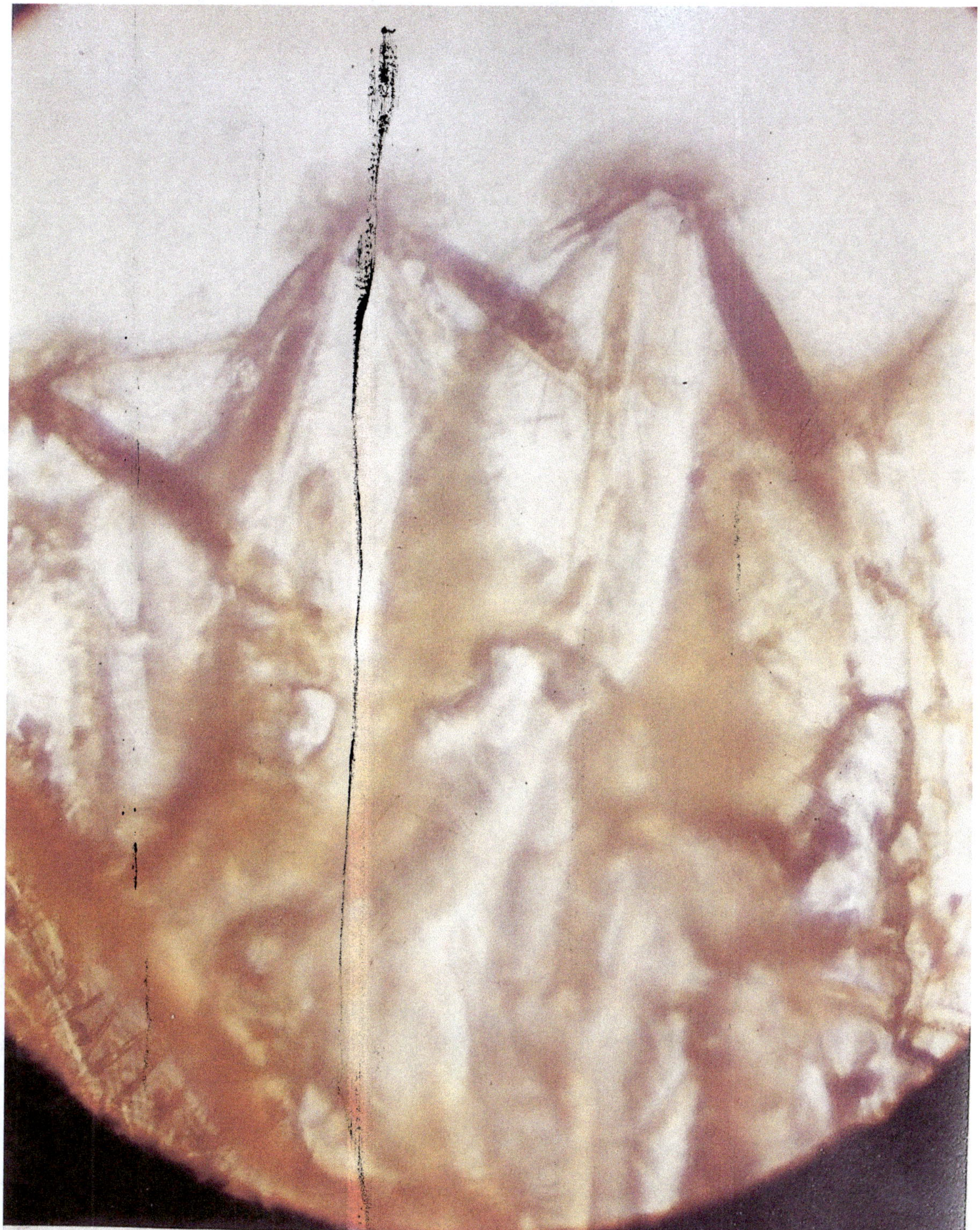

ALUMINUM: Natural spectrum, with more internal crystalline growth, detailed from one infinitesimal section of outer edge of crystal as shown in black & white, with edges of crystals clearly visible. Further note molecular chains, with centralized nucleus.

ALUMINUM: Nemescope. Note internal resolution, revealing presence of the molecular chains and shadows, with directional internal groups.

AIUMINUM OXIDE: Enlarged to 53,000 X, by Electron Microscope (black & white). Note the poor resolution, which reveals no data for definite identification or study of the material and its basic nature.

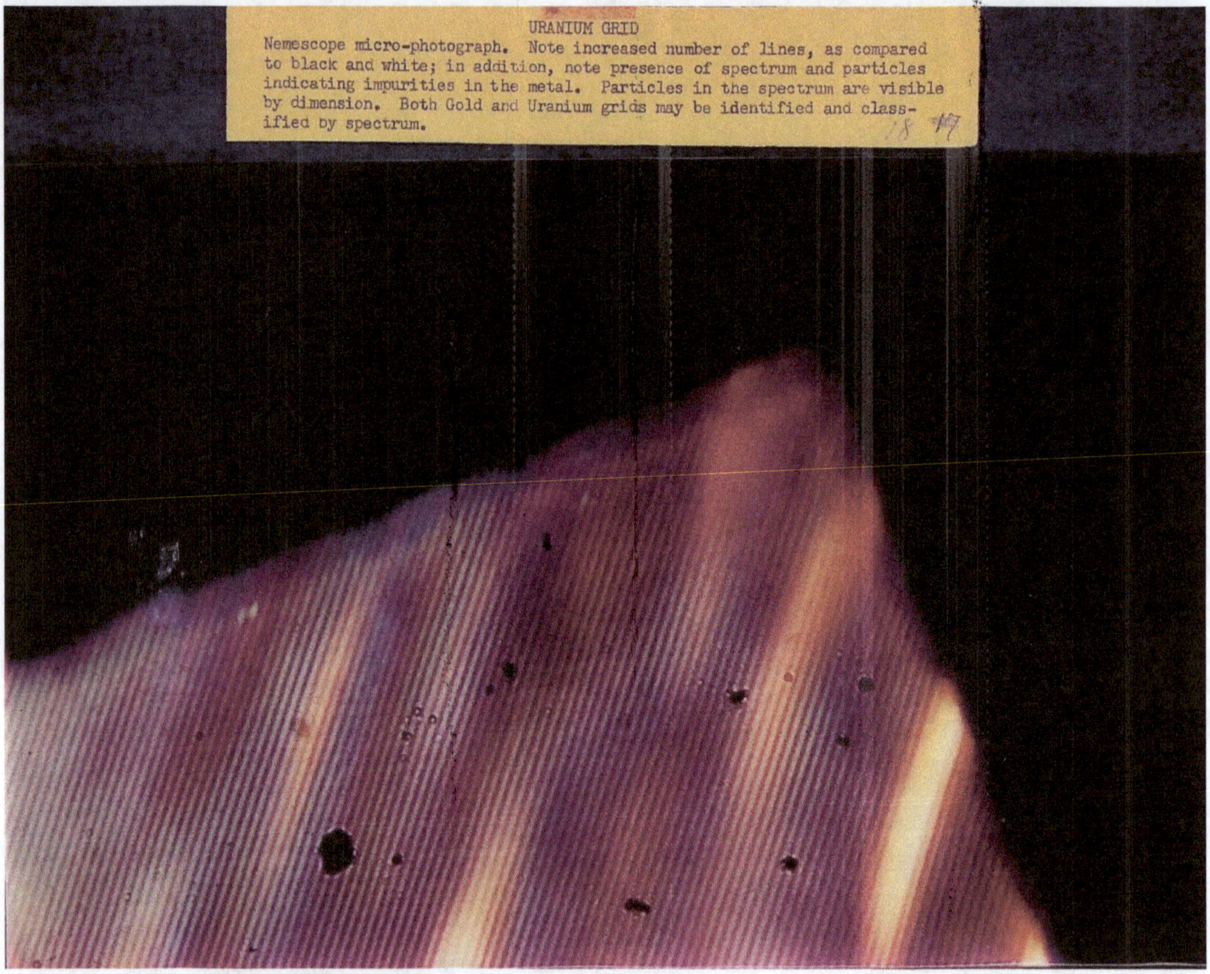

URANIUM GRID

Nemescope micro-photograph. Note increased number of lines, as compared to black and white; in addition, note presence of spectrum and particles indicating impurities in the metal. Particles in the spectrum are visible by dimension. Both Gold and Uranium grids may be identified and classified by spectrum.

URANIUM GRID

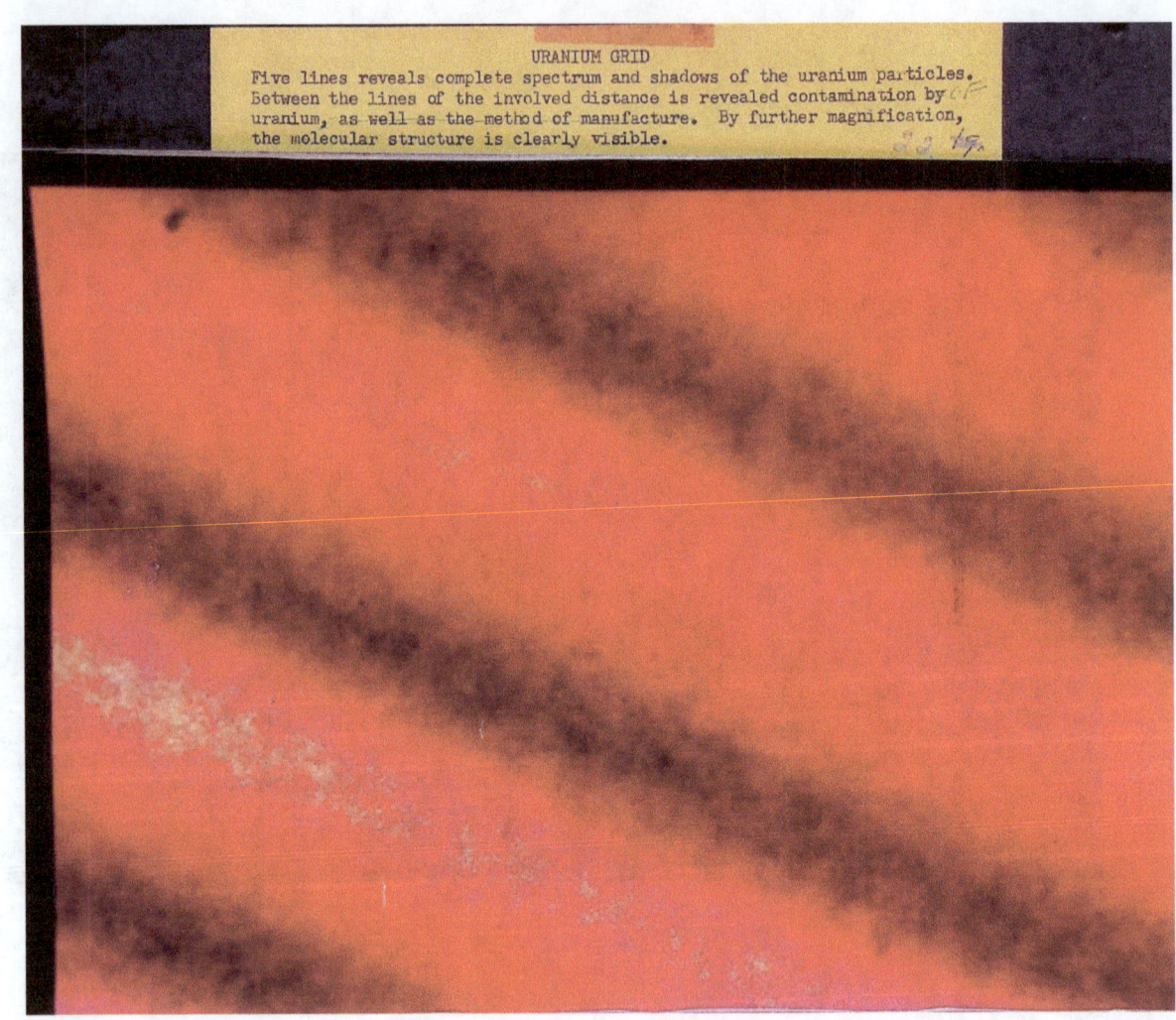

Five lines reveals complete spectrum and shadows of the uranium particles. Between the lines of the involved distance is revealed contamination by uranium, as well as the method of manufacture. By further magnification, the molecular structure is clearly visible.

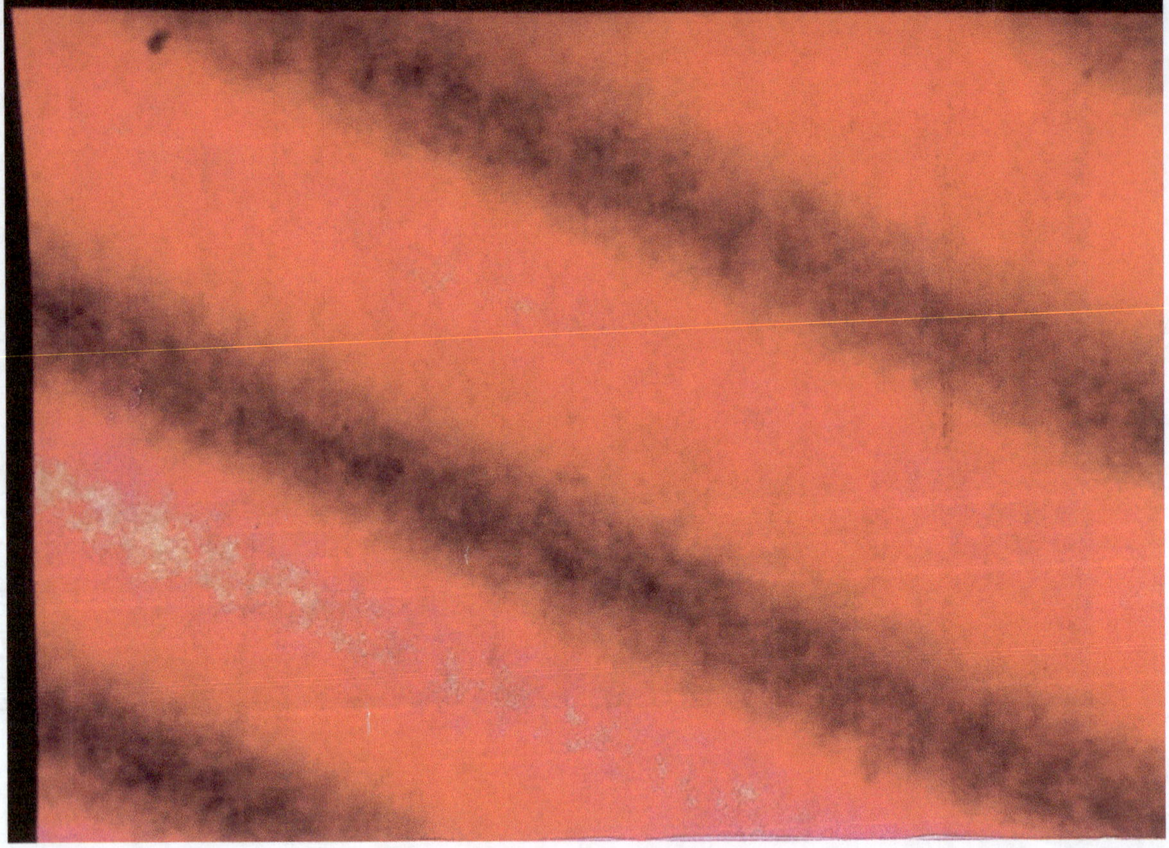

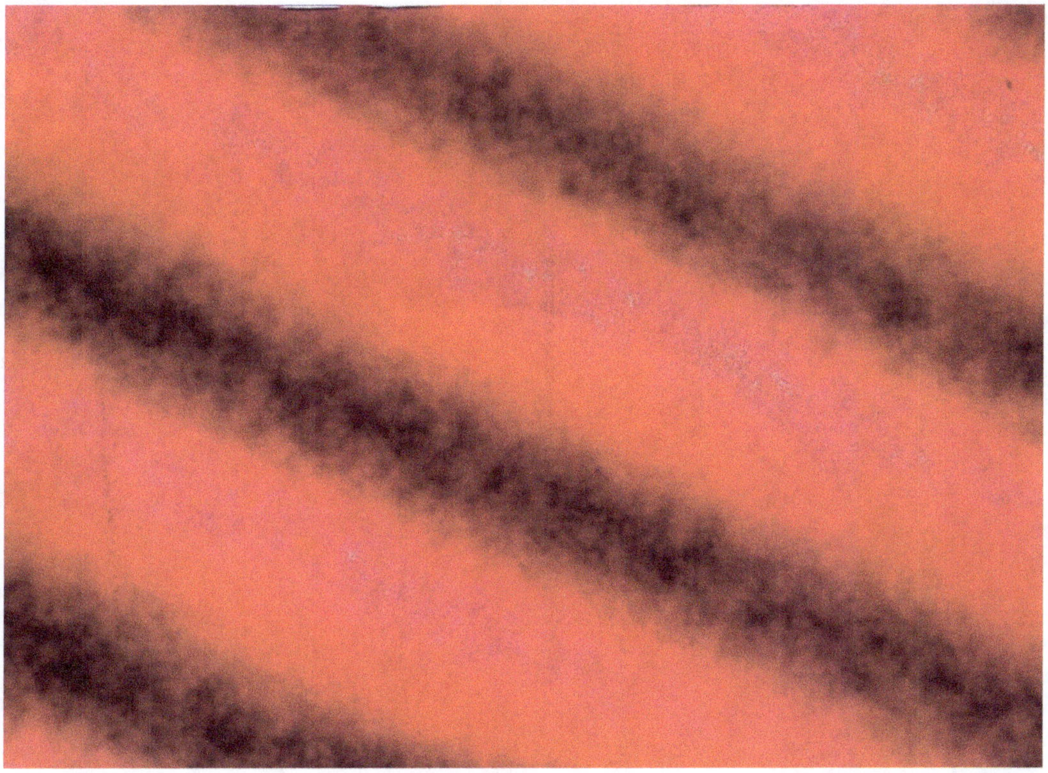

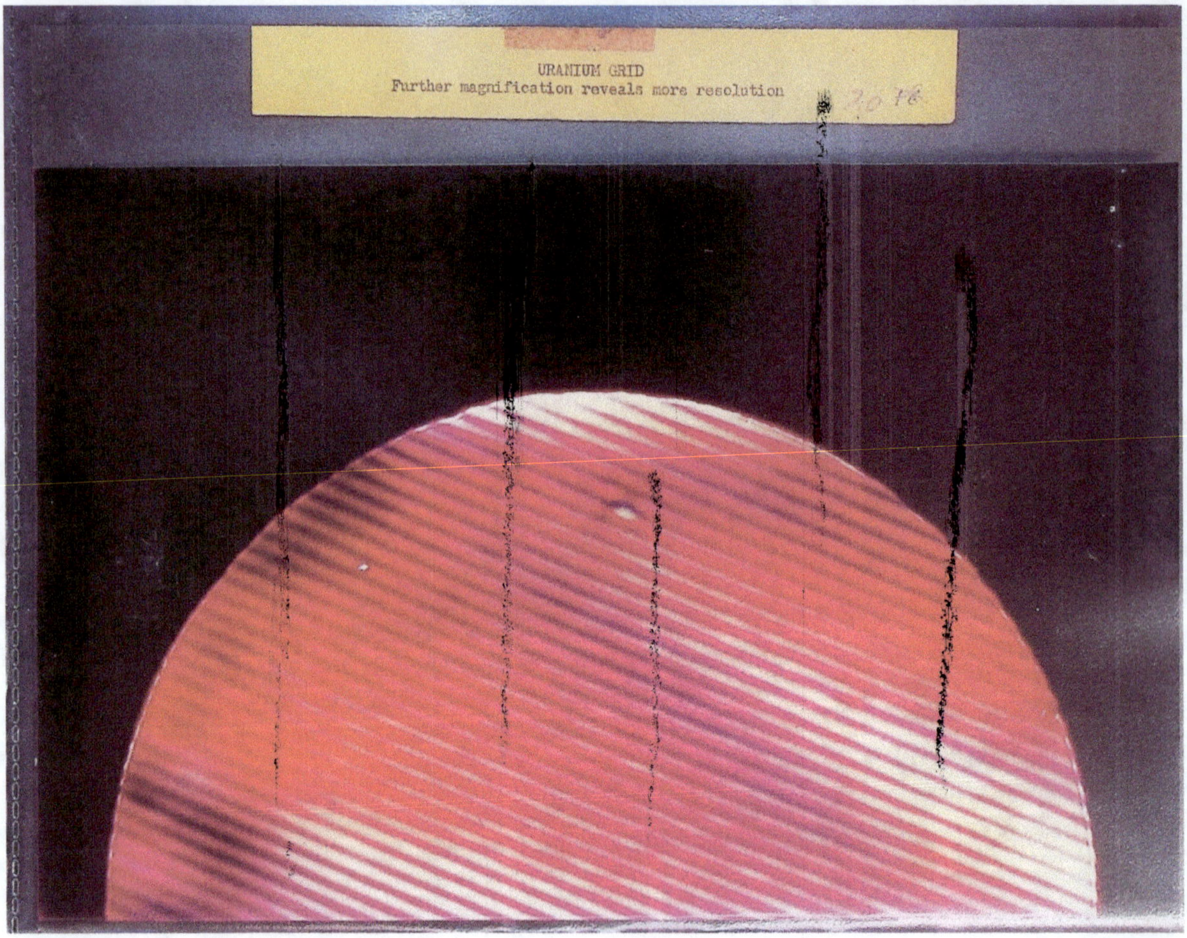
URANIUM GRID
Further magnification reveals more resolution

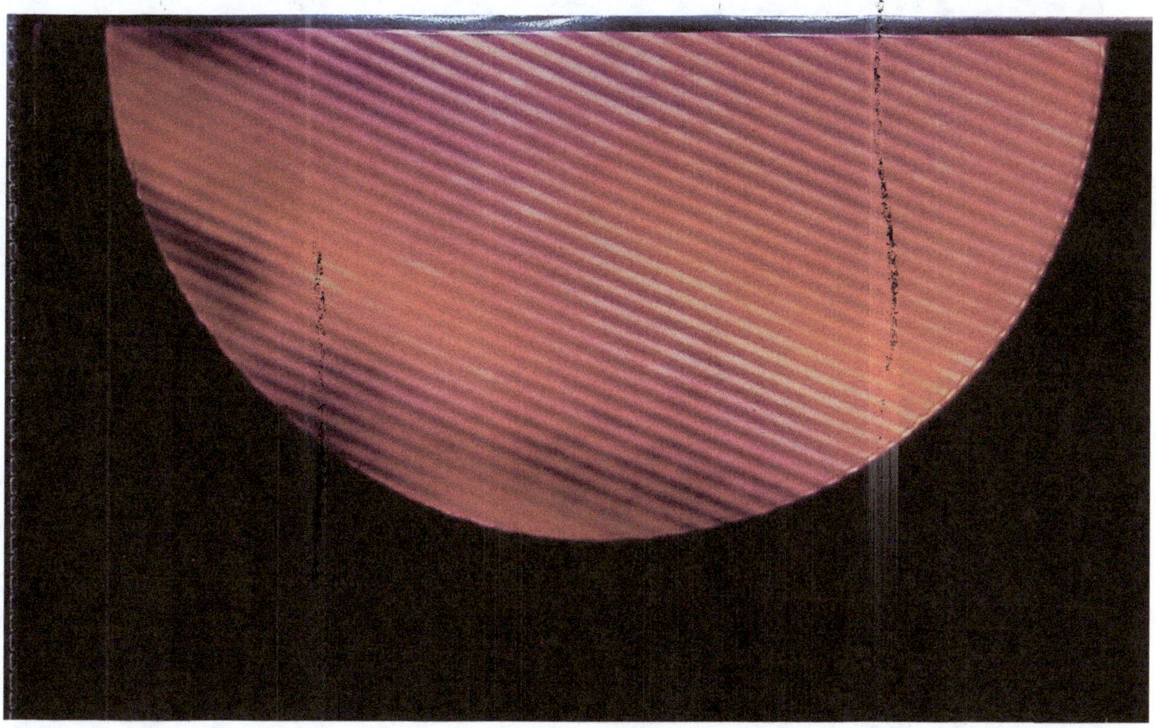

MAGNESIUM: Atomic particles and chain of single crystals, in growth stage.

MAGNESIUM: Crystals, plus or minus 0.1 Angstrom Units in size, and in stage of primary agitation.

MAGNESIUM: Divided growth, with more definition and architecture.

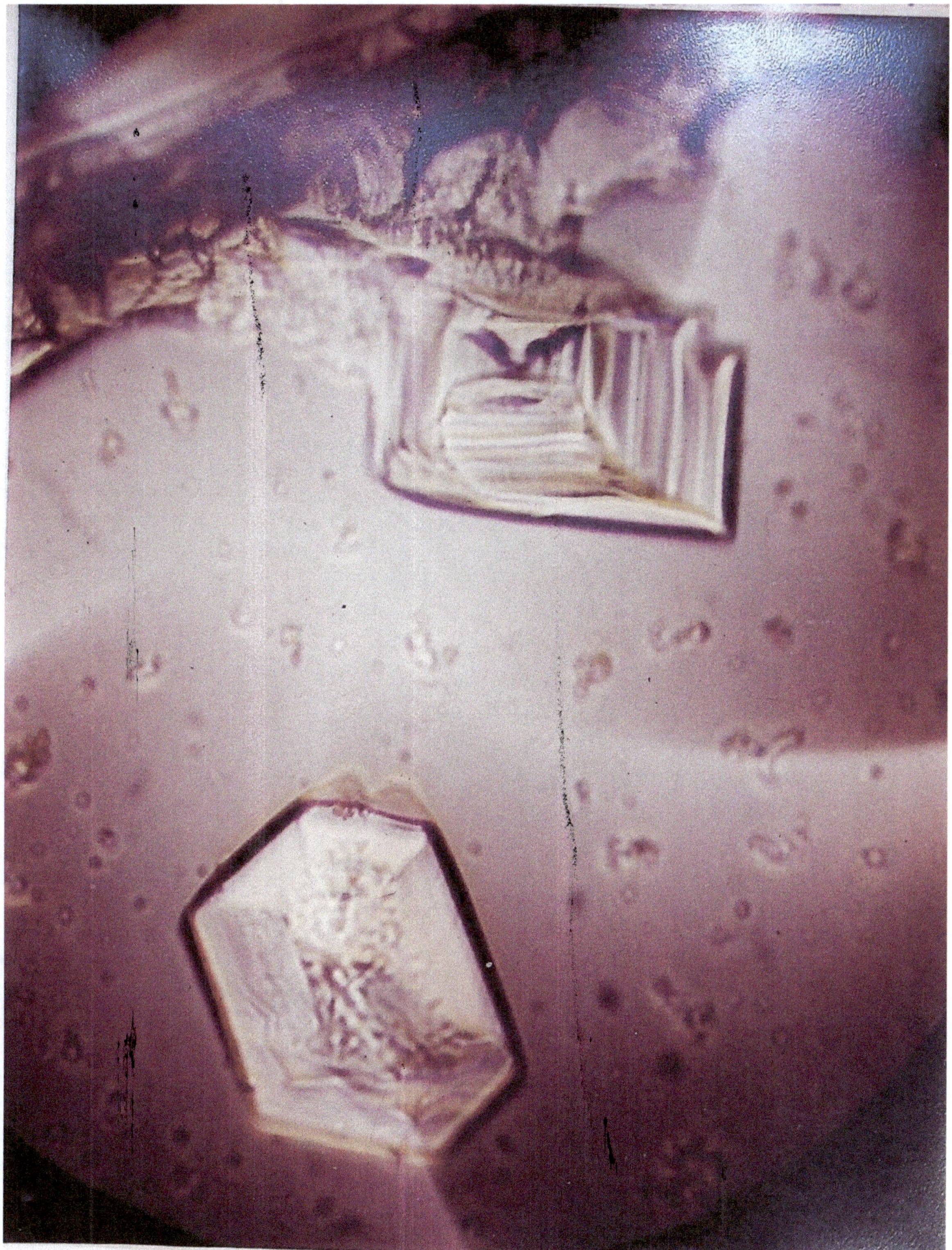

MAGNESIUM: From same crystal as previous; new crystals have grown. Lower left corner detail, 0.1 Angstrom size crystal, with internal atomic chains

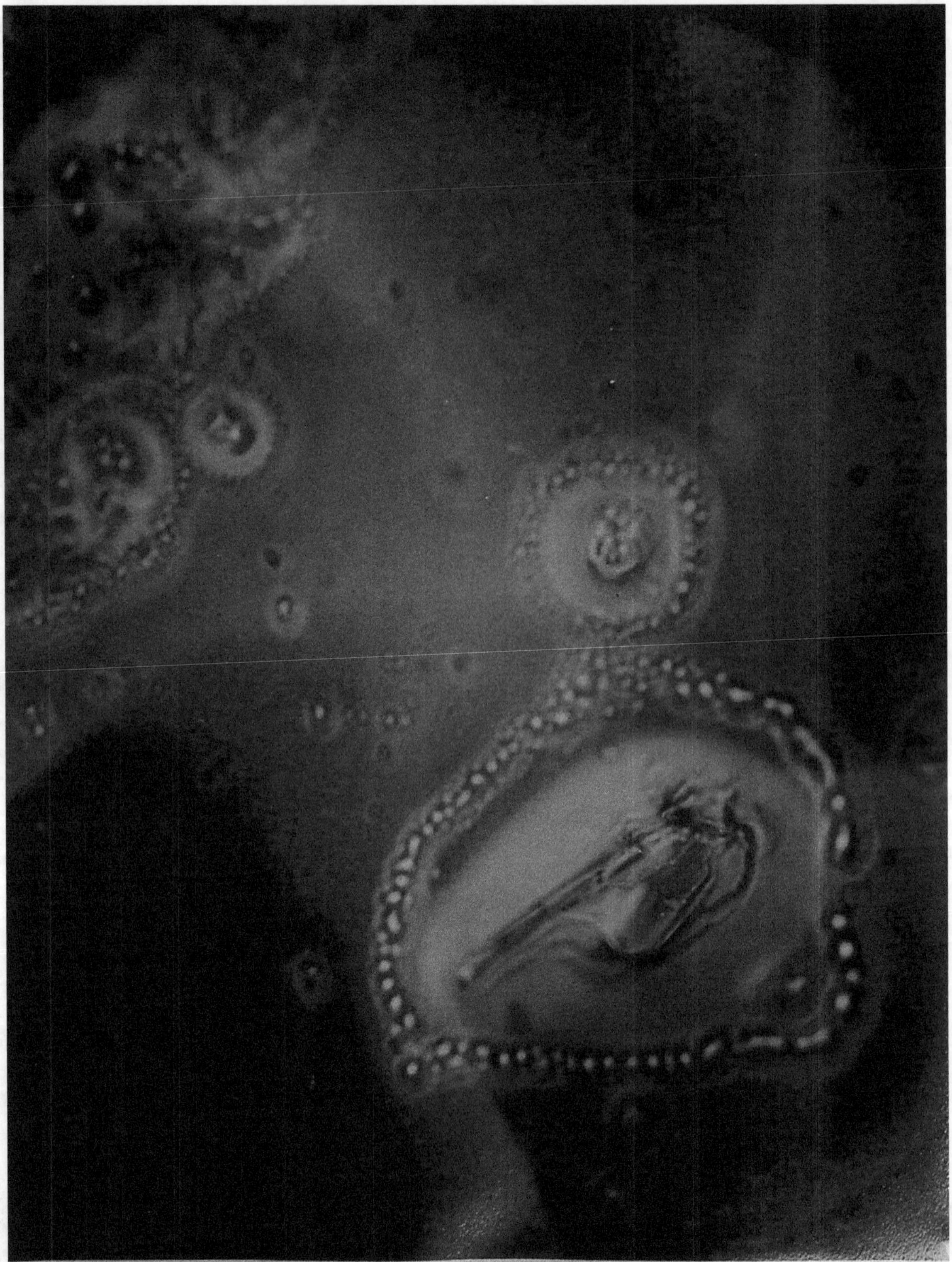

~~ENZYME-RENNET~~: Chains of the same atoms after bombardment with shorter wave length.

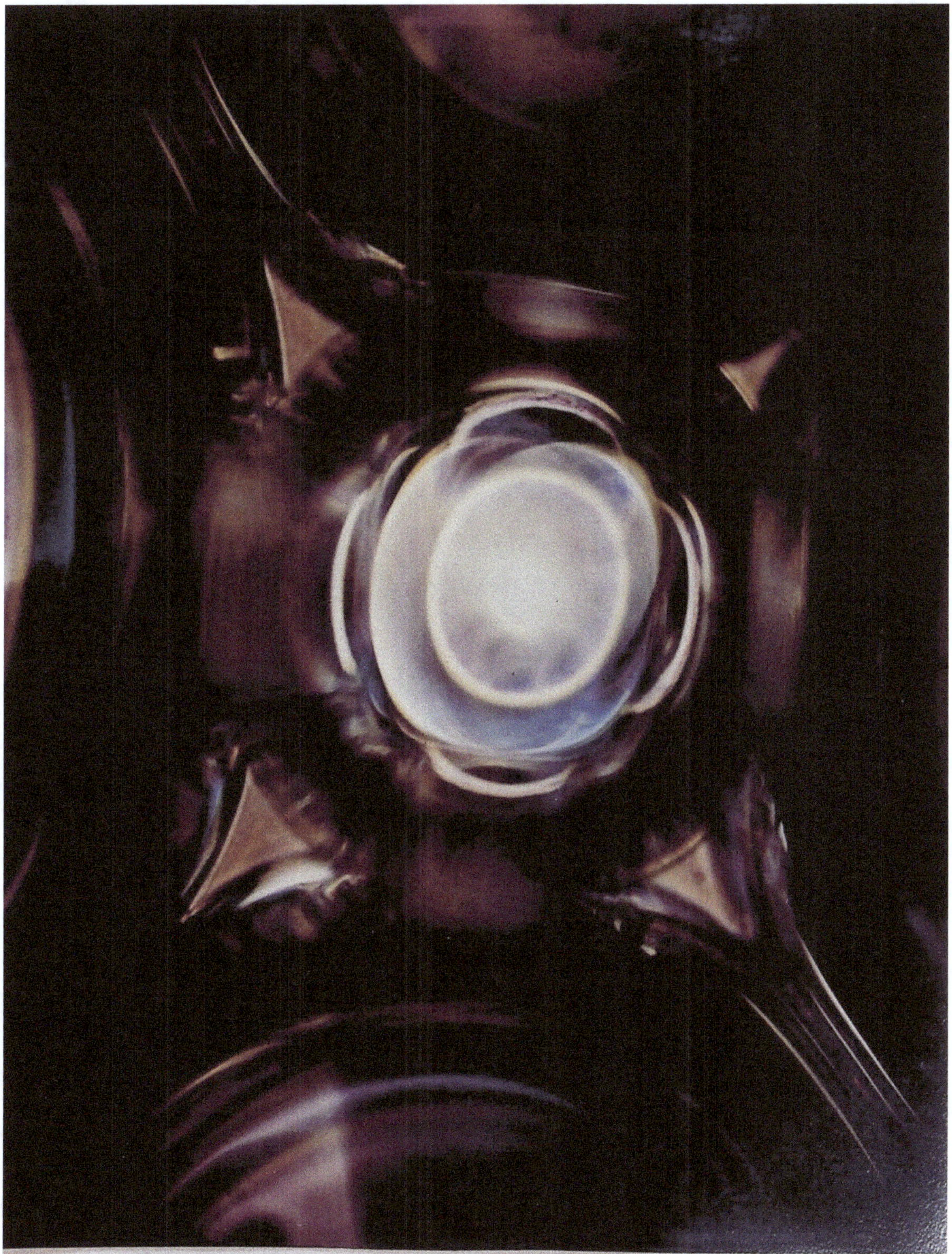

ENZYME OF THE LUNG: Revealing several layers of self-separated gases with basic organic components, suggesting the presence of concentrated energy layers, which radiate out symetrically towards the dilating and invading energy groups.

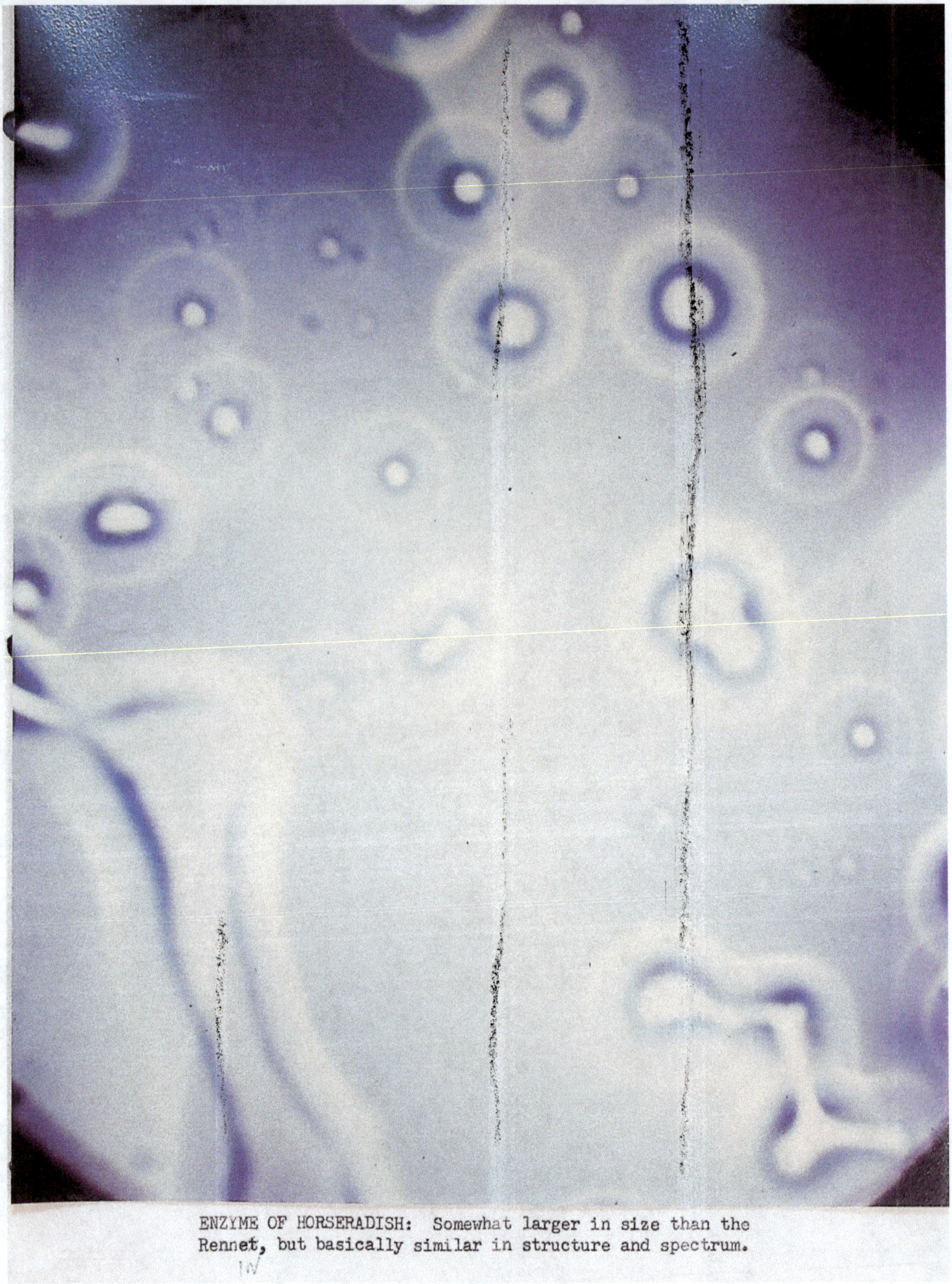

ENZYME OF HORSERADISH: Somewhat larger in size than the Rennet, but basically similar in structure and spectrum.

RADIATED ENZYMES: (Material furnished by Dr. Max Jacobsen) Previously bio-assayed; source of enzymes identified from Horseradish. Bombardment was from 10-20-30-50-100 R. per unit, compared with unradiated enzymes.

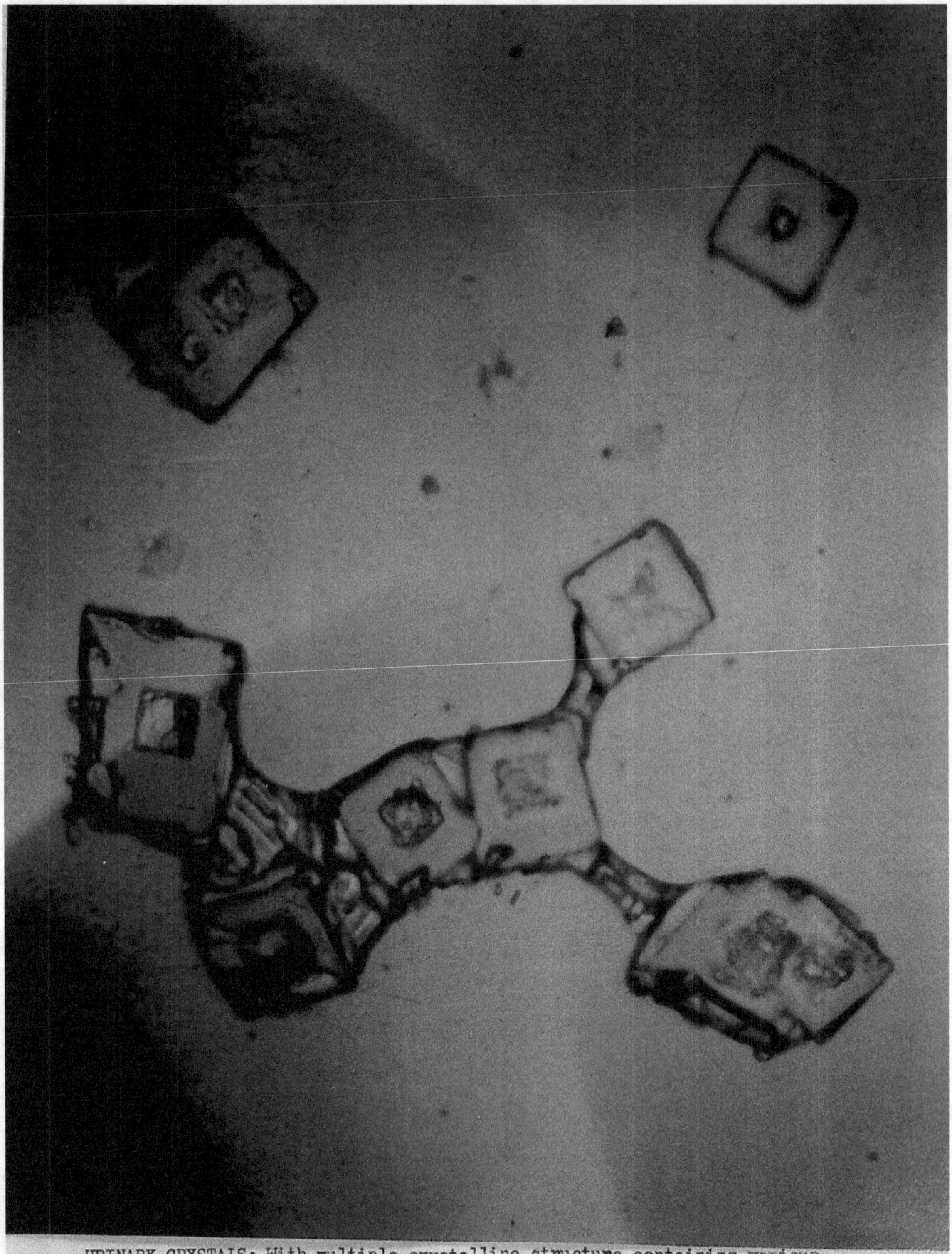

URINARY CRYSTALS: With multiple crystalline structure containing various elements and particles which basically and symetrically grow out, one from the other, carrying impurities, toxins, etc. These crystalline structures appear in most pre-uremia and degenerative atrophy of the liver specimens.

ENZYMES: of Ivy plant after molecular agitation reveals the crystalline structure and same spectrum. (Alice Jennings).

Books by Steven A. Ross

And Nothing Happened...But You Can Make It Happen

Though medical and health cost continue to rise, acceptable solutions are not being offered for any of our major health challenges. Pharmaceutical drugs or repeated surgeries should not be your only option. Is there an alternative to the way that we currently treat disease? Inside this book you will discover better solutions for our health care and why these options have been excluded from common practice. Inside you will learn of...

- A device that heals wounds twice normal speed.
- An African herb that has been shown, in multiple studies, to eliminate the need for heart bypass in 90% of scheduled surgeries.
- How the use of color allowed a little girl with 3rd degree burns on two-thirds of her body to grow new skin without skin grafts or topical applications.
- How an eagle was cured of a health problem, by a therapy that can also be used on humans, but this beneficial and safe therapy is not currently available.
- And many other beneficial therapeutic approaches.

A Grand Design of Dreams: Contemplating Divine Revelation

- "Steven Ross is a modern-day mystic. In the pages of this book, *A Grand Design of Dreams*, he shares both the influences in his life and how he has influenced others to understand the innate nature of our mental and spiritual powers. As Ross shares his dreams and the accompanying interpretations with us, we feel in the presence of an ancient sage, a guide for our spirit. I consider this book an Ode to the Spirit." Regina Meredith, Host of Open Minds on Gaia TV.
- "There is no better dreaming advisor that Dr. Steven A. Ross, whose brilliant teachings are in this amazing book. 'A Grand Design of Dreams.' Steve so aptly points out that you don't need to bend and twist to relate to your dreams. Neither do you need to be an established guru saint, or metaphysician. We all dream and this connects us to source." Cyndi Dale, New Your Times best-selling author of *The Subtle Body: An Encyclopedia of Your Energetic Anatomy*.

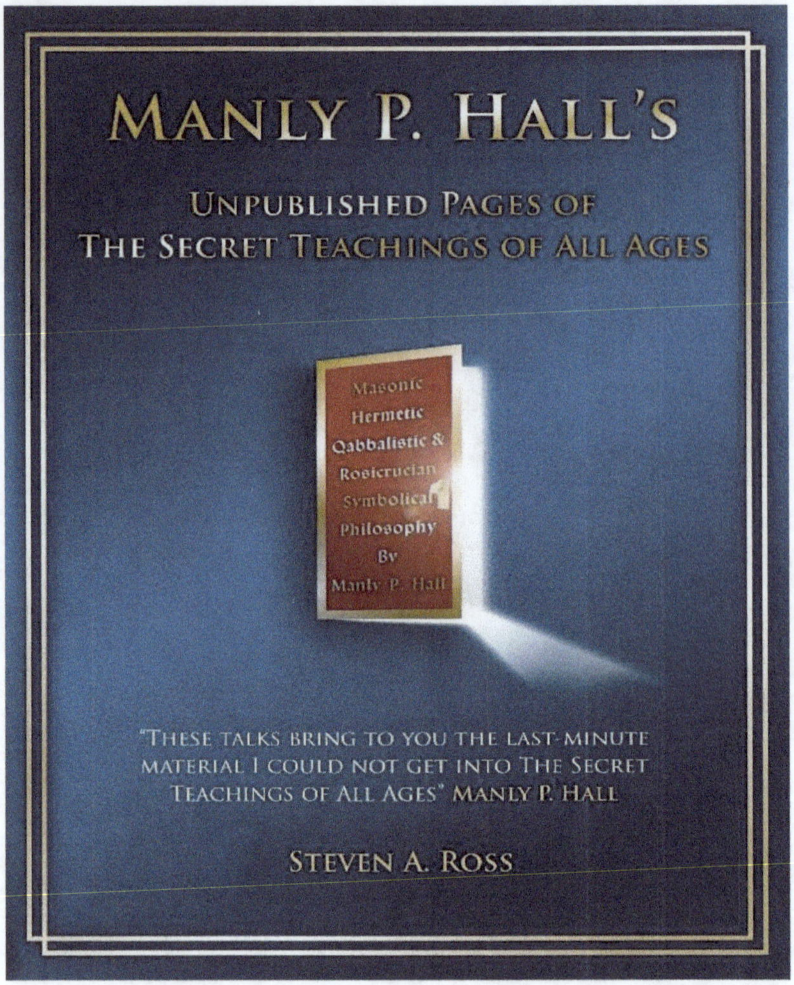

Manly P. Hall's Unpublished Pages of the Secret Teachings of All Ages

Here are the last-minute materials that arrived too late to the printer to be included in Manly Halls great opus, *The Secret Teachings of All Ages*.

Manly hall states in this series of lectures, "What is the most important thing in the Universe? Understanding is the one answer."

In these previously unpublished 20 lectures given my Manly P. Hall in 1928, we learn from the great philosopher how to further our understanding.

In his own words, Manly P. Hall tells us how he intended individuals to approach, read and study the information within his great book, *The Secret Teachings of All Ages*.

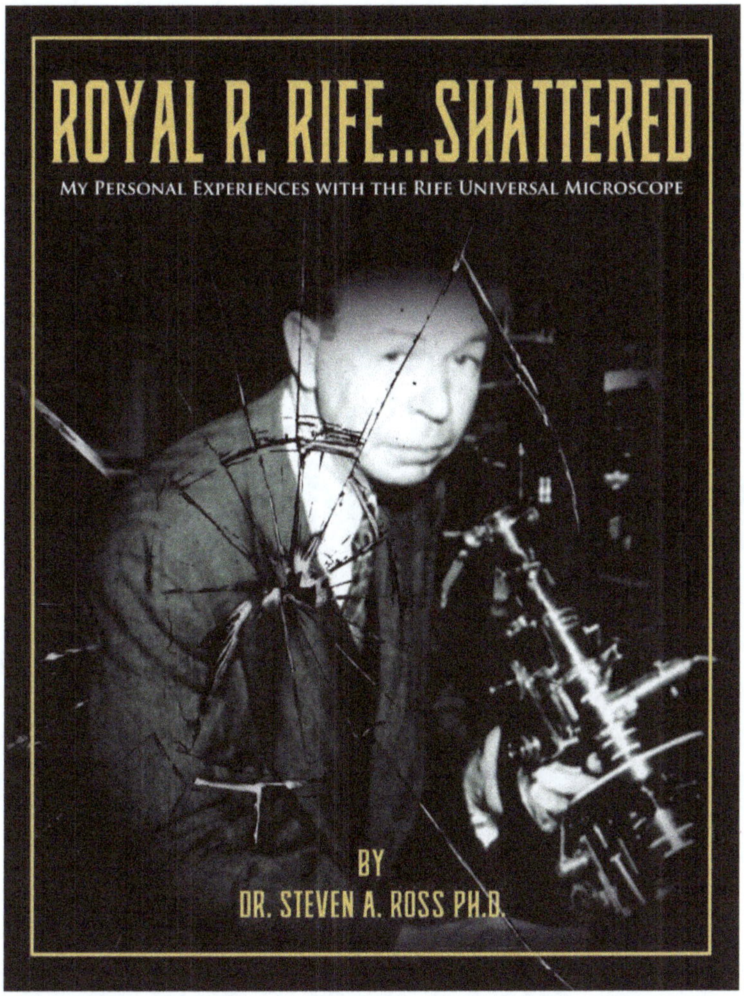

Royal R. Rife Shattered...
My Personal Experiences with the Rife Universal Microscope

In the 1920s and 1930s...

Royal R. Rife discovered the frequencies that destroyed the pathogens for 60 diseases. Rife Microscopes far surpassed the theoretical limiations of light-source microscopes. Rife demonstrated the ability to destroy the virus that was the apparent causitive agent of cancer.

In this book you will find:

- Original letters from Rife's research group.
- Newspaper articles in the 1930s reporting Rife's discoveries.
- How a dream led me to possessing the Universal Microscope.
- Rife's original words regarding his intent and discoveries. (This has never been in print)

Poetry and Channeled Material Through Steven A. Ross

"All that is needed to reach higher enlightenment is a Beautiful Heart, an Open Mind and a Humble Spirit."

"You are not the source...you illuminate the pathway so that others traverse toward the source."

The following poetry and philosophy were channeled between 1994 through 2015. Upon awakening I made no effort to correct wording or sentence structure. Some evenings I would receive six dreams during the night with several poems between the dreams. I have recognized several different spiritual beings delivering the poems to me. I can determine this through the voice that I hear within my head along with the cadence of the words. The spirit guides I recognize are a Native American, a very ancient Chinese Poet, a Greek mythological figure, and an Angelic Female.

To order my books at my website:

Less Complicated.net
https://www.lesscomplicated.net/

Steven A. Ross Presentations on Rife and the Universal

https://globalbem.com/steven-ross-energy-medicine/

Gaia Television: Healing a Criminal Offense with Regina Meredith

https://www.gaia.com/video/healing-criminal-offense-steven-ross

Gaia Television: All Interviews with Dr. Steven Ross

https://www.gaia.com/person/steven-ross

YouTube Channel: LessComplicated with Dr. Steven A. Ross

https://www.youtube.com/channel/UCp6ZdMknojfC4t3xwQjNXdQ

Contact Steven A. Ross

Less Complicated, Inc.
PO Box 20756
Sedona, AZ 86341

dearorpheus@hotmail.com

www.ingramcontent.com/pod-product-compliance
Lightning Source LLC
Chambersburg PA
CBHW082101230426
43670CB00017B/2910
* 9 7 8 1 7 3 5 6 7 4 9 2 6 *